PACEMAKER®

American Literature

GLOBE FEARON
Pearson Learning Group

Pacemaker® American Literature, Second Edition

REVIEWERS
We thank the following educators who provided valuable comments and suggestions during the development of this book:

Pacemaker Curriculum Advisor: Stephen Larson, formerly of the University of Texas at Austin

Teacher Reviewers: Margo McCord, Pewamo-Westphalia Jr./Sr. High School; Jan B. Miller, Providence High School

PROJECT STAFF
Art & Design: Tricia Battipede, Evelyn Bauer, Susan Brorein, Salita Mehta, April Okano, Dan Trush
Editorial: Monica Glina, Brian Hawkes, Emily Shenk
Production/Manufacturing: Karen Edmonds, Jennifer McCormack, Karyn Mueller, Cindy Talocci
Marketing: Ken Clinton
Publishing Operations: Kate Matracia, Debi Schlott

ACKNOWLEDGMENTS
page 58: "SORRY, WRONG NUMBER," Copyright © 1947, 1952, renewed 1980 by Lucille Fletcher. Reprinted by permission of William Morris Agency, Inc. on behalf of the Author.

page 82: THE ALL-AMERICAN SLURP, by Lensey Namioka, copyright © 1987, from VISIONS, ed. by Donald R. Gallo. Reprinted by permission of Lensey Namioka. All rights are reserved by the Author.

page 98: From LAME DEER SEEKER OF VISION by John Fire/Lame Deer. Copyright © 1972 by John Fire/Lame Deer and Richard Erdoes. Reprinted by permission of Simon & Schuster, Inc.

Further acknowledgments appear on page 501, which constitutes an extension of this copyright page.

Photo and Illustration Credits appear on page 502.

ABOUT THE COVER: The images on the cover are connected to the literature in this book in some way. As you read the literature, think about the images on the cover. See if you can make the connections yourself. Ask yourself what other images from the literature in this book could have appeared on the cover.

Globe
Fearon
Pearson Learning Group

1-800-321-3106
www.pearsonlearning.com

Contents

A Note to the Student x

UNIT 1	THE STRANGE AND UNEXPECTED	1
Chapter 1	Short Stories	2

*A*fter Twenty Years 4
by O. Henry, adapted

*A*n Appointment 12
retold by Edith Wharton

*T*he Tell-Tale Heart 16
by Edgar Allan Poe, adapted

▶ **Learn More About It:** Point of View 25

▶ Chapter 1 Review 26

Chapter 2	Poetry	28

*T*he Tide Rises, the Tide Falls 30
by Henry Wadsworth Longfellow

*T*he Cremation of Sam McGee 34
by Robert W. Service

▶ **Learn More About It:** Yukon Gold 40

*T*he Raven 42
by Edgar Allan Poe

▶ **Learn More About It:** The Raven as a Symbol 53

▶ Chapter 2 Review 54

Chapter 3	Drama	56

*S*orry, Wrong Number 58
by Lucille Fletcher, adapted

▶ Chapter 3 Review 76

UNIT 1 REVIEW 78

UNIT 2	LOOKING BACK	79
Chapter 4	Memoirs	80

The All-American Slurp — 82
by Lensey Namioka

Lame Deer Remembers — 98
by John Fire/Lame Deer and Richard Erdoes, adapted

from Prisoner of My Country — 104
by Yoshiko Uchida, adapted

▶ Learn More About It: Japanese Americans and World War II — 115

▶ Chapter 4 Review — 116

Chapter 5	Short Stories	118

The Jacket — 120
by Gary Soto, adapted

A Day's Wait — 128
by Ernest Hemingway

The Circuit — 136
by Francisco Jiménez, adapted

▶ Learn More About It: Migrant Workers and César Chávez — 147

▶ Chapter 5 Review — 148

UNIT 2 REVIEW	150

UNIT 3	**ACCEPTING A CHALLENGE**	**151**
Chapter 6	**Fiction**	**152**
	Thank You, M'am	154
	by Langston Hughes	
	from *The Red Badge of Courage*	162
	by Stephen Crane, adapted	
▶	**Learn More About It:** Civil War Battlefields	173
▶	Chapter 6 Review	174
Chapter 7	**Poetry**	**176**
	The Ballad of John Henry	178
	anonymous	
▶	**Learn More About It:** American Tall Tales	183
	Harriet Tubman	184
	by Eloise Greenfield	
	O Captain! My Captain!	188
	by Walt Whitman	
	Paul Revere's Ride	192
	by Henry Wadsworth Longfellow	
▶	**Learn More About It:** Paul Revere and the Revolutionary War	201
▶	Chapter 7 Review	202
Chapter 8	**Nonfiction**	**204**
	from *Rosa Parks*	206
	by Eloise Greenfield	
	from *Helen Keller: The Story of My Life*	216
	by Helen Keller, adapted	
	Shipwreck of the Whaleship *Essex*	226
	by Owen Chase	
▶	**Learn More About It:** Sperm Whales	237
▶	Chapter 8 Review	238
UNIT 3 REVIEW		**240**

UNIT 4	CLOSE TO THE EARTH	241
Chapter 9	**Fiction**	**242**

River Man   244
by Teresa Pijoan de Van Etten

A Visit to the Clerk of the Weather   252
by Nathaniel Hawthorne, adapted

from The Call of the Wild   262
by Jack London, adapted

▶ **Learn More About It:** The Yukon   273

▶ Chapter 9 Review   274

Chapter 10	**Poetry**	**276**

The Sky Is Low   278
by Emily Dickinson

in Just-   280
by e.e. cummings

Birdfoot's Grampa   284
by Joseph Bruchac

The Road Not Taken   288
by Robert Frost

▶ Chapter 10 Review   292

UNIT 4 REVIEW   **294**

UNIT 5	THE STRUGGLE WITHIN	295
Chapter 11	**Nonfiction**	**296**

*L*ittle Things Are Big — 298
by Jesus Colon, adapted

from *N*arrative of the Life of Frederick Douglass — 304
by Frederick Douglass, adapted

▶ **Learn More About It:** Slavery on Plantations — 315

▶ Chapter 11 Review — 316

Chapter 12	**Short Stories**	**318**

*A*migo Brothers — 320
by Piri Thomas, adapted

*A*mbush — 330
by Tim O'Brien

▶ **Learn More About It:** The Vietnam War — 337

*R*ibbons — 338
by Laurence Yep, adapted

▶ Chapter Review — 354

Chapter 13	**Poetry**	**356**

*B*allad of Birmingham — 358
by Dudley Randall

*T*aught Me Purple — 362
by Evelyn Tooley Hunt

*S*imple-song — 366
by Marge Piercy

▶ Chapter 13 Review — 370

UNIT 5 REVIEW		**372**

UNIT 6	CLOSE TO THE HEART	373
Chapter 14	Memoirs	374

from Childtimes — 376
by Eloise Greenfield and Lessie Jones Little

▶ **Learn More About It:** Autobiographies
and Memoirs — 385

The Medicine Bag — 386
by Virginia Driving Hawk Sneve

▶ Chapter 14 Review — 402

Chapter 15	Poetry	404

Mother to Son — 406
by Langston Hughes

Lament — 410
by Edna St. Vincent Millay

To My Dear and Loving Husband — 414
by Anne Bradstreet

Housecleaning — 416
by Nikki Giovanni

▶ Chapter 15 Review — 420

UNIT 6 REVIEW — 422

UNIT 7	**DANGER AND ADVENTURE**	**423**
Chapter 16	**Autobiographies**	**424**
	*E*scape! *by James W. C. Pennington, adapted*	426
▶	**Learn More About It:** The Mason-Dixon Line	439
	*A*t **Last I Kill a Buffalo** *by Luther Standing Bear, adapted*	440
▶	Chapter 16 Review	454
Chapter 17	**Short Stories**	**456**
	*T*he **Secret Life of Walter Mitty** *by James Thurber, adapted*	458
▶	**Learn More About It:** Similes and Metaphors	469
	*T*he **Invalid's Story** *by Mark Twain, adapted*	470
▶	Chapter 17 Review	482
UNIT 7 REVIEW		**484**
APPENDIX		**485**
	Glossary of Words to Know	**486**
	Keys to Literature: A Handbook of Literary Terms	**496**
	Index of Authors and Titles	**498**
	Index of Fine Art and Artists	**500**
	Acknowledgments	**501**
	Photo and Illustration Credits	**502**

A Note to the Student

In this book, you will read short stories, poetry, memoirs, a play, and much more. These selections represent the experiences of people from many different cultures and backgrounds. You will meet interesting characters. You will be transported to other times and places. You will read about conflicts big and small. What ties together these selections is that they are part of the tradition of American Literature.

Several features will help you along the way. The **Unit Opener** provides you with a snapshot of what you will be reading. The **Chapter Opener** includes a piece of fine art to help set the mood for the chapter. It also lists the **Learning Objectives** and provides a **Preview Activity**. The **Chapter Review** includes summaries of all of the selections in the chapter, a **Vocabulary Review**, a **Chapter Quiz**, and a **Chapter Activity**. Finally, the **Unit Review** covers all of the selections in the unit.

For each selection, you will find a **Before You Read** page. It introduces the **Keys to Literature** with examples, as well as the **Words to Know**. The **Did You Know?** feature will help you build your background knowledge.

As you read each selection, you will find side-column notes that will help you set a purpose for reading, make predictions, understand the Keys to Literature, define confusing words, and think about important questions. In addition, illustrations and photographs visually "tell the story."

For each selection, you will also find an **After You Read** page. It asks key questions to help you think about the selection you just read. In addition, **Learn More About It** pages give you interesting information about something you just read.

We hope you enjoy reading this collection of American Literature. Everyone who put this book together worked hard to make it useful, interesting, and enjoyable. We wish you well in your studies. Our success is in your accomplishment.

Unit 1 ▶ The Strange and Unexpected

Chapter 1 Short Stories

After Twenty Years
by O. Henry, adapted

An Appointment
retold by Edith Wharton

The Tell-Tale Heart
by Edgar Allan Poe, adapted

Chapter 2 Poetry

The Tide Rises, the Tide Falls
by Henry Wadsworth Longfellow

The Cremation of Sam McGee
by Robert W. Service

The Raven
by Edgar Allan Poe

Chapter 3 Drama

Sorry, Wrong Number
by Lucille Fletcher, adapted

Street in Severne by James Abbott McNeill Whistler (1834–1903)

What might happen here? If this were the setting for a story, would it be a mystery? A love story? A horror story? A funny story? Explain.

Learning Objectives

- Understand what a short story is.
- Recognize a story's setting and mood.
- Recognize personification.
- Understand the meaning of irony.
- Recognize who a story's narrator is.
- Identify the first-person point of view.

Preview Activity

Think of something surprising that happened to you. How would you tell the story? Would you save the surprise for the end? List the things that happen in your story. Put them in the order you would tell them. Then, tell your story to someone.

Short Stories and Suspense

A short story is made up from the writer's imagination. It usually has only a few characters and takes place over a short period of time. Short stories all have the following three elements:

characters: the people (or animals) in the story

setting: the place and time of the story

plot: the action or events of the story

In a short story of suspense, the author keeps you wondering what is going to happen next. When the end comes, it is often surprising.

Keys to Literature

mood: the feeling you get from reading a story

> Example: *Chilly gusts of wind with a taste of rain* suggests a gloomy mood.

setting: the time and place of a story

> Example: This story takes place around 10 o'clock at night on a deserted street in New York.

Did You Know?

Policemen "on the beat" work the same area every day. In the early 1900s, the police in New York City often walked the beat alone. Today, the police often ride in cars with partners.

Words to Know

spectators	people who watch something without taking part
intricate	complicated; hard to understand
guardian	protector
reassuringly	in a convincing way
moderately	to do something somewhat, but not too much
submerged	hidden or buried
simultaneously	at the same time

After Twenty Years

BY O. HENRY, *Adapted*

The policeman on the beat moved up the avenue impressively. The way he walked was from habit, and not for show, because **spectators** were few. The time was barely 10 o'clock at night, but chilly gusts of wind with a taste of rain in them had nearly emptied the streets.

Trying doors as he went, twirling his club with many **intricate** and artful movements, turning now and then to cast his watchful eye down the quiet street, the officer made a fine picture of a **guardian** of the peace. The area was one that kept early hours. Now and then you might see the lights of a cigar store or of an all-night lunch counter, but the majority of the business places had long since closed for the night.

READ TO FIND OUT...
What surprise will each friend get after twenty years?

Keys to Literature

Notice how the phrases "chilly gusts of wind" and "a taste of rain" create a sad, gloomy **mood**.

About midway down a certain block, the policeman suddenly slowed his walk. In the doorway of a darkened hardware store, a man leaned, with an unlighted cigar in his mouth. As the policeman walked up to him, the man spoke up quickly.

"It's all right, officer," he said **reassuringly**. "I'm just waiting for a friend. It's an appointment made twenty years ago. Sounds a little funny to you, doesn't it? Well, I'll explain if you'd like to make certain it's all right. About that long ago there used to be a restaurant where this store stands—'Big Joe' Brady's restaurant."

"Until five years ago," said the policeman. "It was torn down then."

The man in the doorway struck a match and lit his cigar. The light showed a pale, square-jawed face with keen eyes, and a little white scar near his right eyebrow. His scarfpin was a large diamond, oddly set.

"Twenty years ago tonight," said the man. "I dined here at 'Big Joe' Brady's with Jimmy Wells, my best friend and the finest chap in the world. He and I were raised here in New York, just like two brothers, together. I was eighteen, and Jimmy was twenty. The next morning, I was to start for the West to make my fortune. You couldn't have dragged Jimmy out of New York—he thought it was the only place on earth. Well, we agreed that night that we would meet again in this spot exactly twenty years from that date and time, no matter what our conditions might be or from what distance we might have to come. We figured that in twenty years each of us ought to have his destiny worked out and his fortune made, whatever they were going to be."

"It sounds pretty interesting," said the policeman. "Rather a long time between meetings, though, it seems to me. Haven't you heard from your friend since you left?"

Keys to Literature

What is the **setting** of this story? Where and when does it take place?

Predict

What has happened in the story so far? What do you think will happen next?

"Well, yes, we corresponded for a time," said the other. "But after a year or two, we lost track of each other. You see, the West is a pretty big place, and I kept hustling around it pretty lively. But I know Jimmy will meet me here if he's alive, for he always was the truest, most loyal chap in the world. He'll never forget. I came a thousand miles to stand in this doorway tonight, and it's worth it if my old partner turns up."

The waiting man pulled out a handsome pocket-watch, its lid set with small diamonds.

"It's three minutes to ten," he announced. "It was at exactly ten o'clock when we parted here at the restaurant door."

"Did pretty well out West, did you?" asked the policeman.

"You bet! I hope Jimmy has done half as well. He was a kind of plodder, though, good fellow as he was. I've had to compete with some of the sharpest wits going to get my pile. A man gets in a groove in New York. It takes the West to put a razor-edge on him."

The policeman twirled his club and took a step or two away.

"I'll be on my way. Hope your friend comes around all right. Going to call time on him sharp?"

"I should say not!" said the other. "I'll give him half an hour at least. If Jimmy is alive on earth, he'll be here by that time. So long, officer."

"Good night, sir," said the policeman, passing on along his beat, trying doors as he went.

There was now a fine, cold drizzle falling, and the wind had risen from its uncertain puffs into a steady blow. The few people moving about in that quarter hurried dismally and silently along with coat collars turned high and pocketed hands. And in the door of the hardware store, the man who had come a thousand

Keys to Literature

What words and phrases continue to create a sad, gloomy **mood**?

miles to keep an uncertain appointment with the friend of his youth, smoked his cigar and waited.

After he waited about twenty minutes more, a tall man in a long overcoat, with the collar turned up to his ears, hurried across from the opposite side of the street. He went directly to the waiting man.

"Is that you, Bob?" he asked doubtfully.

"Is that you, Jimmy Wells?" cried the man waiting in the door.

"Bless my heart!" exclaimed the new arrival, grasping both the other's hands with his own. "It's Bob, sure as fate. I was certain I'd find you here if you were still in existence. Well, well, well! Twenty years is a long time. The old restaurant's gone, Bob, but I wish it had lasted, so we could have had another dinner there. How has the West treated you, old man?"

"It has given me everything I asked it for. You've changed lots, Jimmy. I never thought you were so tall by two or three inches."

"Oh, I grew a bit after I was twenty."

"Doing well in New York, Jimmy?"

"**Moderately**. I have a position in one of the city departments. Come on, Bob. We'll go around to a place I know and have a good long talk about old times."

The two men started up the street, arm in arm. The man from the West, his confidence enlarged by success, was beginning to outline the history of his career. The other, **submerged** in his overcoat, listened to the story with interest.

At the corner stood a drug store, brilliant with electric lights. When they came into the glare of the lights, each of them turned **simultaneously** to gaze upon the other's face.

Predict

O. Henry is known for his surprise endings. What do you think the surprise will be?

The man from the West stopped suddenly and
released his arm.

"You're not Jimmy Wells," he snapped. "Twenty
years is a long time, but not long enough to change a
man's nose from a Roman to a pug."

"It sometimes changes a good man into a bad one,"
said the tall man. "You've been under arrest for ten
minutes, 'Silky' Bob. Chicago thinks you may have
dropped over our way and wires us she wants to have a
chat with you. Going quietly, are you? That's sensible.
Now, before we go on to the station, here's a note I was
asked to hand you. You may read it here at the
window. It's from Patrolman Wells."

▶ Why do you think Bob's hand trembled a little when he read Jimmy's note?

The man from the West unfolded the little piece of paper handed him. His hand was steady when he began to read, but it trembled a little by the time he had finished. The note was rather short.

Bob: I was at the appointed place on time. When you struck the match to light your cigar, I saw it was the face of the man wanted in Chicago. Somehow I couldn't do it myself, so I went around and got a plain-clothes man to do the job.

"JIMMY."

Meet the Author

O. HENRY *(1862–1910)*

O. Henry's real name was William Sydney Porter. He took the name O. Henry when he started writing short stories. He had very little schooling. As an adult, he was a ranch hand and a bank teller before becoming a writer.

O. Henry is famous for his surprise endings, and his own life was full of surprises, too. He was an editor and a prisoner at the same time. He began writing short stories while in jail and eventually wrote more than 600 of them. Two of O. Henry's most famous short stories are "The Ransom of Red Chief" and "The Gift of the Magi."

Check Your Predictions

1. Look back at the answers you gave for the Predict questions. Would you change your answers? Explain.

Understand the Story

2. How do Jimmy and Bob first get to know each other?

3. When does Jimmy figure out who the man from the West really is?

4. Why does Jimmy send the plainclothes man over to Bob?

Think About the Story

5. Why do you think Jimmy sends the note to Bob?

6. Jimmy and Bob had once been best friends. Do you think that Jimmy should have had Bob arrested, or should he have let Bob go free? Why?

7. What words and phrases from the story help you determine the story's setting?

8. What kind of mood does O. Henry create in this story? Give examples from the story.

Extend Your Response

Create a "Wanted" poster for the arrest of 'Silky' Bob. Include information from the story about his appearance, why he is wanted, and where he is wanted. Use your imagination to provide other details. Include a sketch of Bob.

Keys to Literature

personification: giving human characteristics to something that is not human

> Example: *And when Death saw me, he raised his arms ...*

irony: a result that is the opposite of what is expected

> Example: In "An Appointment," the youth tries to escape Death but actually goes to meet him.

Did You Know?

This story takes place long ago when a sultan ruled the Middle Eastern city of Damascus. Now, Damascus is the capital of Syria. Baghdad was another important city in the old Middle East. Today, it is the capital of Iraq.

Words to Know

alarmed	very frightened; afraid
youth	a young person
fly	move quickly
thundered	moved noisily
astonished	greatly surprised; amazed

An Appointment

RETOLD BY EDITH WHARTON

READ TO FIND OUT...
What is the appointment?

One morning the Sultan was resting in his palace in Damascus. Suddenly the door flew open, and in rushed a young man, out of breath and wild with excitement. The Sultan sat up **alarmed**, for the young man was his most skillful assistant.

"I must have your best horse!" the **youth** cried out. "There is little time! I must **fly** at once to Baghdad!"

The Sultan asked why the young man was in such a rush.

"Because," came the hurried reply, "just now, as I was walking in the palace garden, I saw Death standing there. And when Death saw me, he raised his arms in a frightening motion. Oh, it was horrible! I must escape at once!"

Keys to Literature

In this story, Death is a person. This is an example of **personification**.

Albert Pinkham Ryder 1847–1917. *The Race Track (Death on a Pale Horse)*, Oil on canvas, ca. 1886–1908, 70.5 x 90 cm. © The Cleveland Museum of Art, Purchase from the J.H. Wade Fund, 1928.8.

The Sultan quickly arranged for the youth to have his fastest horse. And no sooner had the young man **thundered** out through the palace gate, than the Sultan himself went into the garden. Death was still there.

The Sultan was angry. "What do you mean?" he demanded. "What do you mean by raising your arms and frightening my young friend?"

"Your Majesty," Death said calmly, "I did not mean to frighten him. You see, I raised my arms only in surprise. I was **astonished** to see him here in your garden, for I have an appointment with him tonight in Baghdad."

$\mathcal{M}$eet the $\mathcal{A}$uthor

EDITH WHARTON (1862–1937)

Edith Wharton was born into a wealthy New York family. As a child, she was home-schooled, and she read books from her father's huge library. As an adult, she traveled a great deal and shared ideas with famous writers of the time. She even met President Theodore Roosevelt.

Many of Wharton's novels and short stories are about wealthy New Yorkers. She describes the things they do and the thoughts behind their actions. *Ethan Frome* and *The Age of Innocence* are among her most famous books.

Check Your Predictions

1. Look back at the answers you gave for the Predict question. Would you change your answer? Explain.

Understand the Story

2. Where does the youth see Death?

3. What does Death do when he sees the youth? Why?

4. Why did the youth want a horse?

Think About the Story

5. Why is the Sultan angry with Death?

6. Do you think the youth knows that he has an appointment with Death in Baghdad? How do you know?

7. Wharton uses irony to create an unexpected ending to the story. What happens? Why is it ironic?

8. What effect does personifying Death have on the story?

Extend Your Response

Draw a picture or diagram of the garden. Think about where the youth was standing. Think about where Death was standing. Then, use your picture to describe what happened in the garden.

Keys to Literature

narrator: the person telling the story

> Example: When you tell a story, you are the narrator.

first-person point of view: a story character tells the story, using *I* to refer to himself or herself

> Example: *Finally, I led them to his room.*

Did You Know?

You probably use the word **mad** to mean angry. In this story, *mad* means "crazy or insane." The person telling the story explains again and again that he is not mad. He says he is perfectly sane.

Words to Know

haunted	came back again and again, often in a scary way
passion	a very strong or deep feeling
vulture	a bird of prey
film	a thin coat of something
triumph	an important success
shutters	wooden window covers that swing open and shut
muffled	less loud, as if covered up
furious	very angry
intense	very strong
seized	grabbed suddenly
corpse	a dead body
foul play	dishonest behavior; murder
paced	walked back and forth again and again

The Tell-Tale Heart

BY EDGAR ALLAN POE, *Adapted*

READ TO FIND OUT...
Why would a killer suddenly confess to the police?

Nervous—very, very nervous I had been and am. But why do you say that I am mad? The disease had sharpened my senses—not destroyed or dulled them. Especially sharp was the sense of hearing. I heard all things in heaven and on earth. I heard many things in hell. How, then, am I mad? Listen! See how clearly and calmly I can tell you the whole story.

It is impossible to say how the idea first entered my brain. But once it was born, it **haunted** me day and night. There was no reason for it. There was no **passion** to it. I loved the old man. He had never wronged me. He had never insulted me. I had no desire for his gold.

I think it was his eye! Yes, it was this! He had the eye of a **vulture**. It was a pale blue eye with a **film** over it. Whenever it looked at me, my blood ran cold. And so very gradually I made up my mind to take the life of the old man. This way I would be rid of the eye forever.

Now this is the point. You think I am mad. Madmen know nothing. But you should have seen *me*. You should have seen how wisely, how carefully I went to work. I was never kinder to the old man than during the whole week before I killed him. Every night, about midnight, I turned his door knob. I opened his door—oh, so gently.

Keys to Literature

The man telling the story calls himself *I*. He is the story's **narrator**.

Predict

For seven nights the narrator has done the same thing. What has he done? What do you think he will do on the eighth night?

The opening I made was large enough for my head. I put in a dark lantern, all closed, so that no light shone out. Then I thrust in my head. You would have laughed to see how smartly I thrust it in! I moved it very, very slowly so that I might not disturb the old man's sleep. Ha!—Would a madman have been so wise as this?

Then, when I was in the room, I undid the lantern carefully—oh, so carefully. I undid it just enough so that a single thin ray fell upon the vulture eye. This I did for seven long nights—every night just at midnight. But I found the eye always closed. So it was impossible to do the work. For it was not the old man that annoyed me, but his Evil Eye.

Every morning, when day broke, I went boldly into his room. I spoke bravely to him. I called him by his first name in a friendly tone and asked how he had passed the night. So he would have been a very smart man indeed to suspect what I did every night at midnight.

On the eighth night I was more careful than ever in opening the door. Never before that night had I *felt* the strength of my powers—of my wisdom. I could hardly hold in my feelings of **triumph**. There I had been opening the door little by little each night. He did not even dream of my secret deeds or thoughts.

I almost laughed at the idea, and perhaps he heard me. For he moved on the bed suddenly, as if he were startled. Now you may think that I drew back—but no. His room was pitch black, for the **shutters** were closed. So I knew he could not see the opening of the door. I kept pushing it open steadily, steadily.

I had my head in. I was about to open the lantern, when my thumb slipped on the tin fastening. The old man sprang up in the bed and cried out, "Who's there?"

I kept quite still and said nothing. For a whole hour I did not move a muscle. During that hour I did not hear him lie down. He was sitting up in the bed listening.

Soon, I heard a slight groan. It was not a groan of pain or of grief. Oh, no! It was the low, **muffled** sound that comes up from the soul when it is filled with fear. I knew the sound well. Many a night, just at midnight, it had welled up from my own chest. With its awful echo, it deepened the terrors that disturbed me. I knew what the old man felt, and I pitied him, although I chuckled at heart.

I waited a long time without hearing him lie down. I decided to make a slight opening in the lantern. I did so quietly—you cannot imagine how quietly. Finally, a single dim ray shot out from the opening and fell upon the vulture eye.

Think About It

How does the old man know that someone is in the room with him?

The eye was open, wide open. I grew **furious** as I gazed upon it. I saw it perfectly. It was a dull blue, with a disgusting film over it that chilled my very bones. But I could see nothing else of the old man's body. For I had directed the light right upon the spot.

I have told you that what you mistake for madness is a sharpness of my senses. Now I say that what came to my ears was a low, dull, quick sound. It was a sound such as a watch makes when it is covered with cotton. I knew that sound well, too. It was the beating of the old man's heart. It increased my fury, as the beating of the drum stirs the soldier's courage.

Yet, I kept still. I hardly breathed. I did not move the lantern. I tried to hold the ray of light steadily upon the eye. Meantime the horrible beating of the heart continued. It grew quicker and quicker, and louder and louder. The old man's terror must have been rather **intense**.

It grew louder, I say, louder every moment! Do you hear me? I told you that I am nervous. So I am. Now at this dead hour of the night, in the awful silence of that old house, this strange noise excited me to great terror. The beating grew louder, louder! I thought the heart would burst.

Now a new worry **seized** me. The sound would soon be heard by a neighbor! The old man's hour had come. With a loud yell, I threw open the lantern and jumped into the room.

He cried out once—only once. In an instant, I dragged him to the floor and pulled the heavy bed over him. I then smiled happily to find the deed done. But for many minutes the heart beat on with a muffled sound. This, however, did not bother me. It would not be heard through the wall. Finally it stopped. The old man was dead.

I removed the bed and examined the **corpse**. Yes, he was stone dead. I placed my hand upon the heart and

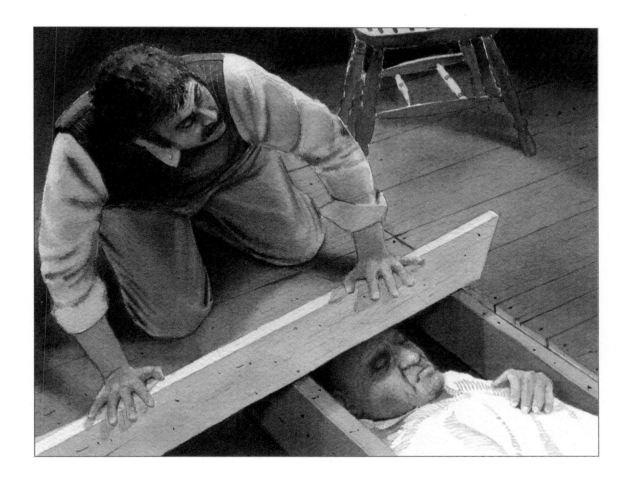

held it there for many minutes. There was no pulse. He was dead. His eye would trouble me no more.

Do you still think me mad? You will think so no longer when I describe how I hid the body. I worked quickly, but in silence. I took up three planks from the floor. Then I placed the body under the boards and replaced them. I did this so cleverly that no human eye—not even his—could have found anything wrong.

When I had finished, it was four o'clock, still dark as midnight. There came a knocking at the street door. I went down to open it with a light heart. For what had I *now* to fear?

Predict

Now that the police have
come, what do you think
the narrator will do?

Three men entered. They introduced themselves as
officers of the police. A cry had been heard by a
neighbor during the night. Someone suspected **foul
play**. The police had been called, and these men were
ordered to search the house.

I smiled, for *what* had I to fear? The cry, I said, was
my own in a dream. The old man, I said, was away in
the country. I took my visitors all over the house. I told
them to search—search well.

Finally, I led them to *his* room. I showed them his
treasures, safe and secure. I brought chairs into the
room and told them to rest *here*. I placed myself in a
chair above the very spot where the victim was buried!

The officers were satisfied. I was at ease. They sat
and talked of familiar things. But before long, I felt
myself getting pale and wished them gone. My head
ached, and I thought I heard a ringing in my ears. The
ringing became clearer. I talked more freely to get rid of
the sound. But it continued. Finally, I found that the
noise was not within my ears.

The sound increased—and what could I do? It was *a low, dull, quick sound, much like a watch makes when it is covered with cotton.* I gasped for breath—yet the officers did not hear it. I talked more quickly, more forcefully. But the noise steadily increased.

I **paced** the floor. But the noise steadily increased. Oh, God! What could I do? I swung the chair upon which I had been sitting and scraped it upon the boards. But the noise continued.

It grew louder—louder—*louder!* And still the men talked pleasantly. Was it possible they did not hear it? No! They heard. They suspected. They *knew.* They were making a fool of me.

Anything was better than this agony! I could bear those awful smiles no longer. I felt I must scream or die! And now again, listen! louder! louder! *louder!*

"Villains!" I cried. "Search no more! I admit the deed. Tear up the planks! Here—here! It is the beating of his awful heart!"

Think About It

Do you think the police officers could hear the beating of the heart?

Think About It

Is "The Tell-Tale Heart" a good title for this story? Explain.

Meet the Author

EDGAR ALLAN POE *(1809–1849)*

Edgar Allan Poe lived a sad life. He was often unhappy and had little money. When his wife, Virginia, died at the age of 25, Poe had a mental breakdown. He became ill, drank too much, and died two years later at the age of 40.

Poe's stories are famous for horror, strange plots, and surprise endings. His characters often suffer from mental illness. Among his most famous short stories are "The Black Cat," "The Pit and the Pendulum," and "The Tell-Tale Heart."

Check Your Predictions

1. Look back at the answers you gave to the Predict questions. Would you change your answers? Explain.

Understand the Story

2. What does the narrator do in the old man's room each night?

3. Why does the narrator decide to kill the old man?

4. How does the narrator hide the body?

Think About the Story

5. The narrator explains that he is sane. Why would you suspect that he is not?

6. Why do you think that the narrator believes that the police know what he did?

7. Why do you think the narrator tells the police that he has killed the old man?

8. What if this story was not told from the narrator's point of view? What if someone else told it? Explain.

Extend Your Response

Write a headline and the first paragraph of a news article about the murder that took place in this story. Include the answers to the questions Who? What? When? Where? Why? and How? Use your imagination to supply any missing information.

Learn More About It

POINT OF VIEW

When you tell a story about something that happened to you, you use the words *I* and *we*. You explain how it felt to be there. You tell the story from your point of view.

Since you are the person telling the story, you are the narrator, and since you are using *I* and *we*, you are telling it from the first-person point of view.

When you tell a story about something that happened to other people—something you have heard about or read about—you use the words *he*, *she*, and *they*.

You are still the narrator, since you are telling the story, but this time you are telling it from the third-person point of view. You are no longer telling what you did or how you felt about it.

Apply and Connect

Which story in this chapter is told from the **first-person** point of view? Which stories are told from the third-person point of view?

First-person point of view

Third-person point of view

Summaries

After Twenty Years Two friends, Bob and Jimmy, had planned to meet after twenty years. Twenty years have passed. Bob is waiting. A policeman comes, talks to Bob, and walks away. Then, another man comes to meet him. Bob finds out that the man is not Jimmy. The man arrests Bob. The policeman had been Jimmy, but he could not arrest his old friend.

An Appointment The Sultan's assistant is upset at seeing Death in the garden in Damascus. He begs the Sultan to help him escape to Baghdad. When the Sultan asks Death why he scared the assistant, Death says he had been surprised to see the assistant there, since he had an appointment with him in Baghdad that night.

The Tell-Tale Heart A narrator says that an old man's evil eye is driving him to murder. He kills the old man and hides the body under the floorboards. When the police come, the narrator believes he hears the old man's heart beating loudly. He thinks the police can hear it, too, so he confesses to the murder.

thundered
spectators
seized
intense
submerged
alarmed

Vocabulary Review

Match each word in the box with its meaning. Write the word and its matching number on a separate sheet of paper.

1. onlookers
2. moved noisily
3. grabbed suddenly
4. frightened
5. hidden or covered over
6. very strong

Chapter Quiz

Answer the following questions in one or two complete sentences. Use a separate sheet of paper.

1. After Twenty Years Why doesn't Bob realize that the policeman is actually his friend Jimmy?

2. After Twenty Years How does Bob finally realize that the man he thought was Jimmy is not really him?

3. An Appointment Why does the young man need the Sultan's fastest horse?

4. An Appointment What is the difference between the way the young man and the Sultan feel about Death?

5. The Tell-Tale Heart Why does the narrator hate the old man?

6. The Tell-Tale Heart How do the policemen find out who murdered the old man?

Critical Thinking

7. After Twenty Years How would the story be different if it was written from the first-person point of view? What new information might we learn?

8. The Tell-Tale Heart The narrator constantly tells us he is not mad. Why do you think he does that?

Chapter Activity

Write a "Who Am I?" riddle to describe one of the characters in this chapter. Include three clues about the character. Use words that tell how the person looks, sounds, and feels. Write your riddle in the first person. For example, a riddle could begin, "I am nervous, but I am not crazy."

Illustration from "The Salem Wolf" by Howard Pyle (1853–1911)

What unexpected thing has happened to this man?

Chapter 2 ▷ Poetry

THE STRANGE AND UNEXPECTED

Learning Objectives

- Understand what a poem is.
- Identify the stanzas of a poem.
- Identify rhyme in a poem.
- Recognize the meter of a poem.
- Understand the story in a narrative poem.
- Analyze the rhyme scheme of a poem.
- Identify repetition in a poem.
- Recognize alliteration.

Preview Activity

Think of a song that has words or phrases that are repeated over and over. What kind of mood do they create? With a partner, make a list of these words and phrases. Share them with others. If you wish, perform the song. Ask others to decide what the mood is.

Poetry and the Unexpected

A poem is arranged in separate lines on a page. Poems often have rhythm and sometimes rhyme. The words are colorful and strong. They help create strong images, and they stir up feelings in the reader.

In many poems about strange and unexpected things, the poet sets a mood by doing the following things:

- repeating words and phrases over and over
- creating a rhythm
- using words in unexpected ways

Keys to Literature

rhyme: words that sound alike

Example: *falls* and *calls; brown* and *town*

stanza: a group of lines in a poem set apart from other groups of lines

Example: The poem on the opposite page has three stanzas.

Did You Know?

The rise and fall of the tides is caused by the pull of the Moon's and the Sun's gravity. This takes place twice a day. In some places on Earth, the difference between high and low tide can be very great.

Words to Know

hastens	hurries
efface	wipe out, erase
steeds	horses
stamp	to bring one's foot down hard

The Tide Rises, the Tide Falls

BY HENRY WADSWORTH LONGFELLOW

READ TO FIND OUT...
What happens to
the traveler?

The tide rises, the tide falls,
The twilight darkens, the curlew calls;
Along the sea-sands damp and brown
The traveler **hastens** toward the town,
5   And the tide rises, the tide falls.

Darkness settles on roofs and walls,
But the sea, the sea in the darkness calls;
The little waves, with their soft, white hands,
Efface the footprints in the sands,
10   And the tide rises, the tide falls.

The morning breaks; the **steeds** in their stalls
Stamp and neigh, as the hostler calls;
The day returns, but nevermore
Returns the traveler to the shore,
15   And the tide rises, the tide falls.

Keys to Literature

What words **rhyme** in
the third and fourth
lines of each stanza?

Each **stanza** ends with
the same line. This
shows that nature
keeps repeating itself
endlessly.

Meet the Author

HENRY WADSWORTH LONGFELLOW *(1807–1882)*

Longfellow was America's most popular poet ever! His fans looked forward to each new poem he wrote, and his works were translated into dozens of languages. For many years, Longfellow taught at Harvard University. After that, he wrote poetry full-time.

Longfellow loved to write about American history. His long poems such as *The Song of Hiawatha* and *Evangeline* show how he taught history through poetry. In telling about America's past, Longfellow included plenty of action and romance.

Understand the Poem

1. What time of day is it when the poem begins?

2. Where is the traveler going?

3. What time of day is it when the poem ends?

4. In Line 8, what has *soft, white hands*?

Think About the Poem

5. In Stanza 2, the traveler's footprints are quickly washed away. What do you think this means?

6. Why do you think the traveler does not return to the shore?

7. How many stanzas are there in this poem? How do you know?

8. Which lines in each stanza of the poem rhyme?

Extend Your Response

Do you think it is important for people to leave footprints on the sands of time? What would you like other people to remember about you? Make a list of three things you would like to achieve in your life. Number your list in order from the most important to the least important.

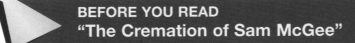
Keys to Literature

narrative poem: a poem that tells a story

Example: The "Cremation of Sam McGee" tells the story of something that happened in the Far North.

meter: the rhythm, or beat, of a poem

Example: *The Arctic **trails** have their secret **tales***

Words to Know

cremated	burned a dead body
mushing	traveling on a sled pulled by dogs
whimper	whine or cry
heed	pay attention to
ghastly	awfully
brawn	strength
loathed	hated
grub	food
harkened	listened
derelict	something left behind or thrown away
trice	a very short time; a moment
grisly	terrifying; horrible

The Cremation of Sam McGee

BY ROBERT W. SERVICE

READ TO FIND OUT...
What is strange about Sam McGee's cremation?

There are strange things done in the midnight sun
    By the men who moil for gold;
The Arctic trails have their secret tales
    That would make your blood run cold;
5 The Northern Lights have seen queer sights,
    But the queerest they ever did see
Was that night on the marge of Lake Lebarge
    I **cremated** Sam McGee.

Keys to Literature

A **narrative poem** tells a story. Line 4 hints that this poem tells a story that will make our blood run cold.

Now Sam McGee was from Tennessee,
10   where the cotton blooms and blows.
Why he left his home in the South to roam
      'round the Pole, God only knows.
He was always cold, but the land of gold
      seemed to hold him like a spell;
15 Though he'd often say in his homely way
      that "he'd sooner live in hell."

Think About It

What words and
phrases in this stanza
help you feel the cold
of the Yukon?

On a Christmas Day we were **mushing** our way
      over the Dawson trail.
Talk of your cold! Through the parka's fold
20   it stabbed like a driven nail.
If our eyes we'd close, then the lashes froze
      till sometimes we couldn't see;
It wasn't much fun, but the only one
      to **whimper** was Sam McGee.

25 And that very night, as we lay packed tight
      in our robes beneath the snow,
And the dogs were fed, and the stars o'erhead
      were dancing heel and toe,
He turned to me, and "Cap," says he,
30   "I'll cash in this trip, I guess;
And if I do, I'm asking that you
      won't refuse my last request."

Predict

What do you think
Sam McGee's last
request will be?

Well, he seemed so low that I couldn't say no;
      then he says with a sort of moan:
35 "It's the cursèd cold, and it's got right hold
      till I'm chilled clean through to the bone.
Yet 'tain't being dead—it's my awful dread
      of the icy grave that pains;
So I want you to swear that, foul or fair,
40   you'll cremate my last remains."

A pal's last need is a thing to **heed**,
    so I swore I would not fail;
And we started on at the streak of dawn;
    but God! he looked **ghastly** pale.
45 He crouched on the sleigh, and he raved all day
    of his home in Tennessee;
And before nightfall a corpse was all
    that was left of Sam McGee.

There wasn't a breath in that land of death,
50   and I hurried, horror driven,
With a corpse half hid that I couldn't get rid,
    because of a promise given;
It was lashed to the sleigh, and it seemed to say:
    "You may tax your **brawn** and brains,
55 But you promised true, and it's up to you
    to cremate those last remains."

Now a promise made is a debt unpaid,
    and the trail has its own stern code.
In the days to come, though my lips were dumb,
60   in my heart how I cursed that load.
In the long, long night, by the lone firelight,
    while the huskies, round in a ring,
Howled out their woes to the homeless snows—
    O God! how I **loathed** the thing.

65 And every day that quiet clay
    seemed to heavy and heavier grow;
And on I went, though the dogs were spent
    and the **grub** was getting low;
The trail was bad, and I felt half mad,
70   but I swore I would not give in;
And I'd often sing to the hateful thing,
    and it **harkened** with a grin.

> **Keys to Literature**
>
> Read aloud this stanza of the poem. Some words are spoken louder than others. This creates the beat, or rhythm in a poem. The regular rhythm of a poem is called its **meter**.

Keys to Literature

Like a story, a **narrative poem** has characters and a plot. In this poem, the plot involves what to do with Sam's body. How do you think the problem will be solved?

Till I came to the marge of Lake Lebarge,
    and a **derelict** there lay;
75 It was jammed in the ice, but I saw in a **trice**
    it was called the "Alice May."
And I looked at it, and I thought a bit,
    and I looked at my frozen chum;
Then "Here," said I, with a sudden cry,
80   "is my cre-ma-tor-eum."

Some planks I tore from the cabin floor,
    and I lit the boiler fire;
Some coal I found that was lying around,
    and I heaped the fuel higher;
85 The flames just soared, and the furnace roared—
    such a blaze you seldom see;
And I burrowed a hole in the glowing coal,
    and I stuffed in Sam McGee.

Then I made a hike, for I didn't like
90   to hear him sizzle so;
And the heavens scowled, and the huskies howled,
        and the wind began to blow.
It was icy cold, but the hot sweat rolled
        down my cheeks, and I don't know why;
95 And the greasy smoke in an inky cloak
        went streaking down the sky.

I do not know how long in the snow
        I wrestled with **grisly** fear;
But the stars came out and they danced about
100   ere again I ventured near;
I was sick with dread, but I bravely said:
        "I'll just take a peep inside.
I guess he's cooked, and it's time I looked,"
        … then the door I opened wide.

105 And there sat Sam, looking cool and calm,
        in the heart of the furnace roar;
And he wore a smile you could see a mile,
        and he said: "Please close that door.
It's fine in here, but I greatly fear
110   you'll let in the cold and storm—
Since I left Plumtree, down in Tennessee,
        it's the first time I've been warm."

There are strange things done in the midnight sun
        By the men who moil for gold;
115 The Arctic trails have their secret tales
        That would make your blood run cold;
The Northern Lights have seen queer sights,
        But the queerest they ever did see
Was that night on the marge of Lake Lebarge
120   I cremated Sam McGee.

Predict

What will Sam's friend
see when he looks
inside the furnace door?

Think About It

Why is Sam happy
at last?

Meet the Author

ROBERT W. SERVICE *(1874–1958)*

Robert W. Service moved to the Yukon in Northwestern Canada in 1894 when there was a gold rush. Service was not a gold miner, though. He worked in a bank. Service liked to listen to the miners' tall tales. He then turned some of them into colorful poems. "The Cremation of Sam McGee" is his most famous poem.

After the gold rush, Service left the Yukon. He traveled all over the world. His poems about his travels are called *Tales of a Rolling Stone*. During World War I, Service drove an ambulance. He wrote poems about that experience, too.

Learn More About It

YUKON GOLD

It is a warm summer day in 1897. You are standing by the docks of Seattle, Washington. A group of men gets off a ship. They are pulling heavy bags full of gold!

This really happened. These men were returning from the gold fields of the Yukon Territory in Canada. They announced to the world that the rivers there were filled with gold.

Thousands of men and women all over the country quit their jobs and went to Canada. They wanted to return home with heavy bags of gold. By the time the gold-seekers made it to the Yukon, most of the land was already claimed. Many people suffered—like Sam McGee—because they were not prepared for life in the Far North.

Check Your Predictions

1. Look back at the answers you gave for the Predict questions. Would you change your answers? Explain.

Understand the Poem

2. Where does this poem take place?

3. What does Sam ask his friend Cap to do? Why?

4. How does Cap cremate Sam's body?

Think About the Poem

5. What struggle does Sam's friend Cap have in this poem?

6. How does Cap feel about carrying out Sam's last request?

7. As a narrative poem, does "The Cremation of Sam McGee" tell a serious or comic story? Explain.

8. How would you describe the meter, or rhythm, of this poem? What sort of feeling does it create?

Extend Your Response

Retell the story of Sam McGee as a comic strip. Draw five pictures that show the key scenes. Write short captions that explain what happens in each scene.

Keys to Literature

rhyme scheme: the pattern of words that sound alike

Example: In "The Raven," the last words in Lines 4, 8, 10, and 11 of each stanza create a rhyme scheme.

repetition: words or sentences used over and over to create a feeling or mood

Example: The word *Nevermore* is repeated at the end of most stanzas in the poem.

alliteration: repeating the same consonant sound

Example: *While I nodded, nearly napping,*

Did You Know?

This is one of the most famous poems in American Literature. It has been translated into other languages and illustrated by famous artists.

Words to Know

dreary	gloomy and dull; depressing
quaint	old-fashioned; out of date
bleak	not cheerful; harsh, cold, and cutting
surcease	end
entreating	asking
implore	beg for; ask for in a serious way
mortals	human beings
token	sign
obeisance	a sign of respect, such as a bow
pallid	pale or light in color

The Raven

BY EDGAR ALLAN POE

READ TO FIND OUT...
What is the only word the Raven says?

Once upon a midnight **dreary**, while I pondered,
    weak and weary,
Over many a **quaint** and curious volume of forgotten
    lore—
5 While I nodded, nearly napping, suddenly there came
    a tapping,
As of someone gently rapping, rapping at my
    chamber door.
"'Tis some visitor," I muttered, "tapping at my
10   chamber door—
          Only this, and nothing more."

Keys to Literature

Each stanza of this poem has eleven lines. The last words in the fourth, fifth, tenth, and eleventh lines all rhyme. This is the poem's **rhyme scheme**. Which words rhyme in this stanza?

Ah, distinctly I remember it was in the **bleak**
    December,
And each separate dying ember wrought its ghost
15   upon the floor.
Eagerly I wished the morrow;—vainly I had tried to
    borrow
From my books **surcease** of sorrow—sorrow for the
    lost Lenore—
20 For the rare and radiant maiden whom the angels
    name Lenore—
            Nameless here for evermore.

And the silken sad uncertain rustling of each purple
    curtain
25 Thrilled me—filled me with fantastic terrors never felt
    before;
So that now, to still the beating of my heart, I stood
    repeating:
"'Tis some visitor **entreating** entrance at my
30   chamber door—
Some late visitor entreating entrance at my
    chamber door;
            This it is and nothing more."

Presently my soul grew stronger; hesitating then no
35   longer,
"Sir," said I, "or Madam, truly your forgiveness I
    implore;
But the fact is I was napping, and so gently you came
    rapping,
40 And so faintly you came tapping, tapping at my
    chamber door,
That I scarce was sure I heard you"—here I opened
    wide the door; —
            Darkness there and nothing more.

▶ The narrator does not open the door until the fourth stanza. This builds suspense because we keep wondering where the tapping is coming from.

45 Deep into that darkness peering, long I stood there
      wondering, fearing,
  Doubting, dreaming dreams no **mortals** ever dared
      to dream before;
  But the silence was unbroken, and the stillness gave
50   no **token**,
  And the only word there spoken was the whispered
      word, "Lenore!"
  This I whispered, and an echo murmured back the
      word, "Lenore!"—
55   Merely this and nothing more.

Think About It

What does the speaker see when he opens his door? What does he whisper?

  Back into the chamber turning, all my soul within me
      burning,
  Soon again I heard a tapping something louder than
      before.
60 "Surely," said I, "surely that is something at my
      window lattice;
  Let me see, then, what thereat is, and this mystery
      explore—
  Let my heart be still a moment, and this mystery
      explore;—
65   'Tis the wind, and nothing more."

Keys to Literature

The last words in six stanzas are *nothing more*. The speaker is telling himself, "Don't worry. It's nothing." What could be a reason for this **repetition**?

  Open here I flung the shutter, when, with many a flirt
      and flutter,
70 In there stepped a stately Raven of the saintly days of
      yore.
  Not the least **obeisance** made he; not a minute
      stopped or stayed he,
  But, with mien of lord or lady, perched above my
      chamber door—
75 Perched upon a bust of Pallas just above my chamber
     door—
            Perched, and sat, and nothing more.

▶ In Greek myths, Pallas was the goddess of wisdom. When the raven lands on the statue, or bust, of Pallas, you can guess that since the Raven sits there, it will give the narrator wisdom.

Then this ebony bird beguiling my sad fancy into
    smiling,
80 By the grave and stern decorum of the countenance it
    wore,
"Though thy crest be shorn and shaven, thou," I said,
    "art sure no craven,
Ghastly grim and ancient Raven wandering from the
85   Nightly shore—
Tell me what thy lordly name is on the Night's
    Plutonian shore!"
             Quoth the Raven, "Nevermore."

Much I marveled this ungainly fowl to hear discourse
90   so plainly,
Though its answer little meaning—little relevancy
        bore;
For we cannot help agreeing that no living human
        being
95 Ever yet was blessed with seeing bird above his
        chamber door—
Bird or beast upon the sculptured bust above his
        chamber door,
                With such name as "Nevermore."

100 But the Raven, sitting lonely on that placid bust,
        spoke only
That one word, as if his soul in that one word he did
        outpour.
Nothing farther then he uttered; not a feather then he
105   fluttered—
Till I scarcely more than muttered: "Other friends
        have flown before—
On the morrow *he* will leave me as my Hopes have
        flown before."
110   Then the bird said, "Nevermore."

Keys to Literature

Once the Raven comes, each stanza ends with *Nevermore*. What kind of feeling does the **repetition** of *Nevermore* create?

Startled at the stillness broken by reply so aptly
        spoken,
"Doubtless," said I, "what it utters is its only stock
        and store,
115 Caught from some unhappy master whom unmerciful
        Disaster
Followed fast and followed faster till his songs one
        burden bore—
Till the dirges of his Hope that melancholy burden
120   bore
                Of 'Never—nevermore.'"

Predict

What will happen now that the Raven has arrived?

Keys to Literature

Notice the **alliteration** in this stanza of words that start with the same consonant sound—*sad, soul,* and *smiling*. It makes the poem sound like music. Can you find another example of alliteration?

But the Raven still beguiling all my sad soul into
    smiling,
Straight I wheeled a cushioned seat in front of bird
125   and bust and door;
Then, upon the velvet sinking, I betook myself to
    linking
Fancy unto fancy, thinking what this ominous bird of
    yore—
130 What this grim, ungainly, ghastly, gaunt, and ominous
    bird of yore
              Meant in croaking "Nevermore."

This I sat engaged in guessing, but no syllable
    expressing
135 To the fowl whose fiery eyes now burned into my
    bosom's core;
This and more I sat divining, with my head at ease
    reclining
On the cushion's velvet lining that the lamp-light
140   gloated o'er,
But whose velvet violet lining with the lamp-light
    gloating o'er
              She shall press, ah, nevermore!

Think About It

In Line 152, *quaff this kind nepenthe* means "drink this liquid that will make you sleep." Why would the narrator want to drink a liquid that will make him sleep?

Then, methought, the air grew denser, perfumed
145   from an unseen censer
Swung by angels whose foot-falls tinkled on the tufted
    floor.
"Wretch," I cried, "thy God hath lent thee—by these
    angels he hath sent thee
150 Respite—respite and nepenthe from thy memories of
    Lenore!
Quaff, oh quaff this kind nepenthe and forget this lost
    Lenore!"
              Quoth the Raven, "Nevermore."

155 "Prophet!" said I, "thing of evil—prophet still, if bird
or devil—
Whether Tempter sent, or whether tempest tossed
thee here ashore,
Desolate, yet all undaunted, on this desert land
160 enchanted—
On this home by Horror haunted,—tell me truly,
I implore—
Is there—*is* there balm in Gilead—tell me—tell me,
I implore!"
165 Quoth the Raven, "Nevermore."

"Prophet!" said I, "thing of evil—prophet still, if bird
or devil!
By that heaven that bends above us—by that God we
both adore—
170 Tell this soul with sorrow laden if, within the distant
Aidenn,
It shall clasp a sainted maiden whom the angels name
Lenore—
Clasp a rare and radiant maiden whom the angels
175 name Lenore."
Quoth the Raven, "Nevermore."

Think About It

How is the narrator
behaving in this
stanza? Why?

"Be that word our sign of parting, bird or fiend!"
I shrieked, upstarting—
"Get thee back into the tempest and the Night's
180 Plutonian shore!
Leave no black plume as a token of that lie thy soul
hath spoken!
Leave my loneliness unbroken!—quit the bust above
my door!
185 Take thy beak from out my heart, and take thy form
from off my door!"
Quoth the Raven, "Nevermore."

And the Raven, never flitting, still is sitting, still is
    sitting
190 On the **pallid** bust of Pallas just above my chamber
    door;
And his eyes have all the seeming of a demon's that is
    dreaming,
And the lamp-light o'er him streaming throws his
195   shadow on the floor;
And my soul from out that shadow that lies floating
    on the floor
        Shall be lifted—nevermore!

Predict

Will the Raven leave?

Meet the Author

EDGAR ALLAN POE *(1809–1849)*

Edgar Allan Poe's life was tragic. His parents died when he was three, and he did not get along with his foster father. He was sent to West Point, but he was thrown out. He could not hold a job for very long, and even as a writer, he did not earn enough money to live on. At age forty, Poe was found dead on a Baltimore street.

Today, Poe is called the father of the American short story. He is also known as the inventor of the detective story. Poe was a great poet, too. "The Raven" and "Annabel Lee" are two of his best-known poems.

Check Your Predictions

1. Look back at the answers you gave for the Predict questions. Would you change your answers? Explain.

Understand the Poem

2. Who is Lenore?

3. How does the Raven answer each of the speaker's questions?

4. What strange effect does the Raven have on the narrator?

Think About the Poem

5. How does the narrator feel at the beginning of the poem? Why?

6. How does the narrator's state of mind change by the end of the poem? What causes the change?

7. What kind of mood does the repetition of *nevermore* or *nothing more* at the end of the stanzas create?

8. Each stanza of the poem has eleven lines. Which lines rhyme with each other?

Extend Your Response

With your classmates, do a choral reading of "The Raven." If you wish, divide your group in half. One group reads the first half of each stanza. The other group reads the last half. Emphasize the **alliteration**. One person could read the word *Nevermore*.

Learn More About It

THE RAVEN AS A SYMBOL

For thousands of years, the raven has been an important symbol in the myths of different cultures. When Poe wrote "The Raven" in 1845, the raven was a symbol of bad luck, disease, war, and death. However, the raven has had other meanings through the years.

According to Greek mythology, the raven originally had white feathers. The raven told everyone's secrets, so its feathers were blackened as punishment by the Greek god Apollo for talking too much.

In ancient China, a three-legged raven was the sun god's companion. It was the symbol of the Chou Dynasty.

Children growing up long ago in Iceland were warned against using a raven's quill, or the hollow stem of a feather, as a drinking straw. One sip from it, and a child would grow up to be a thief.

The raven is an important figure in many Native American stories. It is responsible for bringing fire and light to the world. The raven is often seen as a trickster—a character who plays tricks on people and other animals.

Apply and Connect

In Poe's poem "The Raven," what is the raven a symbol of?

The raven was respected as a worthy symbol to represent rulers and important families. Throughout Europe, from the time of the Middle Ages, the raven has appeared on many coats of arms, or shields.

Summaries

The Tide Rises, the Tide Falls It is getting dark. A traveler hurries along the seashore to a town. During the night, the waves wash away his footprints. Morning comes. The traveler does not return to the shore.

The Cremation of Sam McGee Sam McGee and his friend Cap are in the Yukon hunting for gold. Sam feels as if he is going to die from the cold. He begs his friend to cremate him if he does. When Sam dies, Cap drags the body to an old boat. He builds a fire in the boat's furnace. He puts the body in the fire and cremates Sam. Sam comes back to life.

The Raven A man is reading in his room at midnight. He feels very sad about his lost love, Lenore. He hears a tapping at his door. A mysterious Raven enters the room. The man keeps asking the bird questions. The Raven always answers, "Nevermore." This seems to drive the man crazy and cause him grief.

Vocabulary Review

For each sentence below, write *true* if the underlined word is used correctly. If it is not used correctly, change the underlined word to make the sentence true. Use a separate sheet of paper.

1. I <u>implore</u> you to come with me because I am afraid to go alone.

2. Because of an emergency, the doctor <u>hastens</u> to the hospital.

3. The sound the sick child made was a <u>whimper</u>.

4. The dead person's body was <u>buried</u>, and all that remained were his ashes.

5. She <u>loathed</u> the people who forced her family to leave town.

Chapter Quiz

**Write your answers in one or two complete sentences.
Use a separate sheet of paper.**

1. The Tide Rises, the Tide Falls What happens to the traveler's footprints on the beach?

2. The Tide Rises, the Tide Falls What happens over and over again in this poem?

3. The Cremation of Sam McGee Why does Sam want to be cremated if he dies?

4. The Cremation of Sam McGee What happens once Sam is cremated?

5. The Raven What does the narrator most want to know from the Raven? What answer does he get?

6. The Raven What does the speaker tell the Raven to do at the end of the poem? Does the Raven do what the speaker asks?

Critical Thinking

7. The Tide Rises, the Tide Falls In what way is this poem about all people, not just one traveler?

8. The Raven Is this a narrative poem? How do you know?

Chapter Activity

Retell the "The Cremation of Sam McGee" or "The Raven" as a short story. If you choose "The Cremation of Sam McGee," write the story from Sam's point of view. If you choose "The Raven," write the story from the point of view of the bird.

Winter Night by Stefan Hirsch (1899–1964)

What is the mood of this scene? What strange or unexpected things might be happening here?

Chapter 3 > Drama

THE STRANGE AND UNEXPECTED

Learning Objectives

- Understand what a play is.
- Recognize dialogue in a play.
- Understand plot.
- Identify the climax of a plot.

Preview Activity

Think of something unexpected that happened to you and someone you know. What did you say to each other? Write down your conversation. First write what you said. Then, write what the other person said. (This is called dialogue.)

Plays

Plays bring stories to life before our eyes. They are performed by actors. They are usually performed in theaters. Plays have the following elements:

- characters
- dialogue
- stage directions

There are different kinds of plays. Some plays are comedies (funny plays). Some are musicals (plays with music). Some are dramas (serious plays).

Suspense builds slowly in a play as the characters deal with a problem. Eventually, the play reaches a high point, or climax. The climax is when we find out what happens to the characters.

Keys to Literature

dialogue: a conversation between characters in a story or play; words that characters actually say

> Example: *First Man: Where are you now?*
> *George: In a phone booth.*

plot: the action of a story or play. Most plots have a problem, and at the end, a solution.

> Example: Tom, the starting pitcher on a baseball team, fails an exam and is cut from the team. He studies all summer, retakes the exam, passes, and returns to the team.

climax: the high point of a story when the outcome is decided

> Example: In the plot above, the climax is when Tom passes.

Did You Know?

Years ago, operators helped with most calls. A caller told the operator what phone number he or she wanted. The operator then connected the call. Telephone numbers began with names, such as Murray Hill and Plaza.

Words to Know

client	a customer
fiends	very evil or cruel people
explicitly	very clearly and plainly
civic	having to do with your fellow citizens
apprehend	capture or arrest
unnerved	caused someone to lose courage
invalid	a sick person
drastic	having a strong effect; harsh
coincidence	two events that seem connected but are not
vague	unclear

Sorry, Wrong Number

BY LUCILLE FLETCHER, *Adapted*

READ TO FIND OUT...
Why is the wrong number in this play important?

CHARACTERS

Mrs. Stevenson

Operator

First Man

Second Man (George)

Chief Operator

Second Operator

Sergeant Duffy

Third Operator

Western Union

Information Woman

ACT I

(**Sound:** *Number being dialed on phone; busy signal.*)

Mrs. Stevenson (*a complaining, self-centered person*): Oh—dear!

(*Slams down receiver. Dials* Operator.)

Operator: Your call, please?

Mrs. Stevenson: Operator? I've been dialing Murray Hill 4-0098 now for the last three quarters of an hour, and the line is always busy. But I don't see how it *could* be busy that long. Will you try it for me, please?

Operator: Murray Hill 4-0098? One moment, please.

Mrs. Stevenson: I don't see how it could be busy all this time. It's my husband's office. He's working late tonight, and I'm all alone here in the house. My health is very poor—and I've been feeling so nervous all day—

Operator: Ringing Murray Hill 4-0098.

(**Sound:** *Phone buzz. It rings three times. Receiver is picked up at other end.*)

Think About It
As you read this play, look at the words and phrases in parentheses. What kinds of information do they give you?

Man: Hello.

Mrs. Stevenson: Hello? (*A little puzzled.*) Hello. Is Mr. Stevenson there?

Man (*into phone, as though he had not heard*): Hello. (*Louder.*) Hello.

Second Man (*slow, heavy voice, faintly foreign accent*): Hello.

First Man: Hello, George?

George: Yes, sir.

Mrs. Stevenson (*louder and more commanding, to phone*): Hello. Who's this? What number am I calling, please?

First Man: We have heard from our **client**. He says the coast is clear for tonight.

George: Yes, sir.

First Man: Where are you now?

George: In a phone booth.

First Man: Okay. You know the address. At eleven o'clock the private patrolman goes around to a place on Second Avenue for a break. Be sure that all the lights downstairs are out. There should be only one light visible from the street. At eleven fifteen a subway train crosses the bridge. It makes a noise in case her window is open and she should scream.

Mrs. Stevenson (*shocked*): Oh—*hello*! What number is this, please?

George: Okay. I understand.

First Man: Make it quick. As little blood as possible. Our client does not wish to make her suffer long.

George: A knife okay, sir?

First Man: Yes. A knife will be okay. And remember— remove the rings and bracelets, and the jewelry in the bureau drawer. Our client wishes it to look like simple robbery.

▶ Somehow, Mrs. Stevenson is overhearing the conversation of two men who are planning a crime.

Predict

What will the phone call she hears mean for Mrs. Stevenson?

George: Okay. I get—

    (**Sound:** *A soft buzzing signal.*)

Mrs. Stevenson (*clicking phone*): Oh! (*Soft buzzing signal continues. She hangs up.*) How awful! How unspeakably—

(**Sound:** *Dialing. Phone buzz.*)

Operator: Your call, please?

Mrs. Stevenson (*uptight and breathless, into phone*): Operator, I—I've just been cut off.

Operator: I'm sorry, madam. What number were you calling?

Mrs. Stevenson: Why—it was supposed to be Murray Hill 4-0098, but it wasn't. Some wires must have crossed—I was cut into a wrong number—and—I've just heard the most dreadful thing—a—a murder—and—(*As an order*) Operator, you'll simply have to retrace that call at once.

Operator: I beg your pardon, madam—I don't quite—

Keys to Literature

Dialogue is a conversation between characters. The dashes in Mrs. Stevenson's dialogue tell you she is too upset to speak in complete sentences.

Mrs. Stevenson: Oh—I know it was a wrong number, and I had no business listening—but these two men—they were cold-blooded **fiends**—and they were going to murder somebody—some poor innocent woman—who was all alone—in a house near a bridge. We've got to stop them—we've got to—

Operator (*patiently*): What number were you calling, madam?

Mrs. Stevenson: That doesn't matter. This was a *wrong* number. And *you* dialed it. And we've got to find out what it was—immediately!

Operator: But—madam—

Mrs. Stevenson: Oh, why are you so stupid? Look, it was obviously a case of some little slip of the finger. I told you to try Murray Hill 4-0098 for me—you dialed it—but your finger must have slipped—and I was connected with some other number—and I could hear them, but they couldn't hear me. Now, I simply fail to see why you couldn't make that same mistake again—on purpose—why you couldn't *try* to dial Murray Hill 4-0098 in the same careless sort of way—

Operator (*quickly*): Murray Hill 4-0098? I will try to get it for you, madam.

Mrs. Stevenson: *Thank* you.

(*Sound of ringing; busy signal.*)

Operator: I am sorry. Murray Hill 4-0098 is busy.

Mrs. Stevenson (*madly clicking receiver*): Operator. Operator.

Operator: Yes, madam.

Mrs. Stevenson (*angrily*): You *didn't* try to get that wrong number at all. I asked **explicitly**. And all you did was dial correctly.

Operator: I am sorry. What number were you calling?

Mrs. Stevenson: Can't you, for once, forget what number I was calling, and do something specific?

Think About It

Mrs. Stevenson calls the operator stupid. What does this tell you about her?

Think About It

How does the operator behave toward Mrs. Stevenson? Why do you think she behaves that way?

Now I want to trace that call. It's my **civic** duty—it's *your* civic duty—to trace that call—and to **apprehend** those dangerous killers—and if *you* won't—

Operator: I will connect you with the Chief Operator.

Mrs. Stevenson: *Please!*

(*Sound of ringing.*)

Chief Operator (*a cool pro*): This is the Chief Operator.

Mrs. Stevenson: Chief Operator? I want you to trace a call. A telephone call. Immediately. I don't know where it came from, or who was making it, but it's absolutely necessary that it be tracked down. Because it was about a murder. Yes, a terrible, cold-blooded murder of a poor innocent woman—tonight—at eleven fifteen.

Chief Operator: I see.

Mrs. Stevenson (*high-strung, demanding*): Can you trace it for me? Can you track down those men?

Predict

Do you think the Chief Operator will be able to trace the call? Why or why not?

Chief Operator: It depends, madam.

Mrs. Stevenson: Depends on what?

Chief Operator: It depends on whether the call is still going on. If it's a live call, we can trace it on the equipment. If it's been disconnected, we can't.

Mrs. Stevenson: Disconnected?

Chief Operator: If the parties have stopped talking to each other.

Mrs. Stevenson: Oh—but—but of course they must have stopped talking to each other by *now*. That was at least five minutes ago—and they didn't sound like the type who would make a long call.

Chief Operator: Well, I can try tracing it. Now—what is your name, madam?

Mrs. Stevenson: Mrs. Stevenson. Mrs. Elbert Stevenson. But—listen—

Chief Operator (*writing it down*): And your telephone number?

Mrs. Stevenson (*more bothered*): Plaza 4-2295. But if you go on wasting all this time—

Chief Operator: And what is your reason for wanting this call traced?

Mrs. Stevenson: My reason? Well—for heaven's sake—isn't it obvious? I overheard two men—they're killers—they're planning to murder this woman—it's a matter for the police.

Chief Operator: Have you told the police?

Mrs. Stevenson: No. How could I?

Chief Operator: You're making this check into a private call purely as a private individual?

Mrs. Stevenson: Yes. But meanwhile—

Chief Operator: Well, Mrs. Stevenson—I seriously doubt whether we could make this check for you at this time just on your say-so as a private individual. We'd have to have something more official.

Keys to Literature

A **plot** contains a problem to be solved. What is the problem Mrs. Stevenson faces in this play?

Mrs. Stevenson: Oh, for heaven's sake! You mean to tell me I can't report a murder without getting tied up in all this red tape? Why, it's perfectly idiotic. All right, then. I *will* call the police. (*She slams down receiver.*) Ridiculous!

(*Sound of dialing.*)

Chief Operator: Your call, please?

Mrs. Stevenson (*very annoyed*): The Police Department—*please.*

Second Operator: Ringing the Police Department.

(*Rings twice. Phone is picked up.*)

Sergeant Duffy: Police Department. Precinct 43. Duffy speaking.

Mrs. Stevenson: Police Department? Oh. This is Mrs. Stevenson—Mrs. Elbert Smythe Stevenson of 53 North Sutton Place. I'm calling to report a murder.

Duffy: Eh?

Mrs. Stevenson: I mean—the murder hasn't been committed yet. I just overheard plans for it over the telephone … over a wrong number that the operator gave me. I've been trying to trace down the call myself, but everybody is so stupid—and I guess in the end you're the only people who could *do* anything.

Duffy (*not too impressed*): Yes, ma'am.

Mrs. Stevenson (*trying to impress him*): It was a perfectly *definite* murder. I heard their plans distinctly. Two men were talking, and they were going to murder some woman at eleven fifteen tonight—she lived in a house near a bridge.

Duffy: Yes, ma'am.

Mrs. Stevenson: And there was a private patrolman on the street. He was going to go around for a break on Second Avenue. And there was some third man—a client—who was paying to have this poor woman murdered—They were going to take her rings and

> **Think About It**
>
> What do you think Sergeant Duffy thinks of Mrs. Stevenson?

bracelets—and use a knife—Well, it's **unnerved** me dreadfully—and I'm not well—

Duffy: I see. When was all this, ma'am?

Mrs. Stevenson: About eight minutes ago. Oh … (*relieved*) then you can do something? You do understand—

Duffy: And what is your name, ma'am?

Mrs. Stevenson (*losing patience*): Mrs. Stevenson. Mrs. Elbert Stevenson.

Duffy: And your address?

Mrs. Stevenson: 53 North Sutton Place. *That's* near a bridge, the Queensborough Bridge, you know—and *we* have a private patrolman on our street—and Second Avenue—

Duffy: And what was that number you were calling?

Mrs. Stevenson: Murray Hill 4-0098. But—that wasn't the number I overheard. I mean Murray Hill 4-0098 is my husband's office. He's working late tonight,

Predict

Mrs. Stevenson lives near Second Avenue and a bridge. What will happen to her?

and I was trying to reach him to ask him to come home. I'm an **invalid**, you know—and it's the maid's night off—and I *hate* to be alone—even though he says I'm perfectly safe as long as I have the telephone beside my bed.

Duffy (*trying to end it*): Well, we'll look into it, Mrs. Stevenson, and see if we can check it with the telephone company.

Mrs. Stevenson (*using more patience*): But the telephone company said they couldn't check the call if the parties had stopped talking. I've already taken care of *that*.

Duffy: Oh, yes?

Mrs. Stevenson (*getting bossy*): Personally I feel you ought to do something far more immediate and **drastic** than just check the call. What good does checking the call do, if they've stopped talking? By the time you track it down, they'll already have committed the murder.

Duffy: Well, we'll take care of it, lady. Don't worry.

Mrs. Stevenson: The whole thing calls for a search—a complete and thorough search of the whole city. I'm very near a bridge, and I'm not far from Second Avenue. And I know *I'd* feel a whole lot better if you sent around a radio car to *this* neighborhood at once.

Duffy: And what makes you think the murder's going to be committed in your neighborhood, ma'am?

Mrs. Stevenson: Oh, I don't know. The **coincidence** is so horrible. Second Avenue—the patrolman—the bridge—

Duffy: Second Avenue is a very long street, ma'am. And do you happen to know how many bridges there are in the city of New York alone? Not to mention Brooklyn, Staten Island, Queens, and the Bronx? And how do you know there isn't some little house out on Staten Island—on some little Second

Think About It
Do you think Duffy really plans to help Mrs. Stevenson? Explain.

Avenue you've never heard about? How do you know they were even talking about New York at all?

Mrs. Stevenson: But I heard the call on the New York dialing system.

Duffy: How do you know it wasn't a long-distance call you overheard? Telephones are funny things. Look, lady, why don't you look at it this way? Supposing you hadn't broken in on that telephone call? Supposing you'd got your husband the way you always do? Would this murder have made any difference to you then?

Mrs. Stevenson: I suppose not. But it's so inhuman— so cold-blooded—

Duffy: A lot of murders are committed in this city every day, ma'am. If we could do something to stop 'em, we would. But a clue of this kind that's so **vague** isn't much more use to us than no clue at all.

Mrs. Stevenson: But surely—

Duffy: Unless, of course, you have some reason for thinking this call is phony—and that someone may be planning to murder *you*?

Mrs. Stevenson: *Me?* Oh, no, I hardly think so. I—I mean—why should anybody? I'm alone all day and night—I see nobody except my maid Eloise—she's a big two-hundred-pounder—she's too lazy to bring up my breakfast tray—and the only other person is my husband Elbert—he's crazy about me—adores me—waits on me hand and foot—he's scarcely left my side since I took sick twelve years ago—

Duffy: Well, then, there's nothing for you to worry about, is there? And now, if you'll just leave the rest of this to us—

Mrs. Stevenson: But what will you *do*? It's so late—it's nearly eleven o'clock.

Duffy (*firmly*): We'll take care of it, lady.

Mrs. Stevenson: Will you broadcast it all over the

Keys to Literature

The **climax**, or high point, is the most exciting part of the play. It is now nearly eleven o'clock. Since the crime is planned for eleven fifteen, the play is near the climax.

city? And send out squads? And warn your radio cars to watch out—especially in suspicious neighborhoods like mine?

Duffy (*more firmly*): Lady, I *said* we'd take care of it. Just now I've got a couple of other matters here on my desk that require my immediate—

Mrs. Stevenson: Oh! (*She slams down receiver hard.*) Idiot. (*Looking at phone nervously.*) Now, why did I do that? Now he'll think I am a fool. Oh, why doesn't Elbert come home? *Why* doesn't he?

(*Sound of dialing operator.*)

ACT II

Operator: Your call, please?

Mrs. Stevenson: Operator, for heaven's sake, will you ring that Murray Hill 4-0098 number again? I can't think what's keeping him so long.

Operator: Ringing Murray Hill 4-0098. (*Rings. Busy signal.*) The line is busy. Shall I—

Mrs. Stevenson (*nastily*): I can hear it. You don't have to tell me. I know it's busy. (*Slams down receiver.*) If I could only get out of this bed for a little while. If I could get a breath of fresh air—or just lean out the window—and see the street—(*The phone rings. She answers it instantly.*) Hello. Elbert? Hello. Hello. Hello. Oh, what's the matter with this phone? *Hello? Hello?* (*Slams down receiver. The phone rings again, once. She picks it up.*) Hello? Hello—Oh, for heaven's sake, who is this? Hello, Hello, *Hello.* (*Slams down receiver. Dials operator.*)

Third Operator: Your call, please?

Mrs. Stevenson (*very annoyed and commanding*): Hello, operator. I don't know what's the matter with this telephone tonight, but it's positively driving me crazy. I've never seen such inefficient, miserable service. Now, look. I'm an invalid, and I'm very

Keys to Literature

In this section of **dialogue**, who does Mrs. Stevenson talk to?

nervous, and I'm *not* supposed to be annoyed. But if this keeps on much longer—

Third Operator (*a young, sweet type*): What seems to be the trouble, madam?

Mrs. Stevenson: Well, everything's wrong. The whole world could be murdered, for all you people care. And now, my phone keeps ringing—

Operator: Yes, madam?

Mrs. Stevenson: Ringing and ringing and ringing every five seconds or so, and when I pick it up, there's no one there.

Operator: I am sorry, madam. If you will hang up, I will test it for you.

Mrs. Stevenson: I don't want you to test it for me. I want you to put through that call—whatever it is— at once.

Operator (*gently*): I am afraid that is not possible, madam.

Mrs. Stevenson (*storming*): Not possible? And why may I ask?

Operator: The system is automatic, madam. If someone is trying to dial your number, there is no way to check whether the call is coming through the system or not—unless the person who is trying to reach you complains to the particular operator—

Mrs. Stevenson: Well, of all the stupid, complicated—! And meanwhile *I've* got to sit here in my bed, *suffering* every time that phone rings, imagining everything—

Operator: I will try to check it for you, madam.

Mrs. Stevenson: Check it! Check it! That's all anybody can do. Of all the stupid, idiotic…! (*She hangs up.*) Oh—what's the use … (*Instantly* MRS. STEVENSON'S *phone rings again. She picks up the receiver. Wildly.*) Hello. HELLO. Stop ringing, do you hear me?

Think About It

What is happening to Mrs. Stevenson at this point in the play?

Answer me? What do you want? Do you realize you're driving me crazy? Stark, staring—

Man (*dull, flat voice*): Hello. Is this Plaza 4-2295?

Mrs. Stevenson (*catching her breath*): Yes. Yes. This is Plaza 4-2295.

Man: This is Western Union. I have a telegram here for Mrs. Elbert Stevenson. Is there anyone there to receive the message?

Mrs. Stevenson (*trying to calm herself*): I am Mrs. Stevenson.

Western Union (*reading flatly*): The telegram is as follows: "Mrs. Elbert Stevenson. 53 North Sutton Place, New York, New York. Darling. Terribly sorry. Tried to get you for last hour, but line busy. Leaving for Boston 11 P.M. tonight on urgent business. Back tomorrow afternoon. Keep happy. Love. Signed. Elbert."

Mrs. Stevenson (*shocked, to herself*): Oh—no—

Western Union: That is all, madam. Do you wish us to deliver a copy of the message?

Mrs. Stevenson: No—no, thank you.

Western Union: Thank you, madam. Good night. (*He hangs up phone.*)

Mrs. Stevenson (*Softly, to phone*): Good night. (*She hangs up slowly, suddenly bursting into tears.*) No— no—it isn't true! He couldn't do it. Not when he knows I'll be all alone. It's some trick—some fiendish—(*She dials operator.*)

Operator (*coolly*): Your call, please?

Mrs. Stevenson: Operator—try that Murray Hill 4-0098 number for me just once more, please.

Operator: Ringing Murray Hill 4-0098. (*Call goes through. We hear ringing at other end. Ring after ring.*)

Mrs. Stevenson: He's gone. Oh, Elbert, how could you? How could you—? (*She hangs up phone, sobbing with pity to herself, turning nervously.*) But I can't be alone

▶ Western Union is a telegraph service. People use it to send messages in telegrams. However, e-mail and faxes are now used much more than telegrams.

Keys to Literature

Most **plots** have twists and turns. When Mr. Stevenson makes a sudden trip, this may give him an alibi for the time of the murder.

tonight. I can't. If I'm alone one more second—I don't care what he says—or what the expense is—I'm a sick woman—I'm entitled—(*She dials Information.*)

Information: This is Information.

Mrs. Stevenson: I want the telephone number of Henchley Hospital.

Information: Henchley Hospital? Do you have the address, madam?

Mrs. Stevenson: No. It's somewhere in the seventies, though. It's a very small, private, and exclusive hospital where I had my appendix out two years ago. Henchley. H-E-N-C—

Information: One moment, please.

Mrs. Stevenson: Please—hurry. And please—what *is* the time?

Information: I do not know, madam. You may find out the time by dialing Meridian 7-1212.

Mrs. Stevenson (*angered*): Oh, for heaven's sake! Couldn't you—?

Information: The number of Henchley Hospital is Butterfield 7-0105, madam.

Mrs. Stevenson: Butterfield 7-0105. (*She hangs up before she finishes speaking, and immediately dials number.*)
(*Phone rings.*)

Woman (*middle-aged, solid, firm, practical*): Henchley Hospital, good evening.

Mrs. Stevenson: Nurses' Registry.

Woman: Who was it you wished to speak to, please?

Mrs. Stevenson (*bossy*): I want the Nurses' Registry at once. I want a trained nurse. I want to hire her immediately. For the night.

Woman: I see. And what is the nature of the case, madam?

Mrs. Stevenson: Nerves. I'm very nervous. I need

soothing—and companionship. My husband is away—and I'm—

Woman: Have you been recommended to us by any doctor in particular, madam?

Mrs. Stevenson: No. But I really don't see why all this catechizing is necessary. I want a trained nurse. I was a patient in your hospital two years ago. And after all, I *do* expect to *pay* this person—

Woman: We quite understand that, madam. But registered nurses are very scarce just now—and our superintendent has asked us to send people out only on cases where the physician in charge feels it is absolutely necessary.

Mrs. Stevenson (*growing very upset*): Well, it is absolutely necessary. I'm a sick woman. I—I'm very upset. Very. I'm alone in this house—and I'm an invalid—and tonight I overheard a telephone conversation that upset me dreadfully. About a murder—a poor woman who was going to be murdered at eleven fifteen tonight—in fact, if someone doesn't come at once—I'm afraid I'll go out of my mind—(*Almost off handle by now.*)

Woman (*calmly*): I see. Well, I'll speak to Miss Phillips as soon as she comes in. And what is your name, madam?

Think About It

Do you think Mrs. Stevenson has a reason to be so upset? Explain.

Keys to Literature

At the **climax**, or high point of the play, we are most interested in what will happen. What do you most want to know right now?

Mrs. Stevenson: Miss Phillips. And when do you expect her in?

Woman: I really don't know, madam. She went out to supper at eleven o'clock.

Mrs. Stevenson: Eleven o'clock. But it's not eleven yet. (*She cries out.*) Oh, my clock has stopped. I thought it was running down. What time is it?

Woman: Just fourteen minutes past eleven.

(*Sound of phone receiver being lifted on same line as* MRS. STEVENSON'S. *A click.*)

Mrs. Stevenson (*crying out*): What's *that*?

Woman: What was what, madam?

Mrs. Stevenson: That—that click just now—in my own telephone? As though someone had lifted the receiver off the hook of the extension phone downstairs—

Woman: I didn't hear it, madam. Now—about this—

Mrs. Stevenson (*scared*): But I did. There's someone in this house. Someone downstairs in the kitchen. And they're listening to me now. They're—(*Hangs up phone. In a hushed voice.*) I won't pick it up. I won't let them hear me. I'll be quiet—and they'll think—(*with growing terror*) But if I don't call someone now—while they're still down there—there'll be no time. (*She picks up receiver. Soft buzzing signal. She dials operator. Ring twice*)

Operator (*a slow, lazy voice*): Your call, please?

Mrs. Stevenson (*a desperate whisper*): Operator, I—I'm in desperate trouble—I—

Operator: I cannot hear you, madam. Please speak louder.

Mrs. Stevenson (*Still whispering*): I don't dare. I—there's someone listening. Can you hear me now?

Operator: Your call, please? What number are you calling, madam?

Mrs. Stevenson (*desperately*): You've got to hear me. Oh, please. You've got to help me. There's someone in this house. Someone who's going to murder me. And you've got to get in touch with the—(*Click of receiver being put down in* Mrs. STEVENSON'S *home. Bursting out wildly.*) Oh, there it is—he's put it down—he's put down the extension—he's coming—(*She screams.*) He's coming up the stairs—(*Wildly.*) Give me the Police Department—(*Screaming.*) The police!

Operator: Ringing the Police Department.

(*Phone is rung. We hear sound of a subway train coming nearer. On second ring,* Mrs. STEVENSON *screams again, but roaring of train drowns out her voice. For a few seconds we hear nothing but roaring of train, then dying away, phone at police headquarters ringing.*)

Duffy: Police Department. Precinct 43. Duffy speaking. (*Pause.*) Police Department. Duffy speaking.

George: Sorry. Wrong number. (*Hangs up.*)

> **Think About It**
> Who is George? Why is he at Mrs. Stevenson's house?

Meet the Author

LUCILLE FLETCHER (1912–2000)

Lucille Fletcher grew up in New York City. After college, she worked as a typist at a radio station. At that time, radio plays were very popular. While typing the scripts of these plays, Fletcher decided she could write better ones. She was right. More than twenty of her plays were performed on the radio.

Lucille Fletcher based her plays on real-life events. Once, a rich woman was extremely rude to her in a store. Fletcher went home and wrote *Sorry, Wrong Number*. She made the rich woman Mrs. Stevenson, the character who faced a terrible fate! *Sorry, Wrong Number* was performed on the radio many times. Later, it was made into a movie.

Summary

Sorry, Wrong Number (Act 1) Mrs. Stevenson is a rich invalid who lives in New York City. One day, she overhears a murder plot. The killers plan to murder a woman who lives near a bridge on Second Avenue. The murder is planned for eleven fifteen that night. She asks the operator to trace the call, but it cannot be done. She calls the police, but they are unable to do anything.

Sorry, Wrong Number (Act 2) Mrs. Stevenson, who is alone in the house, cannot reach her husband. Since she lives near a bridge on Second Avenue, she thinks she might be the murder victim. At eleven fifteen, Mrs. Stevenson hears someone in her house. She tries to reach the police, but cannot. Eventually, the police call her. However, the killer picks up the receiver and says, "Sorry, wrong number."

civic
explicitly
coincidence
apprehend
drastic
client

Vocabulary Review

Complete each sentence with a word from the box. Use a separate sheet of paper.

1. Shanti explained the game very _____ to be sure the team understood all the rules.

2. It was a _____ that all three gifts arrived at the same time.

3. In order to help his _____, the lawyer asked him many questions about the car crash.

4. It was Jamie's _____ duty to be considerate of her neighbors, so she turned down the TV sound.

5. The police were able to _____ the bank robber before he struck again.

6. After trying everything else, the doctors took _____ measures to save the woman's life.

Chapter Quiz

**Write your answers in one or two complete sentences.
Use a separate sheet of paper.**

1. Why can't Mrs. Stevenson leave her house?

2. What plan does Mrs. Stevenson overhear on her telephone?

3. What happens when Mrs. Stevenson tries to warn the police?

4. Why is Mrs. Stevenson worried that she might be murdered?

5. What causes the suspense in this play?

6. When does the climax of the play take place?

Critical Thinking

7. What does Mrs. Stevenson's dialogue tell you about the kind of person she is?

8. Why is the wrong number important in this play?

Chapter Activity

Suppose you were a police detective at Mrs. Stevenson's house after the murder has been committed. Tell what steps you would take to solve the crime.

Unit 1 **Review**

On a separate sheet of paper, write the letter that best completes each sentence below.

1. In "After Twenty Years," two old friends
   A. finally meet out West.
   B. don't recognize each other at first.
   C. never meet again.
   D. have dinner at Big Joe Brady's Restaurant.

2. In "An Appointment," the young man's appointment is with
   A. the Sultan.
   B. a skillful assistant.
   C. a gardener.
   D. Death.

3. In "The Tell-Tale Heart," the old man's eye
   A. frightens the narrator.
   B. has a patch over it.
   C. is a dark shade of brown.
   D. is never open.

4. In "The Cremation of Sam McGee," Cap
   A. cremates Sam next to his sled.
   B. brings Sam to Tennessee.
   C. cremates Sam inside a boat's cabin boiler.
   D. does not cremate Sam.

5. At the end of "The Tide Rises, the Tide Falls," the traveler
   A. returns home.
   B. disappears.
   C. gets on a horse.
   D. goes for a swim in the tide.

6. In "The Raven," the bird symbolizes
   A. pepper trees.
   B. good luck.
   C. the writer.
   D. none of the above.

7. At the end of *Sorry, Wrong Number*,
   A. Mrs. Stevenson faints.
   B. Mrs. Stevenson is killed.
   C. George calls a wrong number.
   D. Mr. Stevenson comes home.

Making Connections
On a separate sheet of paper, write the answers to these questions.

8. Which story in this unit did you find the most suspenseful? Explain.

9. Each of the poems in this unit repeats certain lines or words. Find these lines or words. Tell which is your favorite and why.

Writing an Essay
Choose one of the stories or poems in this unit. Describe the setting and one of the characters.

Unit 2 ▶ Looking Back

Chapter 4 ## Memoirs

The All-American Slurp
by Lensey Namioka

Lame Deer Remembers
*by John Fire/Lame Deer and
Richard Erdoes, adapted*

from Prisoner of My Country
by Yoshiko Uchida, adapted

Chapter 5 ## Short Stories

The Jacket
by Gary Soto, adapted

A Day's Wait
by Ernest Hemingway

The Circuit
by Francisco Jiménez, adapted

What kind of childhood memory does this art show?

Learning Objectives

- Understand what a memoir is.
- Explain what comparison is.
- Identify exaggeration.
- Identify character clues from thoughts, actions, and words.
- Understand a character's motivation.
- Identify atmosphere.
- Recognize details.

Preview Activity

Look back in your life at a childhood event. Write a few colorful details about the memory. Ask yourself why you think you remember this event. Did you learn anything from it? Share your memory with a friend.

Memoirs and Childhood

A memoir is the story of an event or part of a person's life. It is written by the person himself or herself. Memoirs are told from the first-person point of view. The writer uses words like *I* or *my* to refer to himself or herself.

Sometimes, a memoir is about an event that happened when a person was young. That is because events that happen early in life are very important. They can affect you for the rest of your life.

Keys to Literature

exaggeration: making something seem worse or better than it really is

> Example: In this story, when the girl is embarrassed, she says that she *died at least fifty times.*

comparison: showing how two things are alike

> Example: *Our family beat a retreat back to the sofa as if chased by enemy soldiers.*

Did You Know?

When people immigrate to a new country, they have to learn the language and get used to the customs of their new land. Sometimes, these customs are surprising or even shocking. The term for this is *culture shock.*

Words to Know

emigrated	left one country to settle in another
disinfect	sterilize; make clean
relish	foods, such as pickles, olives, and raw vegetables, served as an appetizer
unison	together and at the same time
lavishly	in a way that is much more than enough
mortified	ashamed; embarrassed
elegant	attractive and refined
murky	dark or gloomy
etiquette	good manners; rules of proper behavior
slurp	make a loud sipping or sucking sound
coping	dealing with something in a successful way

The All-American Slurp

BY LENSEY NAMIOKA

READ TO FIND OUT...
Why is slurping important in this story?

The first time our family was invited out to dinner in America, we disgraced ourselves while eating celery. We had **emigrated** to this country from China, and during our early days here we had a hard time with American table manners.

In China we never ate celery raw, or any other kind of vegetable raw. We always had to **disinfect** the vegetables in boiling water first. When we were presented with our first **relish** tray, the raw celery caught us unprepared.

Predict

How will the family fit in when they go to the Gleasons' house for dinner?

We had been invited to dinner by our neighbors, the Gleasons. After arriving at the house, we shook hands with our hosts and packed ourselves into a sofa. As our family of four sat stiffly in a row, my younger brother and I stole glances at our parents for a clue as to what to do next.

Mrs. Gleason offered the relish tray to Mother. The tray looked pretty, with its tiny red radishes, curly sticks of carrots, and long, slender stalks of pale green celery. "Do try some of the celery, Mrs. Lin," she said. "It's from a local farmer, and it's sweet."

Mother picked up one of the green stalks, and Father followed suit. Then I picked up a stalk, and my brother did too. So there we sat, each with a stalk of celery in our right hand.

The narrator sits stiffly on the sofa and watches her parents because she is not sure how to behave. She does not want to make any mistakes.

Mrs. Gleason kept smiling. "Would you like to try some of the dip, Mrs. Lin? It's my own recipe: sour cream and onion flakes, with a dash of Tabasco sauce."

Most Chinese don't care for dairy products, and in those days I wasn't even ready to drink fresh milk. Sour cream sounded perfectly revolting. Our family shook our heads in **unison**.

Mrs. Gleason went off with the relish tray to the other guests, and we carefully watched to see what they did. Everyone seemed to eat the raw vegetables quite happily.

Mother took a bite of her celery. *Crunch.* "It's not bad!" she whispered.

Father took a bite of his celery. *Crunch.* "Yes, it *is* good," he said, looking surprised.

I took a bite, and then my brother. *Crunch, crunch.* It was more than good; it was delicious. Raw celery has a slight sparkle, a zingy taste that you don't get in cooked celery. When Mrs. Gleason came around with the relish tray, we each took another stalk of celery, except my brother. He took two.

There was only one problem: long strings ran through the length of the stalk, and they got caught in my teeth. When I help my mother in the kitchen, I always pull the strings out before slicing celery.

I pulled the strings out of my stalk. *Z-z-zip, z-z-zip.* My brother followed suit. *Z-z-zip, z-z-zip, z-z-zip.* To my left, my parents were taking care of their own stalks. *Z-z-zip, z-z-zip, z-z-zip.*

Keys to Literature

How do you know that the sound of celery "zipping" is an **exaggeration**?

Suddenly I realized that there was dead silence except for our zipping. Looking up, I saw that the eyes of everyone in the room were on our family. Mr. and Mrs. Gleason, their daughter Meg, who was my friend, and their neighbors the Badels—they were all staring at us as we busily pulled the strings of our celery.

That wasn't the end of it. Mrs. Gleason announced that dinner was served and invited us to the dining table. It was **lavishly** covered with platters of food, but we couldn't see any chairs around the table. So we helpfully carried over some dining chairs and sat down. All the other guests just stood there.

Keys to Literature

A **comparison** shows how one thing is like another. The narrator makes a comparison between the family's rush to the sofa and soldiers running from an enemy.

Think About It

Based on the information in this paragraph, what is the message of this story?

Mrs. Gleason bent down and whispered to us, "This is a buffet dinner. You help yourselves to some food and eat it in the living room."

Our family beat a retreat back to the sofa as if chased by enemy soldiers. For the rest of the evening, too **mortified** to go back to the dining table, I nursed a bit of potato salad on my plate.

Next day Meg and I got on the school bus together. I wasn't sure how she would feel about me after the spectacle our family made at the party. But she was just the same as usual, and the only reference she made to the party was, "Hope you and your folks got enough to eat last night. You certainly didn't take very much. Mom never tries to figure out how much food to prepare. She just puts everything on the table and hopes for the best."

I began to relax. The Gleasons' dinner party wasn't so different from a Chinese meal after all. My mother also puts everything on the table and hopes for the best.

Meg was the first friend I had made after we came to America. I eventually got acquainted with a few other kids in school, but Meg was still the only real friend I had.

My brother didn't have any problems with making friends. He spent all his time with some boys who were teaching him baseball, and in no time he could speak English much faster than I could—not better, but faster.

I worried more about making mistakes, and I spoke carefully, making sure I could say everything right before opening my mouth. At least I had a better accent than my parents, who never really got rid of their Chinese accent, even years later. My parents had both studied English in school before coming to America, but what they had studied was mostly written English, not spoken.

Father's approach to English was a scientific one. Since Chinese verbs have no tense, he was fascinated by the way English verbs changed form according to whether they were in the present, past imperfect, perfect, pluperfect, future, or future perfect tense. He was always making diagrams of verbs and their inflections, and he looked for opportunities to show off his mastery of the pluperfect and future perfect tenses, his two favorites. "I shall have finished my project by Monday," he would say smugly.

Mother's approach was to memorize lists of polite phrases that would cover all possible social situations. She was constantly muttering things like "I'm fine, thank you. And you?" Once she accidentally stepped on someone's foot, and hurriedly blurted, "Oh, that's quite all right!" Embarrassed by her slip, she resolved to do better next time. So when someone stepped on *her* foot, she cried, "You're welcome!"

In our own different ways, we made progress in learning English. But I had another worry, and that was my appearance. My brother didn't have to worry, since Mother bought him blue jeans for school, and he dressed like all the other boys. But she insisted that girls had to wear skirts. By the time she saw that Meg and the other girls were wearing jeans, it was too late. My school clothes were bought already, and we didn't have money left to buy new outfits for me. We had too many other things to buy first, like furniture, pots, and pans.

––––––––––––––

The first time I visited Meg's house, she took me upstairs to her room, and I wound up trying on her clothes. We were pretty much the same size, since Meg was shorter and thinner than average. Maybe that's how we became friends in the first place. Wearing Meg's jeans and T-shirt, I looked at myself in the mirror. I could almost pass for an American—from the back, anyway. At least the kids in school wouldn't stop and stare at me in the hallways, which was what they did when they saw me in my white blouse and navy blue skirt that went a couple of inches below the knees.

When Meg came to my house, I invited her to try on my Chinese dresses, the ones with a high collar and slits up the sides. Meg's eyes were bright as she looked at herself in the mirror. She struck several sultry poses, and we nearly fell over laughing.

The dinner party at the Gleasons' didn't stop my growing friendship with Meg. Things were getting better for me in other ways too. Mother finally bought me some jeans at the end of the month, when Father got his paycheck. She wasn't in any hurry about buying them at first, until I worked on her. This is what I did. Since we didn't have a car in those days, I often ran down to the neighborhood store to pick up things for her. The groceries cost less at a big supermarket, but the closest one was many blocks away. One day, when she ran out of flour, I offered to borrow a bike from our neighbor's son and buy a ten-pound bag of flour at the big supermarket. I mounted the boy's bike and waved to Mother. "I'll be back in five minutes!"

Before I started pedaling, I heard her voice behind me. "You can't go out in public like that! People can see all the way up to your thighs!"

"I'm sorry," I said innocently. "I thought you were in a hurry to get the flour." For dinner we were going to have pot-stickers (fried Chinese dumplings), and we needed a lot of flour.

"Couldn't you borrow a girl's bicycle?" complained Mother. "That way your skirt won't be pushed up."

"There aren't too many of those around," I said. "Almost all the girls wear jeans while riding a bike, so they don't see any point in buying a girl's bike."

We didn't eat pot-stickers that evening, and Mother was thoughtful. Next day we took the bus downtown and she bought me a pair of jeans. In the same week, my brother made the baseball team of his junior high school, Father started taking driving lessons, and Mother discovered rummage sales. We soon got all the furniture we needed, plus a dart board and a 1,000-piece jigsaw puzzle (fourteen hours later, we discovered that it was a 999-piece jigsaw puzzle). There was hope that the Lins might become a normal American family after all.

Then came our dinner at the Lakeview restaurant.

The Lakeview was an expensive restaurant, one of those places where a headwaiter dressed in tails conducted you to your seat, and the only light came from candles and flaming desserts. In one corner of the room a lady harpist played tinkling melodies.

Father wanted to celebrate, because he had just been promoted. He worked for an electronics company, and after his English started improving, his superiors decided to appoint him to a position more suited to his training. The promotion not only brought a higher salary but was also a tremendous boost to his pride.

Up to then we had eaten only in Chinese restaurants. Although my brother and I were becoming fond of hamburgers, my parents didn't care much for western food, other than chow mein.

But this was a special occasion, and Father asked his coworkers to recommend a really **elegant** restaurant. So there we were at the Lakeview, stumbling after the headwaiter in the **murky** dining room.

At our table we were handed our menus, and they were so big that to read mine I almost had to stand up again. But why bother? It was mostly in French, anyway.

Predict

What kind of problem might the family have at the Lakeview restaurant?

Think About It

Which details in the next three paragraphs make the story funny?

Father, being an engineer, was always systematic. He took out a pocket French dictionary. "They told me that most of the items would be in French, so I came prepared." He even had a pocket flashlight, the size of a marking pen. While Mother held the flashlight over the menu, he looked up at the items that were in French.

"*Pâté en croûte,*" he muttered. "Let's see … *pâté* is paste…. *croûte* is crust … hmm … a paste in crust."

The waiter stood looking patient. I squirmed and died at least fifty times.

At long last Father gave up. "Why don't we just order four complete dinners at random?" he suggested.

"Isn't that risky?" asked Mother. "The French eat some rather peculiar things, I've heard."

"A Chinese can eat anything a Frenchman can eat," Father declared.

The soup arrived in a plate. How do you get soup up from a plate? I glanced at the other diners, but the ones at the nearby tables were not on their soup course, while the more distant ones were invisible in the darkness.

Fortunately, my parents had studied books on western **etiquette** before they came to America. "Tilt your plate," whispered my mother. "It's easier to spoon the soup up that way."

She was right. Tilting the plate did the trick. But the etiquette book didn't say anything about what you did after the soup reached your lips. As any respectable Chinese knows, the correct way to eat your soup is to **slurp**. This helps to cool the liquid and prevent you from burning your lips. It also shows your appreciation.

Keys to Literature

How does the narrator **exaggerate** her embarrassment at the restaurant?

We showed our appreciation. *Shloop*, went my father. *Shloop*, went my mother. *Shloop, shloop*, went my brother, who was the hungriest.

The lady harpist stopped playing to take a rest. And in the silence, our family's consumption of soup suddenly seemed unnaturally loud. You know how it sounds on a rocky beach when the tide goes out and the water drains from all those little pools? They go *shloop, shloop, shloop*. That was the Lin family, eating soup.

Keys to Literature

Do you think it is an **exaggeration** to say that other diners were "hypnotized" by the slurping? Explain.

At the next table a waiter was pouring wine. When a large *shloop* reached him, he froze. The bottle continued to pour, and red wine flooded the tabletop and into the lap of a customer. Even the customer didn't notice anything at first, being also hypnotized by the *shloop, shloop, shloop.*

It was too much. "I need to go to the toilet," I mumbled, jumping to my feet. A waiter, sensing my urgency, quickly directed me to the ladies' room.

I splashed cold water on my burning face, and as I dried myself with a paper towel, I stared into the mirror. In this perfumed ladies' room, with its pink-and-silver wallpaper and marbled sinks, I looked completely out of place. What was I doing here? What was our family doing in the Lakeview restaurant? In America?

The door to the ladies' room opened. A woman came in and glanced curiously at me. I retreated into one of the toilet cubicles and latched the door.

Time passed—maybe half an hour. Then I heard the door open again, and my mother's voice. "Are you in there? You're not sick, are you?"

There was real concern in her voice. A girl can't leave her family just because they slurp their soup. Besides, the toilet cubicle had a few drawbacks as a permanent residence. "I'm all right," I said, undoing the latch.

Mother didn't tell me how the rest of the dinner went, and I didn't want to know. In the weeks following, I managed to push the whole thing into the back of my mind, where it jumped out at me only a few times a day. Even now, I turn hot all over when I think of the Lakeview restaurant.

But by the time we had been in this country for three months, our family was definitely making progress toward becoming Americanized. I remember my parents' first PTA meeting. Father wore a neat suit and tie, and Mother put on her first pair of high heels. She stumbled only once. They met my homeroom teacher and beamed as she told them that I would make honor roll soon at the rate I was going. Of course Chinese etiquette forced Father to say that I was a very stupid girl and Mother to protest that the teacher was showing favoritism toward me. But I could tell they were both very proud.

The day came when my parents announced that they wanted to give a dinner party. We had invited Chinese friends to eat with us before, but this dinner was going to be different. In addition to a Chinese-American family, we were going to invite the Gleasons.

"Gee, I can hardly wait to have dinner at your house," Meg said to me. "I just *love* Chinese food."

That was a relief. Mother was a good cook, but I wasn't sure if people who ate sour cream would also eat chicken gizzards stewed in soy sauce.

Mother decided not to take a chance with chicken gizzards. Since we had western guests, she set the table with large dinner plates, which we never used in Chinese meals. In fact we didn't use individual plates at all, but picked up food from the platters in the middle of the table and brought it directly to our rice bowls. Following the practice of Chinese-American restaurants, Mother also placed large serving spoons on the platters.

Predict

How will the Gleasons fit in when they go to the Lins' house for dinner?

The dinner started well. Mrs. Gleason exclaimed at the beautifully arranged dishes of food: the colorful candied fruit in the sweet-and-sour pork dish, the noodle-thin shreds of chicken meat stir-fried with tiny peas, and the glistening pink prawns in a ginger sauce.

At first I was too busy enjoying my food to notice how the guests were doing. But soon I remembered my duties. Sometimes guests were too polite to help themselves and you had to serve them with more food.

I glanced at Meg, to see if she needed more food, and my eyes nearly popped out at the sight of her plate. It was piled with food: the sweet-and-sour meat pushed right against the chicken shreds, and the chicken sauce ran into the prawns. She had been taking food from a second dish before she finished eating her helping from the first!

Horrified, I turned to look at Mrs. Gleason. She was dumping rice out of her bowl and putting it on her dinner plate. Then she ladled prawns and gravy on top of the rice and mixed everything together, the way you mix sand, gravel, and cement to make concrete.

I couldn't bear to look any longer, and I turned to Mr. Gleason. He was chasing a pea around his plate. Several times he got it to the edge, but when he tried to pick it up with his chopsticks, it rolled back toward the center of the plate again. Finally he put down his chopsticks and picked up the pea with his fingers. He really did! A grown man!

All of us, our family and the Chinese guests, stopped eating to watch the activities of the Gleasons. I wanted to giggle. Then I caught my mother's eyes on me. She frowned and shook her head slightly, and I understood the message: the Gleasons were not used to Chinese ways, and they were just **coping** the best they could. For some reason I thought of celery strings.

Think About It

Is there anything wrong with the way Meg eats? Explain.

Keys to Literature

What **comparison** describes how Mrs. Gleason eats her meal?

Think About It

Why does the narrator suddenly think of celery strings?

When the main courses were finished, Mother brought out a platter of fruit. "I hope you weren't expecting a sweet dessert," she said. "Since the Chinese don't eat dessert, I didn't think to prepare any."

"Oh, I couldn't possibly eat dessert!" cried Mrs. Gleason. "I'm simply stuffed!"

Meg had different ideas. When the table was cleared, she announced that she and I were going for a walk. "I don't know about you, but I feel like dessert," she told me, when we were outside. "Come on, there's a Dairy Queen down the street. I could use a big chocolate milkshake!"

Although I didn't really want anything more to eat, I insisted on paying for the milkshakes. After all, I was still hostess.

Meg got her large chocolate milkshake and I had a small one. Even so, she was finishing hers while I was only half done. Toward the end she pulled hard on her straws and went *shloop, shloop*.

"Do you always slurp when you eat a milkshake?" I asked, before I could stop myself.

Meg grinned. "Sure. All Americans slurp."

Think About It

Why is the narrator surprised to learn that Americans slurp milkshakes?

Meet the Author

LENSEY NAMIOKA *(Born 1929)*

Lensey Namioka was born in Beijing, China. When she was young, her family moved to Seattle, Washington. As a young woman, Namioka became a math professor. However, that did not stop her from writing stories. One of her first novels was *Who's Hu?* This book describes what it was like for a girl to study math.

Lensey Namioka's husband is Japanese American. After they visited Japan together, she began to write novels about the history of Japan. You might enjoy reading *Island of Ogres.* It tells about two swordsmen who uncover strange things on a mysterious island.

Check Your Predictions

1. Look back at the answers you gave for the Predict questions. Would you change your answers? Explain.

Understand the Memoir

2. Why is the narrator embarrassed at the Gleasons' dinner party?

3. Why is the narrator embarrassed at the Lakeview restaurant?

4. Why does the narrator want to giggle when the Gleasons eat at her house?

Think About the Memoir

5. Why do you think the narrator gets so embarrassed by her family's mistakes?

6. Do you think the narrator changes by the end of the story? Explain.

7. Why do you think the author uses exaggeration in this story?

8. Compare the dinner at the Gleasons' with the dinner at the narrator's house.

Extend Your Response

List three table manners that you think are important. Describe a time when someone ignored one of these table manners. Was it funny or embarrassing?

Keys to Literature

character clues: the thoughts, actions, and words in a story that help you understand what a character is like

> Example: *Father said, "I should punish you and whip you, but I won't. That's not my way. You'll get your punishment later."*

motivation: the reason a character behaves as he or she does

> Example: In this story, Lame Deer's father gives away valuable things. His motivation is to honor his daughter.

Did You Know?

A reservation is an area of land set aside for use by Native Americans. There are about 300 reservations in the United States and more than 2,000 in Canada. Native Americans own their reservations. About half the nation's Native Americans live on reservations.

Words to Know

prairie	a large area of land with rich soil, grass, and very few trees
piercing	making a hole through something
ceremony	a special event
awl	a sharp, pointed tool for making holes in leather
gasped	breathed in loudly and quickly after being shocked or surprised
powwow	a Native American meeting or gathering

Lame Deer Remembers

**BY JOHN FIRE/LAME DEER AND
RICHARD ERDOES,** *Adapted*

I was born a full-blooded Indian. I was born in a log cabin, twelve feet by twelve feet, between Pine Ridge and Rosebud. *Maka tanhan wicasa wan*—I am a man of the earth, as we say. Our people don't call themselves Sioux or Dakota. That's white man talk. We call ourselves Ikce Wicasa—the natural humans. We are the free, wild, common people. I am happy to be called that.

I was brought up by my grandparents—Good Fox and … Plenty White Buffalo. This is the way with most Indian children. With our people, the ties to one's grandparents are as strong as the ties to one's parents. We lived in a little hut way out on the **prairie**, in the back country. For the first few years of my life I had nothing to do with the outside world. Of course we had a few white man's things—coffee, iron pots, a shotgun, an old wagon. But I never thought much about where these things came from, or who had made them….

READ TO FIND OUT…

What event in Lame Deer's childhood will he never forget?

▶ *Pine Ridge* and *Rosebud* are reservations in South Dakota.

Keys to Literature

Character clues tell about a character in a story or memoir. What do the clues in this paragraph tell you about Lame Deer?

I liked to ride on a horse behind my older sister. I held onto her. As I got a little bigger, she would hold onto me. When I was nine years old, I had my own horse to ride. It was a beautiful gray pony. My father had given it to me, along with a fine saddle and a Mexican saddle blanket. That gray was my best friend. I was proud to ride him. But he was not mine for long. I lost him, and it was my own fault.

Nonge Pahloka—the **Piercing** of Her Ears—is a big event in a little girl's life. By this **ceremony**, the girl's parents, and especially her grandmother, want to show her how much they love and honor her. They ask a man who is very wise or brave to pierce the ears of their daughter. The grandmother makes food for everybody. The little girl is placed on a blanket. All around her are the many gifts her family will give away in her name. The man who does the piercing gets the best gift. Then everybody gets down to the really important part—the eating.

Well, one day I watched somebody pierce a girl's ears. I saw the fuss they made over it, and the presents he got. I thought I should do this to my little sister. She was about four years old at the time, and I was nine. I don't remember why I wanted to pierce her ears. Maybe I wanted to feel big and important like the man I watched do the piercing. Maybe I wanted to get a big present. Maybe I wanted to make my sister cry. I don't remember what was in my little boy's mind then. I found some wire and made a pair of "earrings" out of it. Then I asked my sister, "Would you like me to put these on you?" She smiled. "*Ohan*—yes." I didn't have the sharp bone used for piercing. I didn't know the prayer that goes with it. I just had an old **awl**. I thought this would do fine. Oh, how my sister yelled. I had to hold her down. But I got that awl through her earlobes, and I put the "earrings" in. I was proud of the neat job I had done.

Keys to Literature

What **motivation** does Lame Deer have to pierce his sister's ears?

Think About It

Was Lame Deer wrong to pierce his sister's ears the way he did?

When my mother came home and saw those wire loops in my sister's ears she **gasped**. But then she went and told my father. That was one of the few times he talked to me. He said, "I should punish you and whip you, but I won't. That's not my way. You'll get your punishment later."

Well, some time passed. I forgot all about it. One morning my father told me we were going to a **powwow**. He had the wagon ready. It was piled high with boxes and bundles. At the powwow, my father told people he was doing a big *otuhan*—a give-away. He put my sister on a pretty Navaho blanket. Then he laid out things to give away—quilts, food, blankets, a fine shotgun, his own new pair of cowboy boots, a sheepskin coat. It was enough to give a whole family all they needed. Dad was telling the people, "I want to honor my daughter for her ear-piercing. This should have been done in a ceremony, but my son did it at

Predict

How will Lame Deer's parents' react to the piercing of his sister's ears?

Keys to Literature

From the **character clues** in this story, how would you describe Lame Deer?

home. I guess he's too small. He didn't know any better." This was a long speech for Dad. He told me to come closer. I was sitting on my pretty gray horse. I thought Dad and I were looking pretty fine. Well, before I knew it, Dad had given my pony away, along with its beautiful saddle and blanket. I had to ride home in the wagon. I cried all the way. Dad said, "You have your punishment now. But you will feel better later on. All her life your sister will tell about how you pierced her ears. She'll brag about you. I bet you are the only small boy who ever did this big ceremony."

Dad's words did not make me feel better. My beautiful gray horse was gone. For three days, my heart was broken. On the fourth morning, I looked out the door. There stood a little white horse with a new saddle and bit. "It's yours," my father told me. "Get on it." I was happy again....

Meet the Author

JOHN FIRE/LAME DEER *(1903–1976)*

Lame Deer grew up on an Indian reservation in South Dakota. His English name was John Fire. As a child, he went to a strict boarding school. He was very unhappy there. As a teenager, Lame Deer wandered around the country and had many jobs, including a rodeo clown, a sign painter, and a shepherd.

At age sixteen, Lame Deer went on a "vision quest." This led him to become a Sioux holy man, or *wicasa wakan*. He was also a great healer of the sick. In the 1960s, Lame Deer took part in the Civil Rights movements. He worked for the rights of African Americans and Native Americans. His autobiography *Lame Deer: Seeker of Visions* tells about his life and his beliefs.

Check Your Predictions

1. Look back at the answer you gave for the Predict question. Would you change your answer? Explain.

Understand the Memoir

2. How does Lame Deer hurt his younger sister?

3. How does Lame Deer's father punish him for hurting his sister?

4. What is the "Piercing of Her Ears" ceremony?

Think About the Memoir

5. Do you think Lame Deer's punishment was fair? Explain.

6. From what point of view is this story told? How do you know?

7. What do you think motivates Lame Deer's father to give his son a new horse?

8. What character clues tell you what kind of man Lame Deer's father is?

Extend Your Response

Suppose you were a news reporter on the Sioux reservation. Write a short news article about the *otuhan*, or give-away, that Lame Deer's father holds. Describe some of the things he gives away. Tell what is unusual about this give-away. Write a title for your news article.

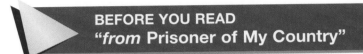

Keys to Literature

details: pieces of information that help to create a picture for the reader

Example: *Our rented house was now an empty shell, with only three mattresses on the floor.*

atmosphere: the general mood of a piece of literature

Example: *I was filled with horror. My knees felt weak, and I almost lost my breakfast.*

Did You Know?

You probably use the word *camp* to mean "a place in the country with outdoor activities for vacationers." In this selection, *camp* refers to a prison where Japanese Americans were held during World War II.

Words to Know

grounds	an area of land around a building
bayonets	rifles with steel knives attached to the end
barracks	buildings used as temporary housing
refugee	a person who leaves his or her country to find safety in another country
degrading	insulting; embarrassing
civil rights	rights that are guaranteed to a person by the U.S. Constitution
betrayed	lied to; broke someone's trust

from Prisoner of My Country

BY YOSHIKO UCHIDA, *Adapted*

READ TO FIND OUT...
How did Yoshiko Uchida become a prisoner of her own country?

Our beautiful garden was now full of holes. Mama had dug up a few favorite plants to give to her friends. Other plants were given to people like the woman who stopped by one day. She asked if she could have some gladiolas. She said, "Since you're leaving anyway ... " She smiled an embarrassed smile.

Our rented house was now an empty shell, with only three mattresses on the floor. In the corner of Mama's room was a large bag we called our Camp Bundle. We tossed into it all the things we had been told to take with us. There were sheets, blankets, pillows, dishes, and knives, forks, and spoons. We also put in other things we thought we'd need. These things were boots, umbrellas, flashlights, tea cups, a hot plate, a kettle, and anything else we thought we could use in camp.

Kay said, "You know, we're supposed to bring only what we can carry."

We tried lifting our suitcases. We found we could each carry two. But what were we going to do about the Camp Bundle? Each day it grew and grew, like some living thing. We had no idea how we would ever get it to camp. There was nothing to do but keep filling it up and hope that somehow things would work out.

The night before we left, our Swiss neighbors invited us to dinner. Mrs. Harpainter made a wonderful chicken dinner. She served it on her best dishes. It made me think of all the times we'd invited guests to our own house in happier days.

When we got home, Marian and Solveig came from next door to say good-bye. They brought gifts for each of us.

They hugged us, saying, "Come back soon!"

Predict

Think about all the things the Uchida family put in their Camp Bundle. How long will the family probably have to stay at the camp?

Keys to Literature

The night before leaving, the Uchida family has dinner with friends. What **details** do we learn about the dinner? Why do you think the author mentions these details?

"We will," we answered. But we had no idea when we would come back. Or even if we would ever come back.

The next morning, Mrs. Harpainter brought us breakfast on a tray full of dishes with bright colors. Then she drove us to the First Congregational Church of Berkeley. The church was a Civil Control Station, where we were supposed to report.

We said our good-byes quickly. We couldn't speak many words. Already the **grounds** of the church were filled with hundreds of Japanese Americans. They held bundles with tags that showed their names and their family's number. At the curb were rows of trucks. They were being loaded with large things that people could not carry by hand.

Kay said in a low voice, "I wish they'd told us there would be trucks. We wouldn't have worried so much about our Camp Bundle."

Think About It

The sight of the soldiers horrifies the narrator. What is happening to the family?

But the army didn't seem to care if we worried or not. To them, we were only prisoners. There were guards all around the church. Their **bayonets** were ready. It wasn't until I saw them that I really knew what was happening to us. I was filled with horror. My knees felt weak, and I almost lost my breakfast.

The First Congregational Church had been good to us. Many of the families in the church had offered to store things for the Japanese Americans while they were gone. Now the church women were serving tea and sandwiches. But none of us could eat.

Soon we were loaded onto waiting buses. We began our one-way trip down streets we knew well. We went across the Bay Bridge and down the Bayshore Highway. Some people were crying quietly, but most of us were silent. We kept our eyes on the window. We watched as sights we knew well slipped away behind us, one by one.

Then we were there—at the Tanforan Racetrack Assembly Center. This was one of the 15 centers at

Japanese Americans boarding buses for internment camps during World War II.

racetracks and fairgrounds along the West Coast where
Japanese Americans were held.

From the bus window, I could see a high fence with
barbed wire that was around the whole area. At each
corner of the camp was a guard tower with soldiers.

The gates swung open to let us in. The guards with
their guns closed them behind us. We were now locked
in. The guards would be there 24 hours a day.

We had never broken the law. We had done
nothing wrong. Yet, we had now become prisoners
of our own country.

Think About It

Why are there guards,
barbed wire, and gates at
the racetrack?

There was a huge crowd of us. It looked as if there
was a horse race that day, except that all the people
there were Japanese of all ages, sizes, and shapes.

Japanese Americans registering at an internment camp during World War II.

Predict

What will Apartment 40 look like?

We looked through the crowd for faces we knew. It felt good to find several friends. They had arrived a few days earlier from Oakland.

They called to us: "Hey, Kay and Yo! Over here!"

Our friends led us through the crowds to a spot where doctors looked down our throats and said we were healthy. Then they helped us find the place we were supposed to be—Barrack 16, Apartment 40.

I asked, "We get apartments?"

My friend said, "Not the kind of apartment you're thinking of, Yo. Wait, you'll see." My friend knew I'd be shocked.

Mama was wearing her hat, gloves, and Sunday clothes. This was because she would never have thought of leaving home any other way. In her good Sunday shoes, she picked her way over the mud puddles that the rain had left the night before.

The army had quickly built dozens of **barracks** around the track for the eight thousand of us. Each barrack was split into six rooms. Each family got one room. But our barrack was not one of these.

Our barrack turned out to be nothing but an old horse stable. Our "apartment" was a small, dark horse stall, 10 feet by 20 feet. I couldn't believe what I saw.

Dirt, dust, and bits of wood were all over the floor. I could smell that horses had lived there. There were two tiny windows on each side of the door.

Tiny bodies of spiders and bugs had been painted onto the walls by army painters. A single light bulb hung from the ceiling. Three army cots lay on the dirty floor. This was to be our "home" for the next five months.

One of our friends found a broom and swept out our stall. Two of the boys went to pick up our mattresses. They had to fill them up with straw themselves.

Another friend loaned us some dishes and silverware until our bundle was delivered. She said, "We'd better leave soon for the mess hall before the lines for dinner get too long."

For now, all meals were being served in the basement. Holding our plates and silverware, we made our way down the muddy racetrack.

When we got to the mess hall, there were already long lines of people waiting to get in. Soon we were separated from our friends. Mama, Kay, and I took our places at the end of one line. We stood close together to keep warm. A cold, sharp wind had begun to blow as the sun went down. It blew dust in our faces.

Keys to Literature

What do the **details** about how Mama is dressed tell you about her?

Keys to Literature

What **details** in the next three paragraphs describe the family's barrack?

Think About It

Why is being in this camp so degrading to the narrator?

I felt like a **refugee** in a strange land. Being here was not only **degrading**, but it did not seem real. It was like an awful dream.

Since we had missed lunch, I was eager for a nice hot meal. But dinner was a piece of bread, a boiled potato, and two sausages from a can. The cooks picked up the food with their fingers and dropped it on our plates.

We ate at picnic tables in the cold, damp basement, along with hundreds of people. Even though I was still hungry, I couldn't wait to get back to our stall.

It was dark now. The north wind was blowing into our stall from all the cracks around the windows and door. We put on our coats and sat on our mattresses, too sad even to talk.

Then we heard a truck outside. A voice called, "Hey, Uchida! Apartment 40!"

Kay and I rushed to the door. "That's us!" we called. We saw two boys trying to get our big Camp Bundle off their truck.

The boys were grinning. They asked us, "What ya got in here, anyways? Did ya bring everything in your whole darn house?"

I was embarrassed. Our bundle was the biggest one in their truck.

I joked, "It's just our pet rhino."

Think About It

The narrator is still able to joke. What does this tell you about her?

While the boys were still laughing, we dragged our huge bundle into the stall. Quickly, we untied all the knots we'd tied just that morning.

Everything we'd put in the bundle rolled out like old friends.

I grabbed the kettle. "I'll go get some water," I said.

I went quickly to the women's toilets and washroom. It was about 50 yards from our stable. While I was gone, Kay and Mama got our sheets and blankets from the bundle to make up our cots.

Japanese American girl waiting to travel with her parents to an internment camp.

When I got back, I had news for them.

"There are no doors for the toilets or showers," I said in horror. "And we have to wash up at long tin sinks. They look like they were used for feeding horses."

I had also taken a look at the laundry barrack. It had rows of tubs for washing. Everything, even sheets and towels, had to be washed by hand. They were still empty, but in the morning there would be long lines of people waiting to use those tubs.

Mama said, "Well, at least we can make some tea now."

We plugged in the hot plate and waited for the water to boil.

Then came a knock at the door. This was the first of many knocks we would hear, as friends found out where we lived.

A voice said, "Hey, Kay and Yo. Are you home?"

Four of my college friends had come by to see how we were doing. They had brought along the only snack they could find. It was a box of dried prunes. The day before, I wouldn't have eaten the prunes. But now they were as welcome as a box of the special chocolates Papa used to bring home from San Francisco.

We sat close to the warmth of the hot plate. We sipped the tea Mama had made for us. We wondered how we had come to be in this awful place.

We were angry that our country had taken away our **civil rights**. But we had been raised up to respect and trust the people in power. We never thought to protest, the way people would today. The world was a totally different place then.

Back then, there had been no freedom marches. No one had heard yet of Martin Luther King, Jr. No one knew about pride for one's own people. Most Americans didn't think much of civil rights. They would have given us no support if we had tried to stop the army from taking us away.

We thought that by going along with our government, we were helping our country. We did not know then how badly our leaders **betrayed** us.

They had put us in prison. They knew it was against the Constitution. And they knew there was no need to put us in prison. We were no danger to anyone.

We wondered how America—our own country—could have done this to us? We tried to cheer up. We talked about steaks and hamburgers and hot dogs as we ate the cold dried prunes.

Meet the Author

YOSHIKO UCHIDA *(1921–1992)*

Yoshiko Uchida grew up in Berkeley, California. During World War II, more than 110,000 Japanese Americans were put in prison camps. The Uchida family was among them. Uchida spent over a year in the camp. Then, she was allowed to go to college.

After the war, Uchida went to Japan where she collected Japanese folktales. When she returned to the United States, she published these stories. She also wrote twenty-seven children's books. Three of her books are *Picture Bride, Journey to Topaz,* and *Desert Exile*.

Check Your Predictions

1. Look back at the answers you gave for the Predict questions. Would you change your answers? Explain.

Understand the Memoir

2. What is life like for the Uchidas before they go to the camp?

3. How does the Uchida family prepare for the move to the camp?

4. How do the Uchidas become prisoners of their country?

5. Who does the narrator say betrayed Japanese Americans? How are they betrayed?

Think About the Memoir

6. Why don't the Japanese Americans protest what the government is doing?

7. What are some details that show the narrator is horrified by her new "apartment"?

8. What is the atmosphere like at the camp?

Extend Your Response

Write a paragraph from the point of view of the narrator's mother or father. How will their experiences be different from hers? How will they be the same?

Learn More About It

JAPANESE AMERICANS AND WORLD WAR II

Before the War

Around 1890, many Japanese began coming to the United States, especially to California and Arizona. These new Americans often lived together. They had their own neighborhoods. They also ran their own stores, banks, and restaurants. Many Japanese Americans became successful farmers, too.

Japanese American children waiting for the bus to travel to an internment camp World War II.

During the War

After the bombing of Pearl Harbor in 1941, Japan and the United States were at war with each other. Some Americans were afraid that Japanese Americans who lived on the West Coast of the United States might help Japan. In 1942, President Roosevelt ordered the U.S. army to take Japanese Americans to internment camps. An internment camp is a prisonlike place in which people are held during a war. Even though their families were held in camps, thousands of Japanese Americans served in the U.S. armed forces. One group, the 442nd Infantry, received many awards for bravery.

After the War

There was never any reason to believe that Japanese Americans were not loyal to the United States. In 1988, the U.S. government paid some Japanese Americans for the loss of their property. However, the money they received covered only about 10 percent of their losses during World War II.

Apply and Connect

Before World War II, where did Yoshiko Uchida's family live? What kind of neighbors did she have?

Summaries

The All-American Slurp The Gleasons, who are American, invite the Lins to dinner. The Lins, who are Chinese, do not know American manners yet, and the narrator becomes embarrassed. Another night, the narrator is embarrassed again when her family slurps soup at a fancy restaurant. Later, the Lins invite the Gleasons to dinner. This time, it is the Gleasons who make mistakes.

Lame Deer Remembers Lame Deer grows up on a Sioux reservation. Piercing a young girl's ears is an important ceremony for his people. One day, Lame Deer pierces his sister's ears himself, before the ceremony. His father punishes him by giving away his pony. Later, his father gives him a new pony.

Prisoner of My Country During World War II, the narrator and her family are forced to leave their home. They are moved, with other Japanese Americans, to a prison camp. The family lives in a horse stall. Life there is difficult. The narrator and her family are angry at their country for making them prisoners.

coping
gasped
degrading
betrayed
mortified

Vocabulary Review

Complete each sentence with a word from the box. Use a separate sheet of paper.

1. Sean lifted his head out of the water and _____ for air.

2. Lisa was _____ to be caught lying in front of all her friends.

3. The spy _____ his country and helped the enemy.

4. Even though their dad had left to fight in the war, the boys were _____ very well.

5. If you can keep your head held high, no experience is _____.

Chapter Quiz

**Write your answers in one or two complete sentences.
Use a separate sheet of paper.**

1. **The All-American Slurp** Why does the Chinese family slurp soup at the Lakeview restaurant?

2. **The All-American Slurp** What does the narrator discover about slurping when eating in the United States?

3. **Lame Deer Remembers** What is the purpose of the ear-piercing ceremony?

4. **Lame Deer Remembers** Why does Lame Deer's father give away the boy's gray pony?

5. **Prisoner of My Country** Why does the Uchida family move into the racetrack barracks?

6. **Prisoner of My Country** How would you describe life at the camp for the Japanese Americans?

Critical Thinking

7. **Lame Deer Remembers** How do you think Lame Deer feels about his childhood? What makes you think so?

8. **Prisoner of My Country** Yoshiko Uchida says that the government took away Japanese Americans' rights. What rights does she mean?

Chapter Activity

Write a paragraph about one of the authors in this chapter. Suggest how events the author describes could have affected the way he or she grew up.

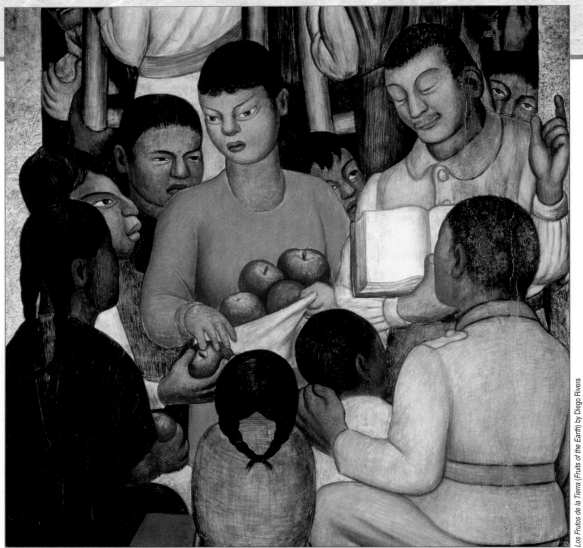

Los Frutos de la Tierra (Fruits of the Earth) by Diego Rivera

What does this painting show?

Chapter 5 — Short Stories
LOOKING BACK

Learning Objectives

- Recognize symbolism and figurative language.
- Identify dialogue.
- Understand a character's internal conflict.
- Recognize irony.
- Identify the rising action of a story.

Preview Activity

Think about a child you know or have seen on TV. What kinds of things did the child have trouble understanding? What was the child unable to control in his or her life? Write three of these things. Share them with a partner. See if your lists are similar or different.

Short Stories and Childhood

Most short stories are only a few pages long and have one or two main characters. All short stories have a setting and a plot. The plot often begins with a problem. The rest of the story shows how the problem gets solved.

In short stories about childhood, problems sometimes come about because children cannot control the things that are happening to them. They do not always understand the world around them. In the end, the child usually solves the problem, learns, and grows from the experience.

Keys to Literature

figurative language: words that describe something by comparing it to something else. It is used to add color and interest to a story.

> Example: *I was a small kid, thin as a young tree.*

symbolism: using something to stand for something else

> Example: In this story, the jacket is a symbol of all the bad things that are happening in the boy's life.

Did You Know?

When people feel happy and sure of themselves, everything seems to go right. When people feel unhappy and unsure of themselves, everything seems to go wrong. The same event can be happening to many people, but some see it one way, and others see it another way.

Words to Know

vinyl	a material made of strong plastic
blurry	not clear
scab	the crust that forms on skin where a sore or cut is healing
camouflage	a disguise made by looking like your surroundings
grunt	a short, deep, hoarse sound

The Jacket

BY GARY SOTO, *Adapted*

READ TO FIND OUT...
What makes one jacket so important?

My clothes have failed me. I remember the green jacket that I wore in fifth and sixth grades. In those grades, some kids danced like champs. But other kids pressed themselves against a greasy wall, feeling bitter as pennies toward the happy couples.

When I needed a new jacket, my mother asked what kind I wanted. I described something like bikers wear. I wanted a jacket with black leather, silver studs, and enough belts to hold down a small town. Mother and I were in the kitchen. Steam was on the windows from her cooking. She listened for a long time while stirring dinner. I thought for sure she knew the kind of jacket I wanted.

Then next day when I came home from school, I saw a jacket hanging on my bedpost. It was the color of day-old guacamole. I threw my books on the bed. I walked up to the jacket slowly, as if it was a stranger's hand I had to shake. I touched the **vinyl** sleeve, the collar, and looked at the mustard-colored lining.

Predict

Will the boy get the black leather jacket he wants? Explain.

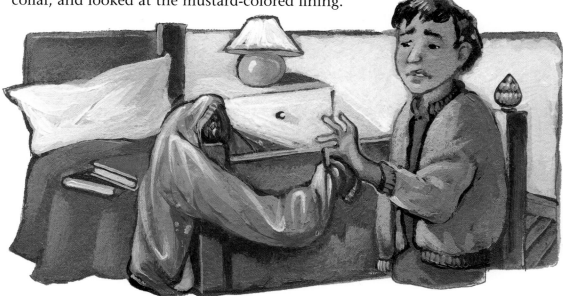

Keys to Literature

What **figurative language** does the narrator use to describe himself?

Think About It

Why do you think the boy does not tell his mother how he feels about the jacket?

From my bed, I stared at the jacket. I wanted to cry because it was so ugly. And it was so big that I knew I'd have to wear it a long time. I was a small kid, thin as a young tree. It would be years before I'd have a new one. I stared at the jacket, like an enemy. Then I took off my old jacket, the sleeves of which climbed halfway up to my elbow.

I put the big jacket on. I zipped it up and down several times. I rolled the cuffs up so they didn't cover my hands. I put my hands in the pockets and flapped the jacket like a bird's wings. I stood and looked in the mirror. Then I combed my hair to see what I would look like doing something natural. I looked ugly. I threw the jacket on my brother's bed and looked at it for a long time.

Then I put the jacket on and went out to the backyard. As I passed the kitchen, I smiled a "thank you" to my mom. Outside, I kicked a ball against a fence. Then I climbed the fence to sit looking into the alley. I threw orange peels at the mouth of an open garbage can. When the peels were gone, I watched the white puffs of my breath thin out to nothing.

I jumped down, hands in my pockets. I stood on my knees and teased my dog, Brownie, by swooping my arms while making bird calls. He jumped at me and missed. He jumped again and again. At last he caught me. One of his teeth sunk deep, making an L-shaped tear in the sleeve. I pushed Brownie away. I looked closely at the tear as if it was a cut on my arm. Darn dog, I thought. I pushed him away hard when he tried to bite again. I got up from my knees and went to my bedroom. I sat with my jacket on my lap, with the lights out.

That was the first afternoon with my new jacket. The next day I wore it to sixth grade and got a D on a math quiz. During the morning recess, Frankie T., the

playground terrorist, pushed me to the ground. He told me to stay there until recess was over. My best friend, Steve Negrete, ate an apple while looking at me. The girls turned away to whisper on the monkey bars. The teachers were no help. They looked my way and talked about how foolish I looked in my new jacket. I saw their heads shake with laughter. Their hands half-covered their mouths.

Even though it was cold, I took off the jacket during lunch. I played kickball in a thin shirt. My arms felt like Braille from goose bumps. When I got back to class, I slipped the jacket on. I shook until I was warm. I sat on my hands, heating them up. My teeth chattered like a cup of crooked dice. When I was finally warm, I slid out of the jacket. But a few minutes later, I put it on when the fire bell rang. We walked out into the

Keys to Literature

The author uses **figurative language** by comparing his goose bumps to Braille. Braille letters are raised dots that people who cannot see use to read.

yard. We sixth graders had to walk past all the other grades to stand against the back fence. Everybody saw me. Nobody said out loud, "Man, that's ugly." But I heard the buzz-buzz of talk and even laughter that I knew was meant for me.

And so I went, in my guacamole jacket. I was so embarrassed, so hurt, I couldn't even do my homework. I got Cs on quizzes. I forgot the state capitals and the rivers of South America, our friendly neighbor. Even the girls who had been friendly blew away like loose flowers. They followed the boys in neat jackets.

I wore that thing for three years, until the sleeves grew short and my arms stuck out like the necks of turtles. All during that time no love came to me. No little dark girl in a Sunday dress she wore on Monday paid attention to me. At lunch I stayed with the ugly boys. We leaned against the fence and looked around with propellers of grass spinning in our mouths. We saw girls walk by alone. We saw couples walking hand in hand. Their heads were like bookends, pressing the air together. We saw them and spun our propellers so fast our faces were **blurry**.

Think About It

Why do you think the boy describes the jacket as "the ugly brother" who tags along with him?

I blame that jacket for those bad years. I blame my mother for her bad taste and her cheap ways. It was a sad time for the heart. With a friend, I spent my sixth-grade year in a tree in the alley. I was waiting for something good to happen to me in that jacket. It had become the ugly brother who tagged along wherever I went.

It was about that time that I began to grow. My chest puffed up with muscle. I even seemed to get a few more ribs. My fingers were already getting hard for coming fights.

But that L-shaped rip in the sleeve of the jacket got bigger. Bits of stuffing came out after a hard day of play. I finally closed the rip with scotch tape. But in rain or cold weather, the tape peeled off like a **scab**. More stuffing came out until the sleeve hung like an arm that had shrunk.

That winter the elbows began to crack. Whole pieces of green began to fall off. I showed the cracks to my mother. She always seemed to be at the stove with steamed-up glasses. She said that there were children in Mexico who would love that jacket. I told her that this was America. I yelled that Debbie, my sister, didn't have a jacket like mine. I ran outside, ready to cry. I climbed the tree in the alley to think bad thoughts and watch the white puffs of my breath float into nothing.

Keys to Literature

The boy compares tape peeling off his jacket to a scab. This **figurative language** helps show his feelings. The jacket has caused him pain, just like a wound.

But whole pieces still flew off my jacket when I played hard, read quietly, or took awful spelling tests at school. When the jacket became so spotted that my brother called me "**camouflage**," I threw it over the fence into the alley. Later, though, I picked it up off the ground. I went inside to lay it across my lap and feel low.

I was called to dinner. Steam made my mother's glasses cloudy as she said grace. My brother and sister bowed their heads and made ugly faces at their glasses of powdered milk. I hated it, too. But I was eager to scoop up beans with big pieces of buttered tortilla. When I finished, I went outside with the jacket across my arm. It was a cold sky. The faces of the clouds were piled up, hurting. I climbed the fence and jumped down with a **grunt**. I started up the alley. Soon, I put on my jacket, that green ugly brother that breathed over my shoulder—that day and ever since.

Keys to Literature

By the end of the story, the boy's feelings about his jacket have changed. What is his jacket now a **symbol** of?

Meet the Author

GARY SOTO *(Born 1952)*

Gary Soto grew up in Fresno, California, where many of his stories take place. Soto usually writes about the sights and sounds of his Mexican American neighborhood. He tells of broken bicycles, baseball mitts, stray dogs, and ugly jackets. His stories show the meaning of these ordinary things.

In addition to short stories, Soto writes novels and poetry. Two of his novels are *Taking Sides* and *Pacific Crossing*. His poetry includes *A Fire in My Hands*.

Check Your Predictions

1. Look back at the answers you gave for the Predict question. Would you change your answer? Explain.

Understand the Story

2. Why does the boy dislike his new jacket?

3. What problems does the boy blame on the jacket?

4. How do the boy and the jacket change as they both get older?

Think About the Story

5. What do you think really causes the boy's problems at school?

6. At the end of the story, why do you think the boy does not throw away the jacket?

7. What figurative language does the boy use in the last paragraph to name his jacket?

8. What is the jacket a symbol of for the boy?

Extend Your Response

What is your favorite or least favorite article of clothing? What does it look like? How does it make you feel? Write a description of it using colorful details to help your readers see it. Explain why you like or dislike it. Then, draw a sketch of yourself wearing this article of clothing.

Keys to Literature

dialogue: a conversation between characters in a story or play; words that characters actually say

Example: *"You go up to bed," I said, "you're sick."*
"I'm all right," he said.

internal conflict: a struggle a person has within himself or herself when trying to make a decision

Example: In this story, the boy struggles to be brave about something difficult he faces.

Did You Know?

A person's normal body temperature is 98.6 degrees F. The *F* stands for Fahrenheit. Most Americans use the Fahrenheit thermometer. In other parts of the world, people use the Celsius thermometer. A person's normal body temperature in Celsius is 36.9 degrees C.

Words to Know

capsules	pills
influenza	a disease usually called "the flu"
epidemic	the quick spread of a disease to many people
pneumonia	a serious lung disease
varnished	smoothed over with a glossy surface
slithered	slid or glided like a snake
flushed	forced out from a hiding place
commenced	began

$\mathcal{A}$ Day's Wait

BY ERNEST HEMINGWAY

READ TO FIND OUT...
What is the boy in this story waiting for?

He came into the room to shut the windows while we were still in bed and I saw he looked ill. He was shivering, his face was white, and he walked slowly as though it ached to move.

"What's the matter, Schatz?"

"I've got a headache."

"You better go back to bed."

"No. I'm all right."

"You go to bed. I'll see you when I'm dressed."

But when I came downstairs he was dressed, sitting by the fire, looking a very sick and miserable boy of nine years. When I put my hand on his forehead I knew he had a fever.

"You go up to bed," I said, "you're sick."

"I'm all right," he said.

When the doctor came he took the boy's temperature.

"What is it?" I asked him.

"One hundred and two."

Downstairs, the doctor left three different medicines in different colored **capsules** with instructions for giving them. One was to bring down the fever, another a purgative, the third to overcome an acid condition. The germs of **influenza** can only exist in an acid condition, he explained. He seemed to know all about influenza and said there was nothing to worry about if the fever did not go above one hundred and four degrees. This was a light **epidemic** of flu and there was no danger if you avoided **pneumonia**.

Back in the room I wrote the boy's temperature down and made a note of the time to give the various capsules.

Keys to Literature

Dialogue is the exact words that characters say to each other. What does Schatz say twice when his father tells him to go back to bed?

Predict

What will happen to Schatz as a result of having influenza?

"Do you want me to read to you?"

"All right. If you want to," said the boy. His face was very white and there were dark areas under his eyes. He lay still in the bed and seemed very detached from what was going on.

I read aloud from Howard Pyle's *Book of Pirates*; but I could see he was not following what I was reading.

"How do you feel, Schatz?" I asked him.

"Just the same, so far," he said.

I sat at the foot of the bed and read to myself while I waited for it to be time to give another capsule. It would have been natural for him to go to sleep, but when I looked up he was looking at the foot of the bed, looking very strangely.

"Why don't you try to go to sleep? I'll wake you up for the medicine."

"I'd rather stay awake."

After a while he said to me, "You don't have to stay in here with me, Papa, if it bothers you."

"It doesn't bother me."

"No, I mean you don't have to stay if it's going to bother you."

I thought perhaps he was a little lightheaded and after giving him the prescribed capsules at eleven o'clock I went out for a while.

It was a bright, cold day, the ground covered with a sleet that had frozen so that it seemed as if all the bare trees, the bushes, the cut brush and all the grass and the bare ground had been **varnished** with ice. I took the young Irish setter for a little walk up the road and along a frozen creek, but it was difficult to stand or walk on the glassy surface and the red dog slipped and **slithered** and I fell twice, hard, once dropping my gun and having it slide away over the ice.

Think About It

How do you think the father feels about his son? How do you know?

Think About It

How would you describe Schatz?

We **flushed** a covey of quail under a high clay bank with overhanging brush and I killed two as they went out of sight over the top of the bank. Some of the covey lit in trees, but most of them scattered into brush piles and it was necessary to jump on the ice-coated mounds of brush several times before they would flush. Coming out while you were poised unsteadily on the icy, springy brush they made difficult shooting and I killed two, missed five, and started back pleased to have found a covey close to the house and happy there were so many left to find on another day.

At the house they said the boy had refused to let anyone come into the room.

"You can't come in," he said. "You mustn't get what I have."

I went up to him and found him in exactly the position I had left him, white-faced, but with the tops of his cheeks flushed by the fever, staring still, as he had stared, at the foot of the bed.

I took his temperature.

"What is it?"

"Something like a hundred," I said. It was one hundred and two and four tenths.

"It was a hundred and two," he said.

"Who said so?"

"The doctor."

"Your temperature is all right," I said. "It's nothing to worry about."

"I don't worry," he said, "but I can't keep from thinking."

"Don't think," I said. "Just take it easy."

"I'm taking it easy," he said and looked straight ahead. He was evidently holding tight onto himself about something.

Think About It

Why do you think the father says the boy's temperature is only one hundred when it is really higher?

"Take this with water."

"Do you think it will do any good?"

"Of course it will."

I sat down and opened the Pirate book and **commenced** to read, but I could see he was not following, so I stopped.

"About what time do you think I'm going to die?" he asked.

"What?"

"About how long will it be before I die?"

"You aren't going to die. What's the matter with you?"

"Oh, yes, I am. I heard him say a hundred and two."

"People don't die with a fever of one hundred and two. That's a silly way to talk."

"I know they do. At school in France the boys told me you can't live with forty-four degrees. I've got a hundred and two."

He had been waiting to die all day, ever since nine o'clock in the morning.

Keys to Literature

What struggle, or **internal conflict**, is going on in Schatz's head all day?

"You poor Schatz," I said. "Poor old Schatz. It's like miles and kilometers. You aren't going to die. That's a different thermometer. On that thermometer thirty-seven is normal. On this kind it's ninety-eight."

"Are you sure?"

"Absolutely," I said. "It's like miles and kilometers. You know, like how many kilometers we make when we do seventy miles in the car?"

"Oh," he said.

But his gaze at the foot of the bed relaxed slowly. The hold over himself relaxed too, finally, and the next day it was very slack and he cried very easily at little things that were of no importance.

Meet the Author

ERNEST HEMINGWAY (1899–1961)

Ernest Hemingway grew up in Oak Park, Illinois. In high school, he liked hunting, boxing, and football. At nineteen, Hemingway was badly wounded in World War I. As he got better, he began to write stories. Often, the characters in his stories face great danger or death.

Hemingway liked adventure in his own life. He hunted big game animals all over the world. He tried to become a bullfighter. Hemingway used events from his life in his short stories and novels. In 1954, Hemingway won the Nobel Prize for literature. You might like to read his novel *The Old Man and the Sea*.

Check Your Predictions

1. Look back at the answer you gave for the Predict question. Would you change your answer? Explain.

Understand the Story

2. What does the doctor say is wrong with Schatz?

3. What does Schatz think is going to happen to him? Why does he think this?

4. What does Schatz's father explain to him about thermometers?

Think About the Story

5. Why doesn't Schatz talk about his fears sooner?

6. If you could change the title of this story, what would it be? Explain your choice.

7. Based on the dialogue in this story, how do the father and son feel about each other?

8. What internal conflict does Schatz face?

Extend Your Response

Write a summary of "A Day's Wait." Place each sentence of your summary on a separate index card. Be sure to write complete sentences. Then, mix up the order of the index cards and exchange them with a partner. Place each other's cards in order.

Keys to Literature

irony: a result that is opposite of what is expected

Example: Living in a garage would make many people unhappy. However, in this story, the mother is glad. The garage is better than other places the family has lived.

rising action: the buildup of excitement in a story

Example: After moving from place to place and hiding from school buses, the boy in this story finally gets to go to school. He hopes nothing will keep him from school this time.

Did You Know?

Migrant workers pick fruits and vegetables. Different crops ripen at different times, so migrant workers move from place to place to find work. Finding a decent place to live is hard for migrant workers. Their children often miss a lot of school.

Words to Know

circuit	a regular trip from place to place taken by people who do a certain kind of work
sharecropper	someone who works on a farm in exchange for a part of the crop
shack	a small house built in a simple, rough way
surplus	more than what is needed
nicks	small cuts, chips, or notches in something
termites	small insects like ants that eat wood and damage buildings

The Circuit

BY FRANCISCO JIMÉNEZ, *Adapted*

READ TO FIND OUT...
What makes a trumpet
so important?

It was that time of year again. The strawberry **sharecropper**, whose name was Ito, did not smile. The time for picking strawberries was almost over. The workers were not picking as many boxes as they had in June or July.

By the time August was almost over, there were fewer workers than before. On Sunday, only one worker—the best one—came to work. I liked him. Sometimes I talked to him during our half-hour lunch break. That is how I found out he was from Jalisco. Jalisco is the same state in Mexico my family was from. That Sunday was the last time I saw him.

At the end of that day, when the sun had gone down behind the mountains, Ito told us to go home. He yelled, *"Ya esora"* (*es hora*, meaning it's time, or

Think About It
What type of workers
are the narrator and
his family?

The Propagandist by Diego Rivera

time's up), in his broken Spanish. Every day at work, those had been the words I had waited to hear. I waited for those words twelve hours a day, every day, seven days a week, week after week. It made me sad to think I would never hear them again.

As we drove home, Papá did not say a word. He drove with both hands on the wheel. He stared at the dirt road. My older brother, Roberto, also said nothing. He leaned his head back and closed his eyes. Once in a while he cleared from his throat the dust that blew in the car window.

Yes, it was that time of year. We had to move on. When I opened the front door to our **shack**, I stopped. Everything we owned had been put in boxes. Suddenly I thought once more of all those hours, days, weeks, and months of work I had just finished. They seemed like the heavy load I was carrying. I sat down on a box. I thought of moving to Fresno and what was waiting for me there. The thought brought tears to my eyes.

That night I could not sleep. I lay in bed thinking about how I hated this move.

A little before five o'clock in the morning, Papá woke everyone up. A few minutes later, the quiet of the new day was broken by the yelling and screaming of my brothers and sisters. To them, moving was a great adventure. Soon, the barking of the dogs added to the noise.

While we packed the breakfast dishes, Papá went outside to start the "Carcanchita." That was the name Papá gave his old black 1938 Plymouth. He had bought it in a used car lot in Santa Rosa in 1949. Papá was proud of his little car. He had a right to be proud of it. He had spent a lot of time looking at other cars before buying this one. Finally, he chose the "Carcanchita." He checked it very carefully before driving it out of the car lot. He looked over every inch of the car. He listened to the motor, holding his head sideways, like a parrot. He listened for any noises that might mean car trouble. At last, Papá thought the car looked and sounded all right. But he wanted to know who the original owner was. He never did find out from the car salesman. Papá bought the car anyway. He figured the original owner must have been an important man. This was because he found a blue necktie behind the back seat of the car.

Papá parked the car out in front and left the motor running. *"Listo,"* he yelled. Without saying a word, Roberto and I began to carry the boxes out to the car. Roberto carried the two big boxes, and I carried the two smaller ones. Papá then threw the mattress on top of the car roof. Then he tied it with ropes to the front and back bumpers.

Everything was in the car except Mama's pot. It was a large, old pot she had bought at an army **surplus** store. She bought it in Santa Rosa the year I was born. The pot had many dents and **nicks**. The more dents and nicks it had gotten, the more Mama liked it. *"Mi olla,"* she would say in a proud voice.

I held the front door of the car open. Mama carefully carried out the pot by both handles. The pot was full of cooked beans. She was careful not to spill them. When she got to the car, Papá reached out to help her with the pot. Roberto opened the back door of the car. Papá put the pot gently on the floor behind the front seat. Then all of us climbed in. Papá sighed. He wiped the sweat off his forehead with his sleeve. In a tired voice, he said, *"Es todo."*

We drove away. I felt a lump in my throat. I turned around and looked at our little shack for the last time.

At sunset, we drove into a labor camp near Fresno. Papá did not speak English so Mama talked to the camp boss. She asked if he needed any more workers.

> ▶ In this story, the author uses many Spanish words. *Listo* means "Ready."

Think About It

Mi olla means "my pot" in Spanish. Why do you think Mama is so proud of this pot?

The camp boss scratched his head. He said, "We don't need no more. Check with Sullivan. He lives down the road. You can't miss his house. It's a big white house with a fence around it."

When we got there, Mama walked up to the house. She went through a white gate, past a row of rose bushes, up the stairs to the front door. She rang the doorbell. A light came on, and a tall man came out. Mama and the man talked for a short time. Then the man went back into his house. Mama came back to the car quickly. She said, "We have work! Mr. Sullivan says we can stay over there the whole season." She pointed to an old garage.

Keys to Literature

Why is it **ironic** that Mama is happy about having the garage to live in?

The garage was very old. It had no windows. The walls had been eaten by **termites**. The roof was full of holes. The dirt floor was the home of many worms. They made the floor look like a gray road map.

That night, by the light of a kerosene lamp, we cleaned our new home. Roberto swept away the loose dirt, so we had a floor of hard ground. Papá plugged the holes in the walls with old newspaper and the tops of tin cans. Mama fed my little brothers and sisters. Then Papá and Roberto brought in the mattress. They put it in the far corner of the garage. Papá said, "Mama, you and the little ones sleep on the mattress. Roberto, Panchito, and I will sleep outside under the trees."

Early next morning, Mr. Sullivan showed us where we would be working. After breakfast, Papá, Roberto, and I went out to pick Mr. Sullivan's grapes.

By about nine o'clock, it was very hot. The temperature was almost one hundred degrees. I was wet all over from sweat. My mouth felt like I had been eating cloth. I walked to the end of the row of grapevines. I picked up the jug of water we had brought and began to drink.

Roberto yelled, "Don't drink too much; you'll get sick." As soon as he said that, I felt sick to my stomach. I dropped down to my knees. I let the jug roll off my hands. I didn't move. I fixed my eyes on the hot, sandy ground. All I could hear was the noise of insects. Slowly, I began to feel better. I poured water over my face and neck. I watched the dirty water run down my arms to the ground.

I still felt a little dizzy when we stopped to eat lunch. It was past two o'clock. We sat under a large walnut tree that was on the side of the road. While we ate, Papá wrote down how many boxes we had picked. Roberto drew in the dirt with a stick. Suddenly Papá's face seemed scared as he looked down the road. He whispered loudly, "Here comes the school bus."

Roberto and I ran and hid behind the grapevines. We did not want to get in trouble for not going to school. Boys about my age, in nice clothes, got off the bus. They carried books under their arms. After they had crossed the street, the bus drove away. Roberto and I came out from behind the grape vines. Papá told us, *"Tienen que tener cuidado."*

After lunch, we went back to work. The sun beat down on us. The buzzing insects, the wet sweat, and the hot dry dust were with us all afternoon. The day seemed to last forever. At last, the sun went down behind the mountains. In an hour, it was too dark to work anymore. The vines covered the grapes like blankets. It was hard to find them. Papá said *"Vámanos."* It was time to quit work. Then Papá took out a pencil. He began to figure out how much money we had made on our first day. He wrote down numbers and crossed some out. Then he wrote down some more. At last, he said, *"Quince,"* in a low voice.

When we got home, we stood under a hose for a cold shower. Then we sat down to eat dinner. We used wooden boxes as a table. Mama had cooked a special dinner for us. We had rice and tortillas with *"carne con chile."* It was my favorite dish.

The next morning, I almost couldn't move. My body hurt all over. My arms and legs wouldn't move the way I wanted them to. I felt this way every morning for days. Then my body finally got used to the work.

It was Monday, the first week in November. Grape picking was finished. Now I could go to school. I woke up early that morning. I lay in bed and looked at the stars. I didn't have to work and that felt good. It also felt good to be starting sixth grade for the first time that year.

Since I couldn't sleep, I had breakfast with Papá and Roberto. I sat at the table across from Roberto. I kept my head down. I did not want to look up and face him. I knew he was sad. He was not going to school today. He was not going tomorrow, or next week, or next month. He would not go until he and Papá had finished picking cotton. That would be sometime in February. I rubbed my hands together. Pieces of my skin, dried out from picking grapes, fell to the floor in little rolls.

I felt better when Papá and Roberto left for work. I walked out to some high ground next to the shack. I watched the "Carcanchita" drive away in a cloud of dust.

Two hours later, around eight o'clock, I stood by the side of the road. I waited for school bus number 20. When it stopped, I climbed in. All the kids were busy talking or yelling. I sat in an empty seat in the back.

The bus stopped in front of the school. I felt very nervous. I looked out the bus window. I saw boys and girls carrying books under their arms. I put my hands in my pants' pockets and walked into the principal's office. When I walked in, I heard a woman's voice say, "May I help you?" The voice made me jump. I had not heard English words for months. For a few seconds, I did not speak. I looked at the lady. She was waiting for an answer. My first thought was to answer her in Spanish, but I held back. Finally, I remembered English words. I was able to tell her I wanted to be in the sixth grade. After I answered many questions, I was taken to the classroom.

Predict

Grape picking is finished. What do you think the narrator and Roberto will do now?

▶ Describe the narrator's feelings on the morning of his first day at school.

Keys to Literature

What is the **rising action** in this paragraph?

Mr. Lema was the sixth grade teacher. He said hello and told me which desk to sit at. Then he told the class who I was. Everyone's eyes were on me. I felt so nervous and scared I wished I were with Papá and Roberto picking cotton.

Mr. Lema took attendance. Then he told the class what they would be doing for the first hour. He said, "The first thing we have to do this morning is finish reading the story we began yesterday." His voice was happy and full of energy.

Mr. Lema walked up to me. He handed me an English book and asked me to read. He said in a polite voice, "We are on page 125." When I heard this, I felt my blood rush to my head. I felt dizzy.

Think About It

Why is it so hard for the narrator to read?

Mr. Lema asked, "Would you like to read?" His voice didn't sound very sure. I opened the book to page 125. My mouth was dry. My eyes began to water. I could not begin. Mr. Lema said in a kind voice, "You can read later."

The rest of reading time, I got more and more angry with myself. I thought to myself: I should have read.

During recess, I went into the restroom. I opened my English book to page 125. I began to read in a low voice. I pretended I was in class. There were many words I did not know. I closed the book and went back to the classroom.

Mr. Lema was sitting at his desk. He was correcting papers. When I came in, he looked up at me and smiled. I felt better. I walked up to Mr. Lema. I asked him if he could help me with the new words. Mr. Lema said, "I would be happy to help you."

The rest of the month I spent my lunch hours working with Mr. Lema. He was my best friend at school.

One Friday during lunch hour, Mr. Lema asked me to walk with him to the music room. As we walked into the building, he asked me, "Do you like music?"

I said, "Yes, I like *corridos.*"

Mr. Lema picked up a trumpet. He blew on it and handed it to me. The sound gave me goose bumps. I knew that sound. I had heard it in many *corridos.*

Mr. Lema said, "How would you like to learn how to play the trumpet?" He must have read my face. Before I could answer, he said, "I'll teach you how to play it during our lunch hours."

I could hardly wait to get home. I wanted to tell Papá and Mama the great news. As I got off the bus, my little brothers and sisters ran up to meet me. They were yelling and screaming. I thought they were happy to see me. But when I opened the door to our shack, I saw that everything we owned was packed up in boxes.

Think About It

If the narrator had stayed in school with Mr. Lema, how might his life have changed?

Meet the Author

FRANCISCO JIMÉNEZ (Born 1942)

Francisco Jiménez went to work at the age of six. He worked from sunrise to sunset, helping his family pick crops. The family moved often. They had to go wherever there was work. In each new place, Jiménez went to a different school.

"The Circuit" is based on Jiménez's memories growing up as a migrant worker. Changing schools taught him the importance of a good education. As an adult, Jiménez became a successful teacher, writer, editor, and administrator. He writes stories in English and in Spanish.

Check Your Predictions

1. Look back at the answers you gave for the Predict questions. Would you change your answers? Explain.

Understand the Story

2. Why does the family leave the strawberry fields?

3. Why does the narrator wait until November to go to school?

4. Why doesn't the narrator get a chance to learn the trumpet?

Think About the Story

5. How does the narrator feel about his family's way of life?

6. Why is Mr. Lema good for the narrator?

7. What incident is part of the rising action?

8. What is the irony at the end of the story?

Extend Your Response

Suppose you are the narrator. You are about to leave the Fresno area with your family. Write a good-bye letter to your teacher, Mr. Lema.

Learn More About It

MIGRANT WORKERS AND CÉSAR CHÁVEZ

Migrant workers live in many areas of the United States. They pick crops on a farm and then move on to other farms. Through the years, migrant workers have not always been treated well by farm owners.

Until the 1960s, migrant workers were not powerful enough to bargain for more pay and better working conditions. At that time, César Chávez, who had been a migrant worker himself, helped form the United Farm Workers Association. This union of about 50,000 members had the power to bargain with farm owners. Chávez often had to face violence as the union got started. He did not use violence, but rather strikes, boycotts, and picketing. In 1994, after Chávez had died, his widow accepted the Medal of Freedom for him from President Clinton.

Today, children of migrant workers still work in the fields. However, their conditions are greatly improved. Programs such as Even Start and Estrella help migrant children. Even Start provides videos that teach math and English. Estrella provides laptop computers that can be taken from farm to farm.

Apply and Connect

What kind of crops do the migrant workers in "The Circuit" pick? How are the narrator and his family treated by the farm owners they work for?

Summaries

The Jacket The boy in this story wants a cool black leather jacket. Instead, his mother buys him an ugly green vinyl one. The boy blames all his unhappiness on the jacket. After three years, the boy accepts the ugly jacket.

A Day's Wait Nine-year-old Schatz has the flu. The doctor tells him he has a temperature of one-hundred-and-two. Schatz thinks he is going to die. Eventually, Schatz shares his fear with his father. His father explains to Schatz that he misunderstood what the temperature means. He is not going to die.

The Circuit The narrator and his family work as fruit and cotton pickers. They move constantly, which the narrator hates. In one town, he goes to school for a few months. His teacher, Mr. Lema, helps him with reading. Mr. Lema offers to teach him the trumpet, too. The narrator is very happy. When he gets home that day, however, his family is about to move again.

commenced
blurry
slithered
camouflage
nicks
surplus

Vocabulary Review

Write the word and its matching number on a separate sheet of paper.

1. not clear

2. a disguise

3. began

4. slid along

5. more than what is needed

6. dents

Chapter Quiz

**Write your answers in one or two complete sentences.
Use a separate sheet of paper.**

1. **The Jacket** Why does the boy's mother buy him such a big jacket?

2. **The Jacket** What problems does the boy blame on his jacket?

3. **A Day's Wait** What does Schatz think is going to happen to him?

4. **A Day's Wait** What does Schatz's father explain to him about his illness?

5. **The Circuit** Why does the narrator's family have to move so often?

6. **The Circuit** Why is the narrator upset at the end of the story?

Critical Thinking

7. **The Jacket** How do you think wearing the green jacket for three years might have changed the boy in the story?

8. **A Day's Wait** What is the internal conflict that Schatz experiences?

Chapter Activity

Which of the three stories in this chapter did you like best? Write a letter to a friend explaining why you liked it. Include character details from the story and discuss at least one of the Keys to Literature from the chapter. Be sure your letter has a heading, a body, and a closing.

Unit 2 **Review**

On a separate sheet of paper, write the letter that best completes each sentence below.

1. In "The All-American Slurp," the narrator is embarrassed by

A. her friend's slurping.
B. the waiter's strange looks.
C. her family's table manners.
D. her mother's dinner party.

2. In "Lame Deer Remembers," Lame Deer is punished because he

A. gives away his gray pony.
B. does not want to live with his grandparents.
C. cries at the give-away ceremony.
D. pierces his sister's ears.

3. In *Prisoner of My Country,* Yoshiko realizes what is happening to her when she

A. says good-bye to the neighbors.
B. packs the Camp Bundle with her mother and sister.
C. sees guards with bayonets.
D. goes to the Harpainter's house.

4. According to the boy in "The Jacket," the green jacket causes

A. his work to be poor in school.
B. the girls in his class to like him.
C. his brother to hate him.
D. his mother to be proud of him.

5. In "A Day's Wait," Schatz is upset because

A. his father goes hunting.
B. he thinks he is going to die.
C. he has to stay in bed.
D. he is missing school.

6. At the end of "The Circuit," the narrator hurries to tell his parents that

A. he knows how to read.
B. he is going to learn to play the trumpet.
C. he is going to move.
D. he is going to become a teacher.

Making Connections
On a separate sheet of paper, write the answers to these questions.

7. The narrators in both *Prisoner of My Country* and "The Circuit" must leave their homes. Explain.

8. Which selection in this unit do you think presented the most interesting memory? Explain.

Writing an Essay
Choose one of the memoirs or short stories in this unit. Describe one of the characters and the internal conflict the character has to deal with.

Unit 3 ▶ Accepting a Challenge

Chapter 6 ## Fiction

Thank You, M'am
by Langston Hughes

from The Red Badge of Courage
by Stephen Crane, adapted

Chapter 7 ## Poetry

The Ballad of John Henry
anonymous

Harriet Tubman
by Eloise Greenfield

O Captain! My Captain!
by Walt Whitman

Paul Revere's Ride
by Henry Wadsworth Longfellow

Chapter 8 ## Nonfiction

from Rosa Parks
by Eloise Greenfield

from Helen Keller: The Story
of My Life
by Helen Keller, adapted

Shipwreck of the Whaleship *Essex*
by Owen Chase

151

Kids on Bikes by David Parks

What challenges are the people in this image facing?

Chapter 6 / Fiction

ACCEPTING A CHALLENGE

Learning Objectives

- Recognize short stories and novel chapters.
- Identify characters in a story.
- Explain a story's theme.
- Identify a story's setting.
- Understand what idioms are.

Fiction and Accepting Challenges

Short stories and novels are both works of fiction. Fiction is about imaginary people and events.

A short story

- has few characters.
- takes place over a short time.
- has a simple plot.
- is several pages long.

A novel

- has many characters.
- takes place over a long time.
- has a complicated plot.
- can be several hundred pages long.
- is made up of chapters.

In a short story or novel about a challenge, the character faces unusual difficulty and has to figure out how to deal with it. The characters struggle with strong feelings as they solve internal and external conflicts.

Keys to Literature

character: a person in a story

Example: This story's characters are a boy and a woman.

theme: the main idea of a story, novel, play, or poem

Example: The theme of this story is that one person's action can make a difference.

Words to Know

permit	allow
frail	weak, thin
contact	two things or people coming together
jerked	gave a quick pull or twist
roomers	people who pay to live in a room of a house
whereupon	after which
suede	leather with the rough side rubbed until it is soft
pause	a stop or short wait
latching	holding together tightly
barren	empty

Thank You, M'am

BY LANGSTON HUGHES

She was a large woman with a large purse that had everything in it but hammer and nails. It had a long strap and she carried it slung across her shoulder. It was about eleven o'clock at night, and she was walking alone, when a boy ran up behind her and tried to snatch her purse. The strap broke with the single tug the boy gave it from behind. But the boy's weight, and the weight of the purse combined caused him to lose his balance so, instead of taking off full blast as he had hoped, the boy fell on his back on the sidewalk, and his legs flew up. The large woman simply turned around and kicked him right square in his blue-jeaned sitter. Then she reached down, picked the boy up by his shirt front, and shook him until his teeth rattled.

READ TO FIND OUT...
Why would someone want to help a person who has just tried to rob her?

Keys to Literature

The **characters** are the people in a story. In this story, the boy and the woman are the characters.

Think About It

How does the woman stop the boy?

Think About It

Why doesn't the woman let the boy go?

Predict

What do you think the woman will do to the boy now?

After that the woman said, "Pick up my pocketbook, boy, and give it here."

She still held him. But she bent down enough to **permit** him to stoop and pick up her purse. Then she said, "Now ain't you ashamed of yourself?"

Firmly gripped by his shirt front, the boy said, "Yes'm."

The woman said, "What did you want to do it for?"

The boy said, "I didn't aim to."

She said, "You a lie!"

By that time two or three people passed, stopped, turned to look, and some stood watching.

"If I turn you loose, will you run?" asked the woman.

"Yes'm," said the boy.

"Then I won't turn you loose," said the woman. She did not release him.

"I'm very sorry, lady, I'm sorry," whispered the boy.

"Um-hum! And your face is dirty. I got a great mind to wash your face for you. Ain't you got nobody home to tell you to wash your face?"

"No'm," said the boy.

"Then it will get washed this evening," said the large woman starting up the street, dragging the frightened boy behind her.

He looked as if he were fourteen or fifteen, **frail** and willow-wild, in tennis shoes and blue jeans.

The woman said, "You ought to be my son. I would teach you right from wrong. Least I can do right now is to wash your face. Are you hungry?"

"No'm," said the being-dragged boy. "I just want you to turn me loose."

"Was I bothering *you* when I turned that corner?" asked the woman.

"No'm."

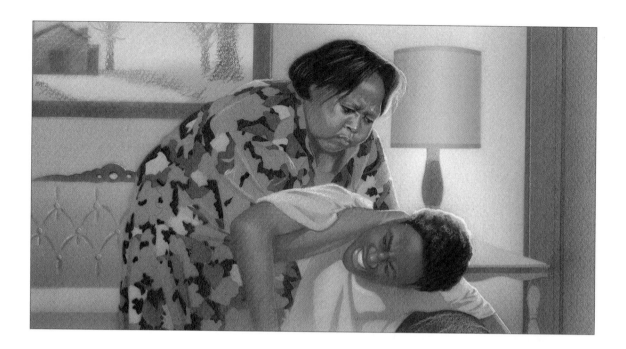

"But you put yourself in **contact** with *me*," said the woman. "If you think that that contact is not going to last awhile, you got another thought coming. When I get through with you, sir, you are going to remember Mrs. Luella Bates Washington Jones."

Sweat popped out on the boy's face and he began to struggle. Mrs. Jones stopped, **jerked** him around in front of her, put a half nelson about his neck, and continued to drag him up the street. When she got to her door, she dragged the boy inside, down a hall, and into a large kitchenette-furnished room at the rear of the house. She switched on the light and left the door open. The boy could hear other **roomers** laughing and talking in the large house. Some of their doors were open, too, so he knew he and the woman were not alone. The woman still had him by the neck in the middle of her room.

She said, "What is your name?"

"Roger," answered the boy.

"Then, Roger, you go to that sink and wash your face," said the woman, **whereupon** she turned him loose—at last. Roger looked at the door—looked at the woman—looked at the door—*and went to the sink.*

"Let the water run until it gets warm," she said. "Here's a clean towel."

"You gonna take me to jail?" asked the boy, bending over the sink.

"Not with that face, I would not take you nowhere," said the woman. "Here I am trying to get home to cook me a bite to eat and you snatch my pocketbook! Maybe you ain't been to your supper either, late as it be. Have you?"

"There's nobody home at my house," said the boy.

"Then we'll eat," said the woman. "I believe you're hungry—or been hungry—to try to snatch my pocketbook."

"I wanted a pair of blue **suede** shoes," said the boy.

"Well, you didn't have to snatch *my* pocketbook to get some suede shoes," said Mrs. Luella Bates Washington Jones. "You could of asked me."

"M'am?"

The water dripping from his face, the boy looked at her. There was a long **pause.** A very long pause. After he had dried his face and not knowing what else to do dried it again, the boy turned around, wondering what next. The door was open. He could make a dash for it down the hall. He could run, run, run, run, *run!*

The woman was sitting on the daybed. After awhile she said, "I were young once and I wanted things I could not get."

There was another long pause. The boy's mouth opened. Then he frowned, but not knowing he frowned.

Think About It

Why is Mrs. Jones so kind to Roger?

The woman said, "Um-hum! You thought I was going to say *but*, didn't you? You thought I was going to say, *but I didn't snatch people's pocketbooks.* Well, I wasn't going to say that." Pause. Silence. "I have done things, too, which I would not tell you, son—neither tell God, if He didn't already know. So you set down while I fix us something to eat. You might run that comb through your hair so you will look presentable."

In another corner of the room behind a screen was a gas plate and an icebox. Mrs. Jones got up and went behind the screen. The woman did not watch the boy to see if he was going to run now, nor did she watch her purse which she left behind her on the daybed. But the boy took care to sit on the far side of the room where he thought she could easily see him out of the corner of her eye, if she wanted to. He did *not* trust the woman not to trust him. And he did not want to be mistrusted now.

"Do you need somebody to go to the store," asked the boy, "maybe to get some milk or something?"

"Don't believe I do," said the woman, "unless you just want sweet milk yourself. I was going to make cocoa out of this canned milk I got here."

"That will be fine," said the boy.

She heated some lima beans and ham she had in the icebox, made the cocoa, and set the table. The woman did not ask the boy anything about where he lived, or his folks, or anything else that would embarrass him. Instead, as they ate, she told him about her job in a hotel beauty shop that stayed open late, what the work was like, and how all kinds of women came in and out, blondes, redheads, and Spanish. Then she cut him a half of her ten-cent cake.

"Eat some more, son," she said.

> ## Think About It
> Why do you think Roger wants Mrs. Jones to trust him?

> ## Keys to Literature
> Mrs. Jones treats Roger very kindly. This helps us understand one of the **themes** of this story: Kindness can be a very powerful thing.

Think About It

What does Mrs. Jones mean when she says that "shoes come by devilish like that will burn your feet"?

Keys to Literature

Think about Roger's **character**. How has meeting Mrs. Jones changed him?

When they were finished eating she got up and said, "Now, here, take this ten dollars and buy yourself some blue suede shoes. And next time, do not make the mistake of **latching** onto *my* pocketbook *nor nobody else's*—because shoes come by devilish like that will burn your feet. I got to get my rest now. But I wish you would behave yourself, son, from here on in."

She led him down the hall to the front door and opened it. "Goodnight! Behave yourself, boy!" she said, looking out into the street.

The boy wanted to say something else other than, "Thank you, m'am," to Mrs. Luella Bates Washington Jones, but he couldn't do so as he turned at the **barren** stoop and looked back at the large woman in the door. He barely managed to say, "Thank you," before she shut the door. And he never saw her again.

Meet the Author

LANGSTON HUGHES *(1902–1967)*

Langston Hughes was born in Joplin, Missouri, and brought up in Cleveland, Ohio. By the time he finished high school, Hughes had already published his first poem. As a young man, he traveled around the world as a sailor. Eventually, he settled in Harlem, in New York City, where he became one of the best-known African American writers in the country.

Hughes's poems describe what it is like to be an African American. He used jazz and blues rhythms in many of his poems. In addition to poetry, Hughes wrote stories, plays, songs, movie scripts, and essays. He also had his own newspaper column. Some of Hughes's poems are "Harlem," "Dreams," and "Mother to Son."

Check Your Predictions

1. Look back at the answer you gave for the Predict question. Would you change your answer? Explain.

Understand the Story

2. What happens to Mrs. Jones as she walks home from work?

3. What does Mrs. Jones do to the boy when he falls to the sidewalk?

4. What is Roger's reason for trying to steal from Mrs. Jones?

Think About the Story

5. At one point in the story, Roger could try to run away. Why do you think he does not do this?

6. At the end of the story, Roger thanks Mrs. Jones. What is he thanking her for?

7. How would you describe Roger after his experience with Mrs. Jones?

8. What is the theme, or main idea, of this story?

Extend Your Response

Think about a different ending for "Thank You, M'am." How else might Roger have said goodbye to Mrs. Jones? What might he have done next? Write a paragraph to explain your ideas.

Keys to Literature

setting: the time and place of a story

> Example: In this story, the time is during the Civil War. The place is in the woods near a road.

idiom: a phrase or an expression that has a different meaning from what the individual words usually mean

> Example: *They stood their ground* means "They did not move away."

Words to Know

dodge	move quickly to get out of the way
gaunt	thin and bony
comrades	friends
volley	a burst of bullets
regiment	a very large unit of soldiers made up of two or more large groups of soldiers
sputtering	making fast, spitting sounds
frenzy	a wild, excited feeling
retreating	running away from an attack
staggered	walked in an unsteady way, as if about to fall
weary	tired; worn out
artillery	large guns

from The Red Badge of Courage

BY STEPHEN CRANE, *Adapted*

Victory

Once again, enemy troops began to pour forth from the woods. Now Henry was full of self-confidence. He stood tall and calm. He looked at the line of troops that formed a blue curve along the side of a hill. He watched the attack begin against a part of the line. He smiled when he saw men **dodge** the shells that were thrown at them.

The youth stood still as he viewed the scene. He still held the flag. But he seemed to have forgotten that he also had a role to play. For the moment he was too busy watching the others. The crash and swing of the great drama made him lean forward. He was not even aware of his breathing. The flag hung silently over him.

READ TO FIND OUT...

What does Henry learn about himself from being in a war?

Predict

From the chapter title "Victory," what do you think this chapter will be about?

A line of the enemy came within dangerous range. The Rebel soldiers could be seen clearly—tall, **gaunt** men with excited faces. They were running with long strides toward a fence.

At the sight of this danger, Henry's **comrades** threw up their rifles and fired a **volley** at the enemy. There had been no order given. The men had immediately sent forth their flock of bullets without waiting for a command.

But the enemy soldiers were quick to gain the protection of the fence. They slid down behind it. From this position, they began to slice up the men in blue.

Henry's **regiment** began to take new losses. One after another, grunting bundles of blue dropped to the ground. The orderly sergeant was shot through the cheeks. His jaw hung down, showing a mass of blood and broken teeth in the wide opening of his mouth. He tried to cry out for help and ran off to the rear of the line.

Others fell down around the feet of their companions. Some of the wounded crawled out and away. But many lay still, their bodies twisted into impossible shapes.

The youth saw the lieutenant holding a position in the rear. The man continued to swear at his troops. But now it was with the air of a man who was using his last box of curses.

The colonel came running along the back of the line. There were other officers following him. "We must charge them!" they shouted. "We must charge them!" they cried with angry voices. They seemed to be afraid that the men might not obey their orders.

Henry studied the distance between him and the enemy. He saw that his regiment would have to go forward. It would be death to stay where they were. Their best hope was to push the enemy away from the fence.

The men of the regiment seemed to agree. At the shouted words of command, the soldiers sprang forward. They bolted ahead in eager leaps. It was as if they knew that this was a last burst of energy. It was as if they had agreed to get the job done quickly so they could go on living.

The blind rush carried the men in dusty and tattered blue across the field toward the fence. From behind the fence the rifles of the enemy kept on **sputtering**.

The youth kept the bright flag to the front. He was waving his free arm in circles, shrieking madly as he ran. It seemed that the mob of men in blue were growing wild as they hurled themselves forward. They were in a state of **frenzy**, shouting and cheering. This made Henry run even faster. Now he thought of the bullets only as things that could stop him from reaching the fence.

As the regiment moved ahead, Henry saw that many of the men in gray were **retreating**. Some of them turned now and then to fire at the advancing blue wave. Just one part of the Rebel line was held by a grim and stubborn group. They stood their ground. Most of them were settled firmly down behind fence posts and rails. Their flag waved over them while their rifles fired fiercely.

The men in blue were now very close to the men in gray. Both groups began to shout insults at each other. Those in blue showed their teeth; their eyes were wide and shone all white.

The youth had fixed his gaze on the Rebel flag. He plunged like a mad horse at it. He would not let it escape him if wild blows could seize it. His own flag was winging toward the other.

Think About It

The author says that the soldiers' blue uniforms are "dusty and tattered." What does it tell you about the battle they are fighting?

Keys to Literature

They stood their ground is an **idiom**. Read the sentences before and after this idiom to help you figure out what it means.

Think About It

Why doesn't Henry seem to be horrified at the awful wounds and death all around him?

Keys to Literature

Why is the fence an important part of the **setting**?

Think About It

Why do you think capturing the enemy's flag is so important?

The men in blue came to a sudden halt at close range. They roared a swift volley. The group in gray was split and broken by this fire. But still they fought. The men in blue yelled again and rushed in upon them.

Henry saw several men stretched upon the ground. Standing among them was the man carrying the Rebel flag. He had been hit and was having trouble staying on his feet. The look of death was on his face. He held onto the flag and **staggered** backward away from the fence.

Wilson leaped over the fence and sprang at the Rebel flag. He pulled at it and grabbed it away from the wounded man with a mad cry. The Rebel soldier, gasping, lurched over and fell down. His dead face was turned to the ground. There was a pool of blood on the grass under his head.

Henry's regiment broke out into wild cheers. Those who still had hats or caps threw them high into the air.

At one part of the line, four enemy soldiers had been taken prisoner. One of the prisoners had been wounded in the foot. He cursed at his captors. Another prisoner, a young boy, was calm and good natured. He was quite willing to talk about the battle with the Union soldiers.

The third prisoner coldly answered any question with, "Ah, go to hell!" And the fourth prisoner said nothing. He acted as if he were ashamed to have been captured.

After the men had celebrated enough, they settled down behind the fence. Since there was some tall grass there, Henry stretched out and rested in it. He leaned his flag against the fence.

Wilson came to him there. He was holding his treasure—the Rebel flag. The two **weary** men sat side by side and congratulated each other.

Glad to Be Alive

The roar of the gunfire slowly died away. The rifles were silent. Every now and then the boom of **artillery** could be heard in the distance. Otherwise it was quiet on the battlefield.

The youth stood up. He shaded his eyes with his grimy hand and gazed over the field. "Well, what now, I wonder?" he said.

His friend also rose and said. "I bet we're going to get along out of here and back over the river."

They waited, watching. Within an hour the regiment received orders to retrace its way. The men grunted as they got up from the grass. They shook their tired legs, and stretched their arms over their heads. One man swore as he rubbed his eyes. They all groaned, "Oh, Lord!"

The men moved slowly back across the field. They kept on marching until they had joined the other regiments of the brigade. The soldiers now marched in a long column through the woods. Finally they reached the road.

At this point the brigade curved away from the woods across a field. The column of soldiers went winding off in the direction of the river. Henry turned his head and looked over his shoulder. Then he said to his friend, "Well, it's all over."

Wilson gazed backward. "By God, it is," he agreed.

Through Henry's mind flashed pictures of all that had happened in the past two days. He kept seeing again the enemy soldiers charging at him. He remembered the roar of the guns and the bullets whizzing by him. He could still hear the shells that had exploded near him.

Keys to Literature

How is the **setting** of this chapter different from the setting of "Victory"?

The longer Henry thought about it, the more amazed he was. Here he was, walking along, talking, breathing. He was still alive. The battle was over, and he had come through it alive. This thought filled him with happiness.

Suddenly Wilson cried, "Good Lord!"

"What?" asked the youth.

"Good Lord!" repeated his friend, "You know Jimmie Rogers? You remember when he was hurt and we tried to find some water for him? Well, he—gosh, I haven't seen him since then. Say, has anybody seen Jimmie Rogers?"

"Seen him? No! He's dead," said the soldier marching in back of Wilson.

Wilson swore. The men kept marching.

Henry began to think about everything he had done. He remembered his brave deeds and thought about the praise he'd received, he was proud of himself.

But then he reminded himself of his failures. Why had he fled from that first battle? He knew he was not a coward. He must have run because he didn't know any better. Yet he felt ashamed.

Henry felt even greater shame when he remembered the tattered soldier who had needed his help. He had left the poor man to die alone in the field. Could he ever forgive himself? He broke out in a chill of sweat and swore out loud.

Wilson turned to him. "What's the matter, Henry?" he asked. The youth's reply was an outburst of curses.

Henry was going over each detail of the scene with the tattered soldier. Finally he calmed down. He knew that he couldn't change the past. Perhaps such a great mistake could be useful to him. It might teach him to

Think About It
The soldiers talk about something from an earlier chapter in the novel. From what they say, what do you think happened in that chapter?

Think About It
Although Henry ran away in the first battle, how do you know he is not a coward anymore?

Keys to Literature

Think about the **idiom**
to see things in balance.
What does it mean?

see things in balance. There was no need for him to feel too guilty nor too proud. He need not be loud or boastful. He was but a man, after all.

It began to rain. The column of weary soldiers marched through a sea of liquid brown mud. The men were muttering and swearing. Yet the youth smiled. He saw that he was going to be all right. He had rid himself of the sickness of battle. The nightmare, the heat and pain of war, was in the past.

Over the river a golden ray of sun came through the dark rain clouds.

Meet the Author

STEPHEN CRANE *(1871–1900)*

Stephen Crane grew up in Newark, New Jersey. In college, he was a star baseball player and almost joined the National Baseball League. Instead, Crane moved to New York City and became a writer. He wrote *The Red Badge of Courage* when he was 24 years old. It is considered one of the best war novels ever written. However, Crane himself, was never a soldier. He was born after the Civil War was over.

The Red Badge of Courage made Crane famous. Newspaper editors sent him to Europe and Cuba to write about the wars there. He became ill and died when he was only 28 years old.

Check Your Predictions

1. Look back at the answers you gave for the Predict questions. Would you change your answers? Explain.

Understand the Story

2. What is Henry's role in the war?

3. What is happening when "grunting bundles of blue dropped to the ground"?

4. After the battle, what flashes through Henry's mind?

Think About the Story

5. Henry is a Union soldier. What does the Rebel flag mean to him?

6. Why is the wooden fence such an important part of the setting of this story?

7. When Henry thinks about the battle, he realizes he "is but a man after all." What do you think this idiom means?

8. The novel ends with a golden ray of sun coming through the dark rain clouds. What does this stand for?

Extend Your Response

Suppose you are Henry. You will soon return home from the war. Write a letter to a friend or relative telling that you are safe and on your way. Describe some of the things you hope to do now that the war is over.

Learn More About It

CIVIL WAR BATTLEFIELDS

Civil War battlefields were huge. One part of a battlefield might be quiet, while not too far away, a bloody struggle might be taking place. Most of the soldiers, like Henry in *The Red Badge of Courage*, saw only what was happening in one small area. Often, the generals could not see the whole battle.

Storming of Fort Wagner by Kurz and Allison

Sometimes, the generals watched from a hill overlooking the battlefield. Then, they sent out riders to give orders. Other riders came back from different areas to report to the generals. In this way, the generals could tell which units needed help. They could see the enemy's strengths and weaknesses and plan how to win.

A soldier in battle, however, could not always hear the orders. The sound of gunfire was very loud, and a soldier might be running. His musket, a gun with a long barrel, had to be reloaded after each shot.

If a soldier was nervous and made a mistake, his musket would not fire. After the Battle of Gettysburg, more than half of the muskets that were found had been loaded incorrectly. They had been useless.

Apply and Connect

The selection from *The Red Badge of Courage* describes a battle. Describe the battlefield that serves as the setting for "Victory."

Summaries

Thank You, M'am Roger tries to steal Mrs. Jones's purse, but she catches him and drags him home with her. She then feeds Roger, and they become friends. Mrs. Jones gives Roger money and tells him not to steal again. When they say goodbye, Roger can say only, "Thank you."

The Red Badge of Courage Henry Fleming is a Union soldier fighting in the Civil War. When Rebel troops fire on his regiment, Henry waves the flag and his unit charges. Henry's regiment defeats the Rebels, and after the battle, Henry feels proud. However, he also feels ashamed of having run away from an earlier battle.

pause

permit

contact

barren

frail

weary

Vocabulary Review

Complete each sentence with a word from the box. Use a separate sheet of paper.

1. I tried to _____ you by e-mail, but you did not answer.

2. There was a _____ before Jan spoke while she thought about what she wanted to say.

3. I was _____ after the 20-mile hike, so I went right to sleep.

4. Jody was so _____ after her operation that she needed help walking.

5. The landowners would not _____ us to hike on their property.

6. The family had moved out, and the house was _____.

Chapter Quiz

Answer the following questions in one or two complete sentences. Use a separate sheet of paper.

1. Thank You, M'am Why does Roger try to steal Mrs. Jones's purse?

2. Thank You, M'am What does Mrs. Jones tell Roger he could have done instead of trying to steal from her?

3. Thank You, M'am What does Mrs. Jones give Roger?

4. The Red Badge of Courage What does Henry's regiment try to do in the battle?

5. The Red Badge of Courage What does Henry do to help his regiment during the charge?

6. The Red Badge of Courage Why does Henry feel both ashamed and proud after the battle?

Critical Thinking

7. Thank You, M'am Why do you think Mrs. Jones does not call the police after Roger tries to steal her purse?

8. The Red Badge of Courage At the beginning of the novel, Henry thinks a wound is like "a red badge of courage." By the end, do you think Henry feels this way? Why or why not?

Chapter Activity

Write a poem that has five lines about one of the characters in this chapter.
Line 1: one word—the character's name
Line 2: two adjectives that describe him or her
Line 3: three verbs that tell what the character does
Line 4: four words that tell how you feel about him or her
Line 5: one word—the character's name or another name for him or her

Sonny's Quilt by Faith Ringgold (born 1930)

What does this picture say about challenges?

Chapter **7** Poetry

ACCEPTING A CHALLENGE

Learning Objectives

- Recognize dialect.
- Understand what a ballad is.
- Recognize rhythm and repetition in a poem.
- Identify the use of symbolism.
- Explain the story in a narrative poem.
- Recognize imagery in a poem.

Preview Activity

Think of a famous person who faced a great challenge. Make a list of words and phrases to describe this person. Do not write down the person's name. Share your list with others. Have them try to guess who the person is.

Poetry and Accepting Challenges

A poem can express strong feelings by awakening our senses.

sense of sight: We see how the poem's lines are arranged.

sense of hearing: We hear the poem's rhythms and rhymes.

all our senses: We experience the poem through colorful language.

The poems in this chapter are about people who meet challenges. These poems may

- repeat sentences to remind us of a hero's greatness.
- have symbols that stand for a hero and the things he or she does.
- use colorful words to describe a hero.

Keys to Literature

dialect: the form of a language that is spoken by people living in a certain place.

> Example: *"I'd hammer my fool self to death, Lawd, Lawd."*

ballad: a song that tells a story

> Example: "The Ballad of John Henry" is a song about a contest between a man and a machine.

Did You Know?

Most people agree that John Henry was a real person. He was an African American railroad worker who lived in West Virginia around 1870. The men he worked with were amazed by his size and strength. One of them probably made up this ballad about him.

Words to Know

steel-drivin'	using a hammer to pound a pointed piece of steel into rock
drive	force a piece of metal into a rock with a hammer
steam drill	a steam-powered machine used to cut through rock
yonder	in the distance; over there
choke	clog or block
locomotive	an engine used to pull railroad cars

The Ballad of John Henry

AN ANONYMOUS POEM

READ TO FIND OUT…
Can a man beat
a machine?

John Henry was a little baby boy
You could hold him in the palm of your hand.
He gave a long and lonesome cry,
"Gonna be a steel-drivin' man, Lawd, Lawd,
5   Gonna be a **steel-drivin'** man."

They took John Henry to the tunnel,
Put him in the lead to **drive**,
The rock was so tall, John Henry so small,
That he laid down his hammer and he cried,
10   "Lawd, Lawd,"
Laid down his hammer and he cried.

▶ Notice the repeated
words at the end of
each stanza. Look for
more repeated words
as you read.

Keys to Literature

In line 18, what do you think the words *ain't nothin' but* are **dialect** for?

John Henry started on the right hand,
The **steam drill** started on the left,
"Fo' I'd let that steamdrill beat me down,
15 I'd hammer my fool self to death, Lawd, Lawd,
Hammer my fool self to death."

John Henry told his captain,
"A man ain't nothin' but a man,
Fo' I let your steamdrill beat me down
20 I'll die with this hammer in my hand, Lawd,
     Lawd,
Die with this hammer in my hand."

Now the Captain told John Henry,
"I believe my tunnel's sinkin' in."
25 "Stand back, Captain, and doncha be afraid,
That's nothin' but my hammer catchin' wind,
     Lawd, Lawd,
That's nothin' but my hammer catchin' wind."

Predict

Who do you think will win the contest—John Henry or the steam drill?

John Henry told his Cap'n,
30 "Look **yonder**, boy, what do I see?
Your drill's done broke and your hole's done
       choke,
And you can't drive steel like me, Lawd, Lawd,
You can't drive steel like me."

35 John Henry hammerin' in the mountain,
Till the handle of his hammer caught on fire,
He drove so hard till he broke his po' heart,
Then he laid down his hammer and he died,
       Lawd, Lawd,
40 He laid down his hammer and he died.

They took John Henry to the tunnel,
And they buried him in the sand,
An' every **locomotive** come rollin' by
Say, "There lies a steel-drivin' man, Lawd, Lawd,
45 There lies a steel-drivin' man."

▶ Reread the poem aloud.
Notice how the repeated
words at the end of each
stanza create the rhythm
of the swinging hammer.

Keys to Literature

Why would someone
sing this **ballad** slowly
and in a sad voice?

Meet the Author

No one knows the name of the person who wrote "The Ballad of
John Henry." It may have been someone who worked on the railroad
with John Henry, but this person did not write down the words to the
song. He just sang it for the workers.

As years went by, other people started singing the ballad. As it
became more and more popular, singers added more stanzas. They
changed some of the facts too. Years later, somebody wrote down
the words and music. By that time, however, the name of the original
author was forgotten.

Check Your Predictions

1. Look back at the answer you gave for the Predict question. Would you change your answer? Explain.

Understand the Poem

2. What does John Henry say when he is a baby?

3. What does John Henry promise his captain?

4. What happens to John Henry after he beats the steam drill?

5. Where is John Henry buried?

Think About the Poem

6. Is beating the steam drill important to John Henry? How do you know?

7. Why do you think people made up and sang this ballad?

8. Dialect is used in Line 15. What do you think "I'd hammer my fool self to death" means?

Extend Your Response

Rewrite this ballad as a short story. Tell about the contest between John Henry and the steam drill. Use dialogue to explain what John Henry says to the captain. Tell what the other workers see and hear, too.

Learn More About It

AMERICAN TALL TALES

"The Ballad of John Henry" is based on an American tall tale. A tall tale is a story in which the facts and details are exaggerated, or made to seem more than they really are.

Paul Bunyan carrying a tree on his shoulder and an ax in his hand.

Exaggeration is an important part of a tall tale. In "Pecos Bill," a tall tale about an American cowboy, Bill was not just a *big* man; he was bigger than a mountain. In "Paul Bunyan," this American logger could chop down an entire forest in a day.

Many American tall tales were told by the pioneers along the U.S. frontier, where life was hard and dangerous. Storytelling was a way for people to have fun. It made people laugh at the end of a hard day, and it took their minds off their troubles.

Tall tales do not have just one author. They have dozens of them. As a tall tale was told, the teller would add more and more to it. Then, the listeners would add their ideas, too.

Tall tales are popular all over the world. Wherever you live, someone is probably telling one. Ask around!

Apply and Connect

In what ways is "The Ballad of John Henry" a tall tale?

Keys to Literature

rhythm: a sound pattern of stressed syllables, or beats, in a poem

   Example: *"Farewell!" she **sang** to her **friends** one **night** ...*

repetition: words or sentences used over and over to create a feeling or mood

   Example: *And didn't stay one either*
   And didn't stay one either

Did You Know?

Harriet Tubman was born into slavery in Maryland in 1820. When she was a child, her owner beat her so badly that for the rest of her life she had dizzy spells. Tubman escaped when she was 29 years old. She helped more than 300 other people to escape.

Words to Know

farewell	goodbye
mighty	very
slave catchers	people who captured runaway slaves and returned them to their owners for money

Harriet Tubman

BY ELOISE GREENFIELD

Harriet Tubman didn't take no stuff
Wasn't scared of nothing neither
Didn't come in this world to be no slave
And wasn't going to stay one either

5 "**Farewell**!" she sang to her friends one night
She was **mighty** sad to leave 'em
But she ran away that dark, hot night
Ran looking for her freedom

READ TO FIND OUT...
Why would someone who had escaped slavery return to the South again and again?

Keys to Literature

Read the poem aloud. Listen to the beats in each line. Those beats give the poem its **rhythm**.

Harriet Tubman by William H. Johnson

She ran to the woods and she ran through the woods
10 With the **slave catchers** right behind her
And she kept on going till she got to the North
Where those mean men couldn't find her

Nineteen times she went back South
To get three hundred others
15 She ran for her freedom nineteen times
To save black sisters and brothers

Harriet Tubman didn't take no stuff
Wasn't scared of nothing neither
Didn't come in this world to be no slave
20 And didn't stay one either

And didn't stay one either

Think About It

The last stanza of this poem is almost the same as the first stanza. Why do you think the author repeats the stanza?

$\mathcal{M}$eet the $\mathcal{A}$uthor

ELOISE GREENFIELD *(Born 1929)*

Eloise Greenfield was born in North Carolina and raised in Washington, D.C. She has been writing books for young people for more than thirty years. Greenfield has won many awards and honors for her poetry, biographies, and fiction.

Greenfield's first collection of poems is called *Honey, I Love* (1978). It contains poems about the beauty of everyday life. She also has written a three-generation memoir called *Childtimes* and *For the Love of the Game: Michael Jordan and Me.*

Understand the Poem

1. Why does Harriet Tubman run away?

2. How does Harriet Tubman feel about leaving her friends?

3. Describe how Harriet Tubman escapes from the slave catchers.

4. How many times does Harriet Tubman return to the South?

Think About the Poem

5. The poem says Harriet Tubman "didn't take no stuff." What do you think this means?

6. What part of the poem proves that Harriet Tubman is very brave?

7. Describe the rhythm of the poem. How many strong beats are in each line?

8. After the last stanza, the poet repeats a line. What does that line say? Why do you think she repeats it?

Extend Your Response

Write another stanza for this poem. Tell something more about Harriet Tubman. Look back at "Did You Know?" on page 184 for ideas. Write four lines and include some repeated words.

Keys to Literature

symbolism: using something to stand for something else

Example: The ship's captain stands for Abraham Lincoln.

This poem was written when the Civil War had just ended. People were feeling happy to be at peace. However, that same month President Lincoln was shot and killed. Walt Whitman wrote "O Captain! My Captain!" soon afterward. The captain in the poem is Lincoln.

Words to Know

weather'd	passed through safely (This word is a contraction for *weathered*.)
rack	hardship; torture
exulting	rejoicing; showing great joy
keel	the center piece of timber along the bottom of a ship
victor	winner
tread	step; walk

O Captain! My Captain!

BY WALT WHITMAN

READ TO FIND OUT...
What happens to the captain in this poem?

O Captain! my Captain! our fearful trip is done,
The ship has **weather'd** every **rack**, the prize we
    sought is won,
The port is near, the bells I hear, the people
5   all **exulting**,
While follow eyes the steady **keel**, the vessel grim
    and daring;
    But O heart! heart! heart!
        O the bleeding drops of red,
10   Where on the deck my Captain lies,
             Fallen cold and dead.

Keys to Literature

The ship is a **symbol** for the United States. The prize is a **symbol** for saving the Union from breaking apart. The port is a **symbol** for the end of the Civil War.

O Captain! my Captain! rise up and hear the
    bells;
Rise up—for you the flag is flung—for you the
15   bugle trills,
For you bouquets and ribbon'd wreaths—for you
    the shores a-crowding
For you they call, the swaying mass, their eager
    faces turning;
20   Here Captain! dear father!
      This arm beneath your head!
        It is some dream that on the deck,
          You've fallen cold and dead.

My Captain does not answer, his lips are pale and
25   still,
My father does not feel my arm, he has no pulse
    nor will,
The ship is anchor'd safe and sound, its voyage
    closed and done,
30 From fearful trip the **victor** ship comes in with
    object won;
    Exult O shores, and ring O bells!
      But I with mournful **tread**,
        Walk the deck my Captain lies,
35   Fallen cold and dead.

Think About It

What has happened
in this poem so far?

*M*eet the *A*uthor

WALT WHITMAN (1819–1892)

    Walt Whitman grew up in Brooklyn, New York. As a
young man, he was a newspaper reporter. He began
writing a collection of poems about America called
Leaves of Grass. During the Civil War, Whitman went to
Washington, D.C., where he became a nurse in a soldiers'
hospital. Whitman printed *Leaves of Grass* himself.
Since then, his poetry has become world famous.

AFTER YOU READ "O Captain! My Captain!"

Understand the Poem

1. According to the first stanza of the poem, what has been won?

2. What do the people do as the ship nears port?

3. Where is the captain? What has happened to him?

4. What is the condition of the ship in the third stanza?

Think About the Poem

5. Does the captain die naturally or is he murdered? How can you tell?

6. Why do you think the narrator calls the captain his "father"?

7. What mood does this poem express? Which line in the poem do you think expresses this mood best?

8. What does the ship symbolize? What storm has it come through?

Extend Your Response

Suppose you were going to write a poem about a famous leader. Who would it be? Write a few sentences that tell why you admire this person. Use the information to create the first four lines of your poem.

Keys to Literature

narrative poem: a poem that tells a story

Example: This poem tells the story of a plan to warn American people about a British attack.

imagery: colorful words that appeal to the senses

Example: *felt the damp of the river fog*

Did You Know?

Paul Revere lived in Boston. He rode out of town on the night of April 18, 1775, to warn people that the British were coming. He headed for the town of Concord, about 20 miles away, where guns and bullets had been stored in preparation for a British attack.

Words to Know

lantern	a lamp that can be covered and carried or hung up
moorings	a place where a boat is tied up
dread	great worry or fear
impetuous	acting in a sudden way without thinking about what might happen
defiance	refusing to do something you are told to do
peril	great danger

Paul Revere's Ride

BY HENRY WADSWORTH LONGFELLOW

READ TO FIND OUT...
What happened on Paul Revere's midnight ride? Did he make it?

Listen, my children, and you shall hear
Of the midnight ride of Paul Revere,
On the eighteenth of April, in Seventy-five;
Hardly a man is now alive
5 Who remembers that famous day and year.

He said to his friend, "If the British march
By land or sea from the town tonight,
Hang a **lantern** aloft in the belfry-arch
Of the North Church tower as a signal light,—
10 One, if by land, and two, if by sea;
And I on the opposite shore will be,
Ready to ride and spread the alarm
Through every Middlesex village and farm,
For the country folk to be up and to arm."

Keys to Literature

In this **narrative poem**, the story begins with Paul Revere asking his friend to do something. What is his friend to do?

15 Then he said, "Good night!" and with muffled oar
Silently rowed to the Charlestown shore,
Just as the moon rose over the bay,
Where swinging wide at her **moorings** lay
The *Somerset*, British man-of-war;
20 A phantom ship, with each mast and spar
Across the moon like a prison bar,
And a huge black hulk, that was magnified
By its own reflection in the tide.

Meanwhile, his friend, through alley and street,
25 Wanders and watches with eager ears,
Till in the silence around him he hears
The muster of men at the barrack door,
The sound of arms, and the tramp of feet,
And the measured tread of the grenadiers,
30 Marching down to their boats on the shore.

Then he climbed the tower of the Old North
    Church,
By the wooden stairs, with stealthy tread,
To the belfry-chamber overhead,
35 And startled the pigeons from their perch
On the somber rafters, that round him made
Masses and moving shapes of shade,—
By the trembling ladder, steep and tall,
To the highest window in the wall,
40 Where he paused to listen and look down
A moment on the roofs of the town,
And the moonlight flowing over all.

Beneath, in the churchyard, lay the dead,
In their night-encampment on the hill,
45 Wrapped in silence so deep and still
That he could hear, like a sentinel's tread,
The watchful night-wind, as it went
Creeping along from tent to tent,
And seeming to whisper, "All is well!"

50 A moment only he feels the spell
Of the place and the hour, and the secret **dread**
Of the lonely belfry and the dead;
For suddenly all his thoughts are bent
On a shadowy something far away,
55 Where the river widens to meet the bay,—
A line of black that bends and floats
On the rising tide, like a bridge of boats.

Meanwhile, impatient to mount and ride,
Booted and spurred, with a heavy stride
60 On the opposite shore walked Paul Revere.
Now he patted his horse's side,
Now gazed at the landscape far and near,
Then, **impetuous**, stamped the earth,
And turned and tightened his saddle-girth;
65 But mostly he watched with eager search
The belfry-tower of the Old North Church,
As it rose above the graves on the hill,
Lonely and spectral and somber and still.
And lo! as he looks, on the belfry's height
70 A glimmer, and then a gleam of light!
He springs to the saddle, the bridle he turns,
But lingers and gazes, till full on his sight,
A second lamp in the belfry burns!

A hurry of hoofs in a village street,
75 A shape in the moonlight, a bulk in the dark,
And beneath, from the pebbles, in passing, a
    spark
Struck out by a steed flying fearless and fleet;
That was all! And yet, through the gloom and the
80   light,
The fate of a nation was riding that night;
And the spark struck out by that steed in his
    flight,
Kindled the land into flame with its heat.

Predict

In lines 53 and 54, the friend sees *a shadowy something far away*. What do you think it will be?

▶ So far, you have read the introduction to the story. Now, Paul Revere is about to begin his ride.

▶ Read this stanza aloud to yourself. Notice that the rhythm, or beat, of the lines sounds like a horse galloping down a road.

85 He has left the village and mounted the steep,
And beneath him, tranquil and broad and deep,
Is the Mystic, meeting the ocean tides;
And under the alders that skirt its edge,
Now soft on the sand, now loud on the ledge,
90 Is heard the tramp of his steed as he rides.

It was twelve by the village clock,
When he crossed the bridge into Medford town.
He heard the crowing of the cock,
And the barking of the farmer's dog,
95 And felt the damp of the river fog,
That rises after the sun goes down.

Think About It

What happens at twelve midnight?

It was one by the village clock,
When he galloped into Lexington.
He saw the gilded weathercock
100 Swim in the moonlight as he passed,
And the meeting-house windows, blank and bare,
Gaze at him with a spectral glare,
As if they already stood aghast
At the bloody work they would look upon.

105 It was two by the village clock,
When he came to the bridge in Concord town.
He heard the bleating of the flock,
And the twitter of birds among the trees,
And felt the breath of the morning breeze

Think About It

What do the first six lines of this stanza describe? What do the last four lines describe?

110 Blowing over the meadows brown.
And one was safe and asleep in his bed
Who at the bridge would be first to fall,
Who that day would be lying dead,
Pierced by a British musket-ball.

115 You know the rest. In the books you have read,
How the British Regulars fired and fled,—
How the farmers gave them ball for ball,

From behind each fence and farmyard wall,
Chasing the redcoats down the lane,
120 Then crossing the fields to emerge again
Under the trees at the turn of the road,
And only pausing to fire and load.

So through the night rode Paul Revere;
And so through the night went his cry of alarm
125 To every Middlesex village and farm,—
A cry of **defiance** and not of fear,
A voice in the darkness, a knock at the door,
And a word that shall echo forevermore!
For, borne on the night-wind of the Past,
130 Through all our history, to the last,
In the hour of darkness and **peril** and need,
The people will waken and listen to hear
The hurrying hoofbeats of that steed
And the midnight message of Paul Revere.

Think About It

What do you think the last six lines mean?

Meet the Author

HENRY WADSWORTH LONGFELLOW *(1807–1882)*

Henry Wadsworth Longfellow grew up in Maine. His grandfather fought in the American Revolution and was a friend of Paul Revere. Longfellow based some of "Paul Revere's Ride" on stories he heard from his grandfather.

During the nineteenth century, Americans liked to read poetry aloud for entertainment. Longfellow was one of their favorite poets. Many of Longfellow's poems were about America's history. Some of his most famous poems are *Song of Hiawatha*, *The Courtship of Miles Standish*, and *Evangeline*.

Check Your Predictions

1. Look back at the answer you gave for the Predict question. Would you change your answer? Explain.

Understand the Poem

2. Why does Paul Revere ride at midnight on April 18, 1775?

3. What plan do Paul Revere and his friend decide upon?

4. How does Revere spread the alarm?

Think About the Poem

5. Line 81 says, "The fate of a nation was riding that night." What do you think this means?

6. What colorful words describe Paul Revere's arrival in Lexington at one o'clock in the morning?

7. What does the rhythm of this poem sound like? Why do you think the poet created such a rhythm?

8. Why do you think Longfellow wrote this narrative poem?

Extend Your Response

Prepare a news story, dated April 19, 1775, the day after Paul Revere's famous ride. Include a headline. Tell the facts about the event. Remember to answer the questions *Who? What? Where? When? Why?* and *How?*

Learn More About It

PAUL REVERE AND THE REVOLUTIONARY WAR

Paul Revere risked his life to warn American colonists that the British were coming. At the time, Great Britain ruled the American colonies. Many colonists were angry at the British and wanted to be free. The British were ready to fight to keep control.

In real life, Revere did not ride alone. When he reached Lexington, he was joined by William Dawes and Samuel Prescott. The three men shouted the alarm as they rode toward Concord. Both Revere and Dawes were captured by the British along the way. Prescott continued the ride and warned other towns. Because of these riders, the colonists were ready when the British soldiers arrived.

The Revolutionary War started on April 19, 1775, the day after Paul Revere's ride. No one knows who fired the first shot. However, in minutes, eight colonists were dead and one British soldier was hurt.

After six long years, the colonists finally defeated the British at the Battle of Yorktown. Two years later, the American colonies became the United States of America.

Paul Revere. ca 1768–70. John Singleton Copley, U.S., 1738–1815. Oil on Canvas, 35 1/8 x 28 1/2 in. (88.9 x 72.3 cm.) Gift of Joseph W. Revere, William B. Revere and Edward H.R. Revere, 30.781. Courtesy, Museum of Fine Arts, Boston. Reproduced with permission. © 1999 Museum of Fine Arts, Boston. All Rights Reserved.

Apply and Connect

Why do you think Longfellow did not tell that Paul Revere never finished his ride and that he did not ride alone?

Summaries

The Ballad of John Henry John Henry is a steel-drivin' man. When a new steam drill is invented, John Henry refuses to believe it can drill holes faster than a man. In a contest, he beats the machine. However, John Henry dies.

Harriet Tubman This poem shows how brave and determined Harriet Tubman is. She escapes slavery but goes back to the South many times to help other enslaved people escape. Although slave catchers try to get her, they never can.

O Captain! My Captain! The captain (Abraham Lincoln) has safely taken a ship (the United States) through a terrible storm (the Civil War). Now the captain is dead, lying on the deck of the ship. The narrator is very sad. He wants the captain to rise and enjoy the celebration.

Paul Revere's Ride On April 18, 1775, the British are about to attack Concord. Paul Revere agrees to spread this news. A friend lets him know how the British are on the way. Between midnight and 2:00 A.M., Revere wakes up the people. They gather and defeat the British.

Vocabulary Review

For each sentence below, write *true* if the underlined word is used correctly. If it is not used correctly, change the underlined word to make the sentence true. Use a separate sheet of paper.

1. A person who swims in shark-infested water faces great <u>peril</u>.

2. Heavy traffic can <u>choke</u> the main roads.

3. When my aunt arrived, the first thing she said was, "<u>Farewell</u>."

4. The <u>victor</u> of the six-mile race is the one who wins.

5. A <u>locomotive</u> is a kind of plane engine.

Chapter Quiz

Answer the following questions in one or two complete sentences. Use a separate sheet of paper.

1. The Ballad of John Henry What challenge is John Henry involved in?

2. The Ballad of John Henry What causes the death of John Henry?

3. Harriet Tubman What does Harriet Tubman do after escaping to freedom?

4. O Captain! My Captain! Why is the narrator in this poem so sad? Why is the crowd so happy? Do they know the captain is dead?

5. Paul Revere's Ride Why does Paul Revere make his famous ride?

6. Paul Revere's Ride What is the setting of this poem?

Critical Thinking

7. The Ballad of John Henry Why is the ballad of John Henry considered a narrative poem?

8. Paul Revere's Ride The last part of the poem is about the future. What do you think it means?

Chapter Activity

Compare two poems from this chapter. Draw two overlapping circles, or a Venn Diagram. Label each outer circle part with the title of a poem you select. Label the overlapping part of the circles Both Poems. Think of ways the poems are different from each other. Write your ideas in the outer circles. Think of how the poems are alike. Write those ideas in the overlapping part.

Acrobats by Charles Demuth

What challenges do these performers face?

Chapter 8 ▷ Nonfiction
ACCEPTING A CHALLENGE

Learning Objectives

- Understand what a biography is.
- Recognize external conflict.
- Identify details.
- Define an autobiographical essay.
- Recognize the narrative hook of a story.

Nonfiction and Accepting Challenges

Biographies are nonfiction. They are based on facts. A biography is the story of someone's life.

- It is written by another person.
- It is told from the third-person point of view.
- It uses *he* or *she* to refer to the person.

Autobiographies are also nonfiction. An autobiography is also the story of a person's life.

- It is written by that person.
- It is told from the first-person point of view.
- It uses *I* or *me* to refer to the person.

In both kinds of books, people face challenges. They make decisions that change their lives forever.

Keys to Literature

biography: the story of a person's life written by another person

> Example: This story is about the life of Rosa Parks. It was written by Eloise Greenfield.

external conflict: a struggle that a person has with another person or with society

> Example: In this biography, Rosa Parks struggles with the police and the bus company.

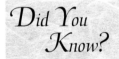

Did You Know?

Rosa Parks became famous by working toward peacefully ending segregation. Segregation forces people of different racial groups to live apart from each other and to go to separate schools.

Words to Know

ached	hurt
bond	money paid to free someone from jail before a trial
citizens	people who have rights under the laws of the city or country in which they live
courteously	politely; with good manners
pulpit	a raised platform from which a person leads a worship service
guilty	proven to have committed a crime
protest	an action against something that seems unfair
hymn	a religious song of praise

from Rosa Parks

BY ELOISE GREENFIELD

READ TO FIND OUT...
What one action by Rosa Parks changed a whole city?

On Thursday evening, December 1, 1955, Mrs. Parks left work and started home. She was tired. Her shoulders **ached** from bending over the sewing machine all day. "Today, I'll ride the bus," she thought.

She got on and sat in the first seat for blacks, right behind the white section. After a few stops the seats were filled. A white man got on. He looked for an empty seat. Then he looked at the driver. The driver came over to Mrs. Parks.

"You have to get up," he said.

All of a sudden Mrs. Parks knew she was not going to give up her seat. It was not fair. She had paid her money just as the man had. This time she was not going to move.

"No," she said softly.

"You'd better get up, or I'll call the police," the driver said.

It was very quiet on the bus now. Everyone stopped talking and watched. Still, Mrs. Parks did not move.

"Are you going to get up?"

"No," she repeated.

The driver left the bus and returned with two policemen.

"You're under arrest," they told her.

Mrs. Parks walked off the bus. The policemen put her in their car and drove to the police station. One policeman stuck a camera in her face and took her picture. Another took her fingerprints. Then she was locked in a cell.

Keys to Literature

The **biography** of Rosa Parks starts with an actual date. Facts are important in a biography.

Predict

What will Rosa Parks do?

Mrs. Parks felt very bad, sitting in that little room with iron bars. But she did not cry. She was a religious woman, and she thought of her faith in God. She said a silent prayer. Then she waited.

Someone who had seen Mrs. Parks arrested called Edgar Daniel Nixon of the NAACP. Mr. Nixon went right away to the police station and posted a hundred dollar **bond** for Mrs. Parks. This meant that she could leave, but that she promised to go to court on Monday for her trial.

Mrs. Parks left the police station. She had been locked up for two and a half hours. Mr. Nixon drove her home. At her apartment Mrs. Parks, her husband, Mr. Nixon, and Fred Gray, a lawyer, talked about what had happened. They thought they saw a way to solve the problem of the buses.

▶ The NAACP is the National Association for the Advancement of Colored People. This civil rights group was formed in 1909 to win equal rights for African Americans.

Rosa Parks is fingerprinted after she is arrested for refusing to give up her seat on a bus.

Mr. Gray would go into court with Mrs. Parks. He would prove that the bus company was not obeying the United States Constitution. The Constitution is an important paper that was written by the men who started the United States. It says that all the **citizens** of the United States must be treated fairly.

The next morning Mrs. Parks went to her job as usual. Her employer was surprised to see her. He had read about her arrest in the newspaper, and he thought she would be too upset to come in. Some of the white workers gave Mrs. Parks mean looks and would not speak to her. But she went on with her work.

That night Mrs. Parks met with a group of ministers and other black leaders of the city. Dr. Martin Luther King was one of the ministers. The black men and women of Montgomery were angry again. But this time they knew what to do.

"If the bus company won't treat us **courteously**," one leader said, "we won't spend our money to ride the buses. We'll walk!"

After the meeting some of the people printed little sheets of paper. These sheets of paper, called leaflets, said, "DON'T RIDE THE BUS TO WORK, TO TOWN, TO SCHOOL, OR ANYWHERE, MONDAY, DECEMBER 5." They also invited people to a church meeting on Monday night. The leaflets were left everywhere—in mail boxes, on porches, in drugstores.

On Sunday morning black ministers all over the city preached about Mrs. Parks in their churches. Dr. King preached from his **pulpit** at the Dexter Avenue Baptist Church.

The preachers said, "Brothers and sisters, if you don't like what happened to Rosa Parks and what has been happening to us all these years, do something about it. Walk!"

Think About It

The U.S. Constitution says everyone must be treated fairly. How is Rosa Parks treated unfairly?

Think About It

Why do African Americans in Montgomery decide to walk? How will fewer riders affect the bus company?

And the people said, "Amen. We'll walk."

On Monday morning, no one was riding the buses. There were many people on the street, but everyone was walking. They were cheering because the buses were empty.

Mrs. Parks got up early that morning. She went to court with her lawyer for her trial. The judge found her **guilty**. But she and her lawyer did not agree with him. Her lawyer said, "We'll get a higher court to decide. If we have to, we'll take the case to the highest court in the United States."

That night thousands of people went to the church meeting. There were so many people that most of them had to stand outside and listen through a loudspeaker.

Martin Luther King Jr. shakes hands with his lawyer. King was fined for working to boycott segregated city buses.

First there was prayer. Then Rosa Parks was introduced. She stood up slowly. The audience rose to its feet and clapped and cheered. After Mrs. Parks sat down, several ministers gave their speeches. Finally Dr. Martin Luther King started to speak.

"We are tired," he said.

"Yes, Lord," the crowd answered.

"We are tired of being kicked around," he said.

"Yes, Lord," they answered.

"We're not going to be kicked around anymore," Dr. King said. "We walked one day. Now we are going to have a real **protest**. We are going to keep walking until the bus company gives us fair treatment."

After Dr. King finished speaking, the Montgomery Improvement Association was formed to plan the protest. Dr. King was made president.

Then there was **hymn** singing and hand clapping. The people went home feeling good. All that walking was not going to be easy, but they knew they could do it.

The Montgomery Improvement Association and the churches bought as many cars and station wagons as they could afford. There were telephone numbers that people could call when they needed a ride. Women who worked at home answered the phones. Mrs. Parks was one of them. Her employer had told her that she was no longer needed. When someone called for a ride, Mrs. Parks would tell the drivers where to go. But there were not nearly enough cars.

Old people and young people walked. The children walked a long way to school. The men and women walked to work, to church, everywhere. In the morning it was like a parade. People were going to work, some riding on the backs of mules, some riding in wagons pulled by horses, but most of them walking. Sometimes they sang.

Think About It

Do you think it is fair that Rosa Parks is let go from her job?

Think About It

Mrs. Parks gets a death threat, but she keeps protesting anyway. What character traits does she have?

In the evening the parade went the other way, people going home. The newspapers called Montgomery "the walking city."

It was hard. Many people had to leave home long before daylight to get to work on time. They got home late at night. Their feet hurt. But they would not give up. The bus company kept saying it would not change. And black people kept on walking.

The enemies of the blacks tried to frighten them. They threw bottles at the walkers. Some homes were bombed.

One day Mrs. Parks's phone rang. She picked it up.

"Hello," she said.

"You're the cause of all this trouble," a voice said. "You should be killed."

Mrs. Parks hung up. The calls kept coming, day after day. Mrs. Parks was afraid, but she knew she could not stop.

Think About It

How is Mrs. Parks's life changed by the protest?

Rosa Parks arrives at court to face charges for refusing to give up her seat on a bus.

After two months, more than a hundred leaders of the protest were arrested. Mrs. Parks was among them. A court had said that the protest was against the law. The leaders posted bond, and went right back to their work.

Reporters came to Montgomery from all over the United States and from other countries. They wrote stories in their newspapers about the arrests.

Mrs. Parks began to travel to other cities, making speeches. She told about the hardships of the people. Many of the people she spoke to helped. They gave her money to pay for bonds and to buy gas for the cars.

The black citizens of Montgomery walked all winter, all spring, all summer and fall in all kinds of weather. The bus company lost thousands of dollars.

In November, the Supreme Court, the highest court in the United States, said that the bus company had to change. It had not been obeying the Constitution.

That night the Ku Klux Klan paraded past the homes of the blacks. The people stood in their doorways and watched. They were no longer afraid. They had won.

Several weeks later, the bus company obeyed the Supreme Court and changed its rules. A year had passed since Mrs. Parks refused to give up her seat. Now blacks could sit in any seat. They would not have to get up for anyone.

Black people in other places read about Montgomery. They began to work for fair treatment of blacks in their own cities.

They said, "If Rosa Parks had the courage to do this, we can do it too." They called her the "Mother of the Civil Rights Movement."

One day a group of reporters went to Mrs. Parks's home. They took her to ride on the bus. She entered through the front door. For the first time she sat

Keys to Literature

How is Rosa Parks's **external conflict** resolved in the courts?

anywhere she chose. And she would stay there until the end of her ride.

No one could ever ask her to get up again.

Rosa Parks sits in the front of a bus the day after the U.S. Supreme Court bans segregation on public transportation.

$\mathcal{M}$eet the $\mathcal{A}$uthor

ELOISE GREENFIELD *(Born 1929)*

Eloise Greenfield grew up in Washington, D.C. As a girl, she was part of a strong, loving African American family. She remembers segregation, though. When she was young, blacks and white people had separate schools, separate swimming pools, and separate water fountains.

Greenfield began to write in her early twenties. Since then, she has published more than 40 books. She has written novels, biographies, poetry, and picture books. Her 1973 biography, *Rosa Parks*, won the Carter G. Woodson Award. Her picture book *Africa Dream* won the Coretta Scott King Award. Greenfield is a member of the National Literary Hall of Fame for Writers of African Descent.

Check Your Predictions

1. Look back at the answer you gave for the Predict question. Would you change your answer? Explain.

Understand the Biography

2. What event starts the protest against the bus company in Montgomery?

3. What do other African Americans in Montgomery do to protest against the bus company?

4. How do people in the rest of the country find out about Rosa Parks?

5. What does the U.S. Supreme Court decide to do about Rosa Parks's case?

Think About the Biography

6. What important role does Martin Luther King Jr. play in the Montgomery boycott?

7. What external conflict caused Rosa Parks to become known as the "Mother of the Civil Rights Movement"?

8. Why do you think Eloise Greenfield wrote about Rosa Parks?

Extend Your Response

Create a Sequence of Events chart for the story of Rosa Parks. In the first box, write **Rosa Parks refuses to give her seat to a white person on a bus.** In the last box, write **Rosa Parks sits where she wants to on the bus.** In the other boxes, write important events from the selection in the order in which they happened.

Keys to Literature

details: pieces of information that help to create a more complete picture

> Example: *The parallel grooves are like lines and we press the paper into them with the round end of a pencil.*

Words to Know

timid	shy
autograph	something written in a person's handwriting, especially the person's name
grooved	having a long, narrow cut in a surface
parallel	always being the same distance apart
forefinger	the finger next to the thumb
legible	clear enough to be read easily
interpreter	a person who explains the meaning of something to another person
isolated	alone; set apart from others
captivity	prison

from Helen Keller: The Story of My Life

BY HELEN KELLER, *Adapted*

READ TO FIND OUT...
What amazing things can a person do even though she cannot see or hear anything?

Helen Keller could neither see nor hear. She lived in darkness and silence. Then when she was six, a teacher came to live with her and changed her life.

The first thing her teacher did was to give her a doll and spell the word *d-o-l-l* into her hand. Finally, Helen understood that everything had a name. Only three months later, Helen wrote this letter to her cousin Anna.

She hadn't learned yet about capital letters or punctuation.

> *Tuscumbia, Alabama, June 17, 1887.*
>
> helen write anna george will give helen apple simpson will shoot bird jack will give helen stick of candy doctor will give mildred medicine mother will make mildred new dress
>
> (No signature)

Think About It

These letters are part of Helen Keller's autobiography. How can you tell that this first letter is from a young child?

Two years later, when Keller was nine years old, her teacher, Anne Sullivan, was away for three and a half months. This is from a letter that Keller wrote to Sullivan at the time.

> *Tuscumbia, Ala., August 7, 1889.*
>
> Dearest Teacher—
>
> ... I read in my books every day. I love them very, very, very much. I do want you to come back to me soon. I miss you so very, very much. I cannot know about many things, when my dear teacher is not here....
>
> From your affectionate little pupil,
>
> HELEN A. KELLER.

Think About It

Compare the two letters on this page. What progress has Helen Keller made?

Helen Keller holding pet poodle, 1887.

Helen Keller at graduation.

Helen Keller sitting at a desk reading a book.

Helen Keller playing chess with Anne Sullivan at Radcliffe, 1899.

When she was ten, Keller was taught how to speak by another teacher. She wrote this letter to the teacher only one week after she began her lessons.

Predict

Now that Helen Keller can speak, how do you think her life will change?

South Boston, Mass., April 3, 1890.

My dear Miss Fuller,

My heart is full of joy this beautiful morning, because I have learned to speak many new words, and I can make a few sentences.... How glad my mother will be. I can hardly wait for June to come I am so eager to speak to her and to my precious little sister. Mildred could not understand me when I spelled with my fingers, but now she will sit in my lap and I will tell her many things to please her. We shall be very happy together....

My teacher told me that you wanted to know how I came to wish to talk with my mouth.... When I was a very little child, I used to sit in my mother's lap all the time, because I was very **timid**. I would keep my little hand on her face all the while. It amused me to feel her face and lips move when she talked with people. I did not know then what she was doing.

When I was older, I noticed that my friends kept moving their lips just like my mother, so I moved mine too. Sometimes it made me angry ... when I came to school in Boston, I met some deaf people who talked with their mouths like all other people. My teacher promised to take me to see a kind and wise lady who would teach me to speak. That lady was yourself. Now I am as happy as the birds, because I can speak and perhaps I shall sing too. All of my friends will be so surprised and glad.

Your loving little pupil,

HELEN A. KELLER.

Think About It

Why does Helen Keller get angry when she tries to move her lips like other people?

People were curious about how a person who could not see was able to write. Keller explained this in a letter to a children's magazine, *St. Nicholas*. She wrote this when she was twelve.

Keys to Literature

In this letter, what **details** give you a picture of how children who cannot see write?

DEAR ST. NICHOLAS:

It gives me very great pleasure to send you my **autograph** because I want the boys and girls who read *St. Nicholas* to know how blind children write. I suppose some of them wonder how we keep the lines so straight so I will try to tell them how it is done. We have a **grooved** board which we put between the pages when we wish to write. The **parallel** grooves are like lines and we press the paper into them with the round end of a pencil. It is very easy to keep the words even. The small letters are all made in the grooves, while the long ones extend above and below them. We guide the pencil with the right hand. We feel carefully with the **forefinger** of the left hand to see that we shape and space the letters correctly.

It is very difficult at first to form them plainly, but if we keep on trying it gradually becomes easier. After a great deal of practice, we can write **legible** letters to our friends. Then we are very, very happy. Sometime your readers may visit a school for the blind. If they do, I am sure they will wish to see the pupils write.

Very sincerely your little friend,

HELEN KELLER.

When Keller was 14 years old, she attended the Wright-Humanson School for the Deaf in New York City. Her family wanted her to have the best training in speaking and lip-reading. Keller wrote this letter to Caroline Derby during her first year at the school.

The Wright-Humanson School.

New York, March 15, 1895.

... I think I have improved a little in lip-reading. I still find it very difficult to read rapid speech, but I am sure I shall succeed some day if I work hard. Dr. Humanson is still trying to improve my speech. Oh, Carrie, how I should like to speak like other people!... What a joy it would be for all of my friends to hear me speak naturally!! I wonder why it is so difficult for a deaf child to learn to speak when it is so easy for other people....

You know our kind teachers take us to see everything they think will interest us. We learn a great deal in that delightful way.

▶ Lip reading is a way of understanding what a person says by watching the person's lips move. Because Helen Keller cannot see, she has to *feel* a person's lips with her fingers to "read" them.

Think About It

Why do you think it is difficult for a child who cannot hear to learn to speak?

Keller was determined to achieve the same things that people who could see and hear could. After preparing for many years and passing difficult entrance examinations, Keller was accepted to Radcliffe College. This letter to the Chairman of the Academic Board of Radcliffe College was written before the school year began.

138 Brattle Street, Cambridge, Mass.
May 5, 1900.

DEAR SIR:

As an aid to me in planning my studies for the coming year, I wonder if you can answer some questions about the possibility of my taking regular courses in Radcliffe College.

Since I received my certificate of admission to Radcliffe last July, I have been studying with a private tutor....

In college I wish to continue most of my subjects. I would require the presence of Miss Sullivan. She has been my teacher and companion for 13 years. She is my **interpreter** of oral speech and a reader of examination papers. In college she, or possibly someone else, would have to be with me in the lecture-room and I would do all my written work on a typewriter. If a professor could not understand my speech, I could write out all my answers to his questions and hand them to him afterwards.

Is it possible for the College to permit these conditions, and allow me to study at Radcliffe? I realize that the challenge of studying for a college education is great. To others, it may seem impossible, but, dear Sir, a true soldier does not admit defeat before the battle.

Helen Keller works at her desk on a typewriter, September, 1911.

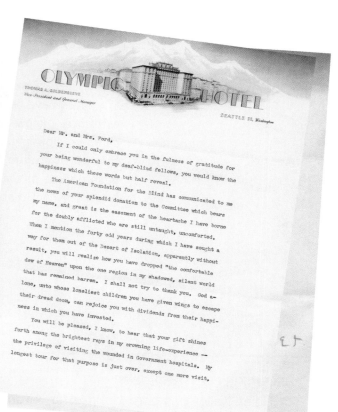

OLYMPIC HOTEL

THOMAS A. GALBRIGHT
Vice-President and General Manager

SEATTLE 11, Washington

Dear Mr. and Mrs. Ford,

If I could only embrace you in the fulness of gratitude for your being wonderful to my deaf-blind fellows, you would know the happiness which these words but half reveal.

The American Foundation for the Blind has communicated to me the news of your splendid donation to the Committee which bears my name, and great is the easement of the heartache I have borne for the doubly afflicted who are still untaught, uncomforted. When I mention the forty odd years during which I have sought a way for them out of the Desert of Isolation, apparently without result, you will realize how you have dropped "the comfortable dew of Heaven" upon the one region in my shadowed, silent world that has remained barren. I shall not try to thank you. God alone, unto whose loneliest children you have given wings to escape their dread doom, can rejoice you with dividends from their happiness in which you have invested.

You will be pleased, I know, to hear that your gift shines forth among the brightest rays in my crowning life-experience -- the privilege of visiting the wounded in Government hospitals. My longest tour for that purpose is just over, except one more visit,

Letter written by Helen Keller to thank Henry Ford, 1948.

Helen Keller hugging a guide dog.

Helen Keller visits President John F. Kennedy, April 8, 1961.

This is from a letter Keller wrote when she was in college.

> ... I have been rescued from the death-in-life existence. I know how **isolated**, how shrouded in darkness, how cramped and powerless a soul is without thought or faith or hope. Words cannot describe the prison-house of that darkness. Nor can they describe the joy of the soul that is released from the dark **captivity**.

Meet the Author

HELEN KELLER *(1880–1968)*

Helen Keller was born in Alabama. At one-and-a-half years old, she suffered a serious illness that left her unable to see or hear. When Helen Keller was seven, Anne Sullivan became her teacher. She taught her to understand language. Anne Sullivan remained with Helen Keller for fifty years.

Helen Keller graduated from Radcliffe College with honors. Later, she worked for organizations that helped the blind. She traveled around the world giving lectures. She also wrote some best-selling books. These include *The Story of My Life* and *The World I Live In*. A play called *The Miracle Worker* tells the story of her life as a young child.

Check Your Predictions

1. Look back at the answer you gave for the Predict question. Would you change your answer? Explain.

Understand the Autobiography

2. What happens to Helen Keller as a very young child?

3. How does Helen Keller first learn about words?

4. What important skill does Helen Keller learn at age ten?

5. How does Anne Sullivan help Helen Keller in college?

Think About the Autobiography

6. Are you surprised that Helen Keller becomes a famous author and speaker? Why or why not?

7. Why do you think many of the details in Helen Keller's letters are about the sense of touch?

8. What are some feelings that Helen expresses in her letters?

Extend Your Response

Complete an Idea Web. In a circle, write Keller's name. Around it, write the qualities you admire most in Helen Keller.

Keys to Literature

narrative hook: a point in the story at which the author grabs your attention

> Example: Readers are curious when they learn that the author was saved *from a horrible death*.

autobiographical essay: writing that focuses on one event in the writer's life

> Example: This essay focuses on an event that almost cost the author his life.

Did You Know?

Whaling was a very important industry in the United States from 1820 to 1850. Whale oil was used for lamps, candles, and perfume. More than 700 American whaling ships hunted whales. About 10,000 whales were killed each year, mostly in the Pacific Ocean.

Words to Know

destiny	fate; what is likely to happen
latitude	the distance north or south of the equator
longitude	the distance east or west of Greenwich, England
harpoon	a spear on a rope used for killing whales
knots	a measurement of a ship's speed
helm	a ship's steering wheel
thrashing	tossing about
steward	the person in charge of food and equipment on a ship
salvation	rescue
casks	barrels or kegs

Shipwreck of the Whaleship *Essex*

BY OWEN CHASE, *Adapted*

READ TO FIND OUT...
Can an animal like a whale take revenge?

A great deal of time has passed since it happened. Still, I cannot remember the scenes which I am about to describe without certain emotions. They are a mixture of horror and amazement at the incredible **destiny** that saved me and my companions from a horrible death.

On November 20th, we were cruising in **latitude** 0° 40' south, **longitude** 119° 0' west. Then a group of whales was discovered off in the distance. The weather at this time was very fine and clear. At 8:00 A.M., the man at the lookout gave the usual cry of "there she blows."

Keys to Literature

Notice how Owen Chase catches your interest in the first paragraph. In this **narrative hook**, he tells you that he was saved "from a horrible death."

Keys to Literature

An **autobiographical essay** focuses on a real event in the writer's life. Owen Chase begins the story by telling exactly when and where this event took place.

Right away, we headed off in the direction where the whales were. Soon we had gotten within a half mile of the place where they'd been seen. All our boats were lowered down, manned, and we chased after them. The ship waited for us.

I had the **harpoon** in the second boat. The captain went in the first. We arrived at the spot where we thought the whales were. At first we could see nothing. We lay on our oars expecting the whales to come up somewhere near us.

Soon, one rose and spouted a short distance ahead of my boat. I sped toward it and struck it. The whale felt the harpoon in him. Then he threw himself, in agony, towards the boat. He gave a heavy blow with his tail. He struck the boat near the edge of the water and drove a hole in her.

I immediately grabbed a hatchet and cut the harpoon line. That separated the boat from the whale, which by this time was running off with great speed. I succeeded in getting clear of him, but we lost the harpoon and line. The water poured into the boat fast. I quickly stuffed three or four of our jackets in the hole. Then I ordered one man to keep bailing water and the other men to row immediately for the ship. We succeeded in keeping the boat afloat and shortly reached the ship.

The captain and the second mate were in the other two boats. They kept up the chase and soon struck another whale. At this time, I went forward, turned the ship around, and sailed in their direction. The boat, which had been damaged, was immediately lifted onto the ship. I examined the hole. I found that I could nail a piece of canvas over it and get her ready to join the chase.

I was in the act of nailing on the canvas when I noticed a very large sperm whale. As far as I could tell, it was about 85 feet in length. He broke water about 100 yards off our ship. He was lying quietly with his head pointed towards the ship.

He spouted two or three times and then disappeared. In less than two or three seconds, he came up again. He made directly for us at a speed of about three **knots**. The ship was then going at about the same speed. The whale's appearance and attitude at first gave us no worry. I stood watching his movements, as he came toward us with great speed. I ordered the boy at the **helm** to turn hard, intending to avoid him.

The words were hardly out of my mouth before he came down upon us with full speed. He struck the ship with his head. He slammed into us so hard that we nearly fell on our faces. The ship stopped suddenly, as if she'd struck a rock. It shook for a few seconds like a leaf.

We looked at each other in amazement. We did not even have the power to speak. Many minutes went by before we realized the awful accident that had taken

Predict

What will the sperm whale do to the *Essex*?

place. During that time, the whale went under the ship and came up alongside her, facing the wind. He lay on top of the water for about a minute. He seemed stunned by the blow. Then suddenly he started off again.

After a few moments, we recovered from the confusion that had grabbed us. I saw that the whale had put a hole in the ship. I knew that it would be necessary to get the pumps going. They were set up and put in operation. However, they'd only been going for about a minute when I noticed something. The head of the ship was gradually settling down in the water.

I then ordered the signal for the other boats to sail off. Right after this, I again saw the whale. He was **thrashing** about on top of the water some 500 yards away. He was covered by the foam of the sea, which he had created by his moving about. I could clearly see him clamp his jaws together in rage and fury. He stayed a short time like this. Then he started off with great speed in the other direction.

By this time, the ship had sunk down quite a bit in the water. I gave her up as lost. However, I ordered the pumps to be kept constantly going. I turned to the two boats that were still with the ship. I intended to get them ready for use, if there were no other choice left. While I was paying attention to that, I heard the cry of a man. "Here he is—he's making for us again."

I turned around. I saw him about 500 yards directly ahead of us. He was coming down with twice his usual speed. And he seemed to be ten times angrier.

The surf flew in all directions about him. His path toward us was marked by white foam about five yards wide, which he made by thrashing his tail. His head was about half out of water. And in that way he came up and again struck the ship.

I yelled up to the helmsman, "hard up." But the ship had barely moved before we took the second

Think About It

Why is the ship settling down in the water?

shock. He completely smashed in her bow. Then he passed under the ship again and went off in the other direction. We saw no more of him.

Our situation at this point is difficult to describe. Misfortune found us at a moment when we did not dream of any accident. We had looked forward to earning money from our work. Now we were faced with disaster.

We were more than a thousand miles from the nearest land. And there was nothing more than a light, open boat to provide safety for myself and my companions.

I ordered the men to stop pumping and everyone to provide for himself. I grabbed a hatchet and cut away the ropes on the spare boat. I cried out to those near me to take her as she came down. They did so and carried her as far as mid-ship.

At the same time, the **steward** had gone down into the cabin twice. He had saved some equipment, and the captain's trunk and mine. All of this was quickly thrown into the boat along with two compasses I had saved. The steward tried to go back down again. But by this time the water had rushed in, and he returned without success.

By this time, the ship had filled with water. She was going down. We shoved our boat as quickly as possible into the water. All hands jumped in her at the same time, and we pushed off clear of the ship. We were barely two boat's lengths distant from her when she fell over and sunk.

Shock and despair now took hold of us. We thought with horror about the sudden tragedy that had overtaken us. None of us spoke a word for several minutes. Everyone seemed to be under a spell of confusion.

From the time we were first attacked by the whale until the ship sunk, not more than ten minutes had passed. My companions had not saved a single thing

Predict

Now that the ship has been rammed, what do you think will happen next?

Think About It

What is going through the sailors' minds as they watch their ship go down?

Think About It

What do the sailors take off the sinking ship?

except what they had on their backs. But I was quite satisfied, if one could be satisfied by such a gloomy situation. We had been lucky enough to save our compasses and other tools.

The first shock of what happened was over. Then I happily thought of these tools as the likely source of our **salvation**. Without them, all would have been dark and hopeless. What a picture of distress and suffering I began to imagine!

The crew of the ship, 20 men, were saved. But all that was left to carry us across the stormy waters, thousands of miles, were three open light boats. The idea of getting any food or water from the ship was now very doubtful. How many long and watchful nights would we have? How many long days of near starvation would we have to suffer through? When could we expect some relief from our troubles?

We lay in our boat about two ship's lengths from the wreck. We were silent and calm, thinking about our lost ship. Soon, we saw the other boats rowing up to us. They had shortly before discovered that some accident had happened to us. But they did not know the nature of the accident.

The ship's sudden and mysterious disappearance was first discovered by the boat steerer in the captain's boat. With horror on his face, he shouted, "Where is the ship?" A general cry of shock and horror came from the lips of every man. They immediately made their way toward us.

Think About It

What kind of person do you think the captain is? Explain.

The captain's boat was the first to reach us. He stopped a short distance away. But he had no power to say a single word. He was overpowered with the sight before him. He sat down in his boat, pale and speechless. I hardly recognized his face. Finally, he was able to ask me a question.

"Mr. Chase, what is the matter?"

"We have been struck by a whale," I answered. I then briefly told him the story.

He thought for a few moments. Then he said we must cut away the ship's masts. This would allow the ship to rise up a bit. Then we could get something out of her to eat. Our thoughts were now set on saving from the wreck whatever we might want. So, for this purpose, we rowed up and got on to her.

We cut away the masts as fast as we could. The ship came up about two-thirds out of the water. We now began to cut a hole through the planks right above two large **casks** of bread. From them, we were able to get about 600 pounds of bread.

Think About It

Why do the sailors cut away the ship's masts?

Other parts of the deck were then torn up. We took as much freshwater as we dared to carry in the boats. Each one was supplied with about 65 gallons. We also got from one of the lockers a gun, some gunpowder, and about two pounds of boat nails. In the afternoon, a wind came up to blow a strong breeze. By then we had taken everything we could think of. So, we began to prepare for our safety during the night.

A boat's line was tied to the ship. One of the other boats was tied to the other end of it about 300 feet away. Another boat was then attached to the first one about 50 feet to one side. Then the third boat was attached to the second about the same distance away.

Night came on just as we had finished our work. And such a night as it was to us! We were worried and distracted. None of us was able to sleep.

After several hours of sorrow, I began to think about the accident. I thought about by what destiny this sudden and deadly attack had been made upon us. It had been made by an animal never before known to attack in such a planned, violent way.

Think About It

Why does Owen Chase think the whale wants revenge?

Every fact made me believe that the attack did not happen by chance. The whale made two attacks upon the ship. Both attacks were designed to do us the most harm. His actions were horrible and filled with fury. He came directly from the group of whales where we had struck three of his companions. It was as if he wanted revenge for their suffering.

However, one point may be made by observers. The whale's usual way of fighting is either with repeated strokes of its tail or by snapping its jaws together. A case similar to this one has never before been heard of among the oldest and most experienced whalers.

To this I have an answer. The build and strength of the whale's head is well-designed for this kind of attack. The whale's head is as hard and tough as iron. A harpoon would not make the slightest dent there. The eyes and the ears are far from this front part of the head. So, they are not in any way put in danger when the attack is made.

All the events taken together, which happened before my eyes, lead me to feel correct in my opinion. It is certainly in all ways, up to now, an unheard of event. Perhaps it is the most extraordinary event in the history of fishing.

Meet the Author

OWEN CHASE *(1797–1869)*

Owen Chase was born on Nantucket Island in Massachusetts. He went to sea at age 14. His first trip on the *Essex* was very successful. His second trip was not. After the whale sank the *Essex*, Chase spent 90 days in an open boat. He was one of eight sailors out of 21 to survive.

After his rescue, Owen Chase made two more whaling trips. His experience on the *Essex*, though, ruined his health. Chase suffered from headaches that became worse and worse. Eventually, he went insane. However, his story had a big impact on American literature. The famous novel *Moby Dick*, by Herman Melville, was based on this story.

Check Your Predictions

1. Look back at the answers you gave to the Predict questions. Would you change your answers? Explain.

Understand the Autobiographical Essay

2. What is the purpose of the _Essex_'s trip?

3. What causes the _Essex_ to sink?

4. Why do the sailors think it will be hard for them to be rescued?

5. Once the _Essex_ sinks, what do the sailors travel in?

Think About the Autobiographical Essay

6. Why are the sailors so horrified by the loss of their ship?

7. What does the author use to grab his readers' attention?

8. Why is "Shipwreck of the Whaleship _Essex_" called an autobiographical essay?

Extend Your Response

The selection you just read is only part of Owen Chase's autobiographical essay. Continue the essay. Describe what may have happened the next day in the open boat. Write your paragraph from the first-person point of view.

Learn More About It

SPERM WHALES

Sperm whales are huge animals. A male sperm whale can grow to more than 60 feet long. Its enormous, square head is its most outstanding feature. The whale's head takes up about one-third of its total body length.

Sperm whales can "talk" to each other with clicks. These clicks can be heard as far as six miles away. Each whale has his or her own special series of clicks called a *coda*. Some scientists believe that these codas are the whales' names.

Although sperm whales live in the sea, they are mammals and must breathe air. Sperm whales, however, can dive more than 3,500 feet and stay underwater for more than an hour. They like to eat squid, but they will also eat octopus and some fish. Although sperm whales generally travel in groups of 25 to 40, some males leave the groups and travel alone.

Many people want to protect sperm whales from hunters. They have formed the International Whaling Commission, which controls the whaling industry. More than 40 countries around the world have agreed to follow its rules and hunt only a certain number of whales and only the kinds of whales the commission allows.

Apply and Connect

What characteristics described here may have made it possible for a sperm whale to attack the *Essex*?

Chapter 8 Review

Summaries

Rosa Parks On December 1, 1955, Rosa Parks refused to give a white person her bus seat. When she was arrested and taken to jail, African Americans in Montgomery, Alabama, showed their support by not riding the buses until the company gave equal treatment to African Americans and white people. Dr. Martin Luther King Jr. led the protest. After a year, the U.S. Supreme Court ruled in favor of Rosa Parks.

Helen Keller: The Story of My Life As a young child, Helen Keller was unable to see or hear. Despite that, she learned the meaning of words and how to write. At 12, she published a letter in a national magazine, and at 14, she learned to speak and read lips. At 20, with the help of an interpreter, she attended college.

Shipwreck of the Whaleship *Essex* Owen Chase was a sailor on a whaleship, hunting whales. When the ship was far from land, a large sperm whale attacked it. As the ship sank, the sailors saved a few things and escaped in small boats. Chase thought the whale attacked for revenge. Years later, he remembered the event with horror.

guilty
isolated
destiny
thrashing
legible
protest

Vocabulary Review

Match each word in the box with its meaning. Write the word on a separate sheet of paper.

1. clear enough to be read easily
2. alone
3. proven to have committed a crime
4. tossing about
5. fate
6. an action against something unfair

Chapter Quiz

Answer the following questions in one or two complete sentences. Use a separate sheet of paper.

1. Rosa Parks Why do the police arrest Rosa Parks?

2. Rosa Parks What does the Supreme Court tell the bus company in Montgomery, Alabama?

3. Helen Keller: The Story of My Life How does Helen Keller first learn to understand language?

4. Helen Keller: The Story of My Life What does Helen Keller use to help her write clearly by hand?

5. Shipwreck of the Whaleship *Essex* Why does Owen Chase think the whale attacked the *Essex*?

6. Shipwreck of the Whaleship *Essex* Why are the sailors so horrified by the loss of their ship?

Critical Thinking

7. Rosa Parks Why is Rosa Parks considered a hero?

8. Helen Keller: The Story of My Life What kind of problems does Helen Keller have to overcome because she cannot see or hear?

Chapter Activity

Choose one of the following heroes or heroines: Rosa Parks, Helen Keller, or Owen Chase. Write a paragraph that tells why you think this person's challenge was more difficult than the others'. Give examples from the selections in this chapter.

Unit 3 **Review**

On a separate sheet of paper, write the letter that best completes each sentence below.

1. In "Thank You, M'am," what does Mrs. Jones do when she hears why Roger wants money?
   A. She says it is foolish to waste money on blue suede shoes.
   B. She offers him a part-time job at the hotel where she works.
   C. She gives him money to buy the shoes.
   D. She says she will talk to Roger's mother about the shoes.

2. In "Harriet Tubman," after she escapes to the North, she
   A. writes articles that argue against slavery.
   B. returns to the South to rescue enslaved people.
   C. returns home to help poor people in the South.
   D. decides to help poor people in the North.

3. In "Paul Revere's Ride," Revere warns the colonists that the British
   A. have entered Boston.
   B. have started fires in Lexington.
   C. are arresting patriots.
   D. none of the above.

4. In *Rosa Parks*, the protests against the Montgomery buses end because
   A. the Supreme Court orders the bus company to change.
   B. the people get tired of walking everywhere.
   C. the bus company is losing too much money.
   D. the police arrest Parks and Martin Luther King Jr.

5. In "Shipwreck of the Whaleship *Essex*," the ship sinks when it is
   A. caught in a storm.
   B. attacked by an enemy ship.
   C. hit by an iceberg.
   D. rammed by a whale.

Making Connections
On a separate sheet of paper, write your answers to the following questions.

6. Which selection in this unit do you like best? Explain why. What did you learn from the selection about accepting a challenge?

7. Describe the external conflict of one of the characters in this unit.

Writing an Essay
Choose one of the stories or poems from this unit. Describe its theme. Give examples from the selection you choose.

Chapter 9 ## Fiction

River Man
by Teresa Pijoan de Van Etten

**A Visit to the Clerk
of the Weather**
by Nathaniel Hawthorne, adapted

from **The Call of the Wild**
by Jack London, adapted

Chapter 10 ## Poetry

The Sky Is Low
by Emily Dickinson

in Just–
by e.e. cummings

Birdfoot's Grampa
by Joseph Bruchac

The Road Not Taken
by Robert Frost

What is the mood of this painting?

Learning Objectives

- Explain what a fable is.
- Identify a character's traits.
- Recognize who a story's narrator is.
- Explain what a myth is.
- Identify sensory details in a story.
- Understand a character's external conflict.

Preview Activity

Think of a time you saw something remarkable in nature. It could be a violent storm or a beautiful sunset. Describe what you saw or experienced in a few sentences. Do not write the name of your experience. Exchange papers with a classmate. Guess what the other person wrote about by the way it is described.

Fiction and Nature

Fiction is about imaginary people and events. In this chapter, you will read different kinds of fiction:

a fable: a story that teaches a lesson.

a myth: an old story that explains how something came to be.

a short story: fiction that usually takes place over a short period of time, has only a few characters, and has a simple plot.

Fiction about nature includes many sensory details to describe the natural world. In some works of fiction, nature is the subject. Then, different parts of nature become the characters.

Keys to Literature

fable: a short story that teaches a lesson. In fables, animals and other natural things act and talk like people.

Example: This fable teaches us to take good care of our rivers.

character traits: qualities that a person has like bravery or honesty

Example: In this fable, the river man's character traits are humor and mischief.

Did You Know?

The main character in this fable is a river. The river can do things a human can do—speak, have feelings, and even play tricks on people. For thousands of years, different cultures have given rivers, lakes, and other parts of nature human traits and abilities. For example, the Roman god Neptune was the sea god.

Words to Know

humor	something funny
channeled	made into passageways
untapped	not used
appliances	household machines like dishwashers and refrigerators
mischievousness	playfulness or naughtiness
pout	frown; be silent and unfriendly
vaults	safes where money or jewels are kept
glimpse	a peek; a quick look
generosity	a willingness to give things to others
balance	evenness
reflection	an image, as from a mirror

River Man

BY TERESA PIJOAN DE VAN ETTEN

READ TO FIND OUT...
What makes the river man sad?

The man in the river has always given each of us a little of himself—a bit of **humor** each time we drank some of his river water. But times change and with the times come new ideas and new devices. Men came here, men with modern ways, and told us not to drink the river water because it was unclean. They were right—people had thrown garbage in the river and the water was unclean.

The men brought in clean, shiny metal pipes. The earth was dug up and **channeled** to hold these metal pipes that contained the water. The river and ditches no longer carried it to the people. River water was forgotten. People even forgot to throw their garbage in the river. The water slowly became clean again.

Keys to Literature

Animals and other natural things are often characters in **fables**.

Predict

What do you think the river man will do to people who forget him?

The river was not used for washing, bathing, drinking, or cooking. The great humor of the river man was **untapped**. We were too busy using modern **appliances**, piped water, and water in bottles to think of river water.

The river man was left with his humor. He was saddened that the people who had once used river water would no longer have that little smile in the morning after drinking a cup of tea or coffee made with it. He worried about the children bathing in such pure, piped water—where would their **mischievousness** go? And the old ones—how would they keep their crooked smiles and sparkling eyes? How would they be now?

The river man waited. He waited for a long time. He listened to the big tractors and trucks that came by. Some of them tried to change his path, but he laughed at them and went the way he wished. While he waited, he worried. The river man knew that laughter and a good sense of humor keep the life alive in each of us.

Keys to Literature

Character traits are the qualities a person has. What character traits has the river man shown so far?

The river man watched from his flowing river. He heard new babies cry—cry a *lot*. He heard small children complain and **pout** around their mothers and each other. The river man saw the old ones dry up in sadness. The river man didn't wait to see the old ones die. Oh, no. He made a plan.

The river man crept out of the river at night and went into people's houses. He went to the fancy new machines and pulled some wires; he went into the children's rooms and moved their toys around; he went to the old people's houses and took their false teeth.

The river man did mischief. He went to the house **vaults** of the rich ones, and he took their money and floated it in the river. The people became angry and irritable. We argued and fought.

Think About It

Why do you think the river man does these things?

One mother took her daughter out of school. She tried to teach her at home, but the little girl sat at the window and stared at the flowing river. The mother let her look, for she did not know what to do with the child.

One night, the river man came out of the river and took everyone's shadow. The children no longer had their shadows to play with. The lonely ones could no longer talk to their shadows. The old ones could no longer watch their shadows walk with them.

The little girl who lived with her mother stopped smiling, for her best friend was her shadow. She called for her shadow; she searched in the trees and the woods for her shadow. She didn't find it.

Think About It

Why does the river man take everyone's shadow?

What do you think the
young man and the little
girl will do?

One afternoon she met a young man who was
looking for his money. He was very rich, and he had
seen his money mysteriously hurrying out the door
toward the river early in the morning.

"Did you take my money?" the youth asked the
little girl.

She laughed. "I would not take your money. I am
searching for my shadow." They talked, and agreed to
spend the night in a tree by the river to find out who
was playing tricks. The mother gave her daughter some
extra food for the young man.

The youth fell asleep, but not the little girl. She
watched. She saw a man with long flowing silver hair
come running from the town to the river. He ran right
into the river and disappeared. She woke the young
man, who just caught a **glimpse** of the old man's hair
floating down into the river. The young man was
greedy, and he wanted his money back. He dived into
the river to get the old man. The girl dived in after
him, for she feared what he would do to the old man.

Down they swam to an underwater house. They
peered through the window. There were black shapes
in the house, and the little girl recognized her shadow.
She pushed open the door, and the young man
followed her. The door slammed behind them. There
stood the old man with the long flowing silver hair.

"What are you doing in my house?" the river man
asked with a big grin.

"We are looking for things that we lost. Who are you?"

"I am the river man. I am the one who brings humor
and joy into the lives of those that use my river water."

They listened to him. His wonderful, warm face
glowed with a grand smile. They were happy to have
found him and almost forgot all about their things.
When at last the river man said he was tired, for he
had had a busy night, they took what they needed.

Think About It

What do the little girl and
the young man see
through the window of the
underwater house?

The young man only took a little of his money, and the girl took her shadow.

"If those who have things here will come to the river and use the river water, they will get their things back." The old man smiled and nodded off to sleep.

The next morning, the young man and the little girl went into town and told their story of the river man and his mischief and of the river water. The people were angry. How dared this river man make so much trouble for them! They went to the river, and those who tried to swim in it were amazed at how happy they felt. Those who washed their faces in the clean

Think About It

Why do you think the young man takes only a little of his money from the river man?

river water felt their lips stretch across their faces in almost-forgotten smiles. Slowly, small items came floating up from the river. The people—all of us—laughed and played in the water.

The river water brought joy, friendship, **generosity**, and good will back to us. The river man did not come up, but the flowing water rippled and slapped against the riverbank. We knew that he was pleased.

Keys to Literature

What lesson does this **fable** teach?

We use the river water every day now for different things, as we used to do, but now we use it and it brings **balance** to our lives. We respect the river and keep it clean.

In the **reflection** of the river water, we can see our own smiles. Look, and you can see yours, too.

Meet the Author

TERESA PIJOAN DE VAN ETTEN *(Born 1951)*

Teresa Pijoan de Van Etten lives in New Mexico, where she is a storyteller, writer, and speaker. Through the years, she has collected many folktales from Native Americans and Spanish Americans who live in New Mexico. The stories she writes are based on these folktales.

Van Etten has given many speeches about her work with folktales. She has lectured at the American Museum of Natural History in New York and at the San Francisco Art Institute. You can read some of her stories in *Spanish American Folktales* and *The Practical Wisdom of Spanish Americans in 28 Eloquent and Simple Stories*.

Check Your Predictions

1. Look back at the answers you gave for the Predict questions. Would you change your answers? Explain.

Understand the Story

2. Who is the river man?

3. Why do the people stop going to the river?

4. What kind of mischief does the river man do?

Think About the Story

5. Why does the river man steal things from the people?

6. What character traits does the river man have?

7. At the end of the story, what does the river bring back to the people?

8. Why is this story called a fable?

Extend Your Response

Suppose you are making a movie about the river man. Create a series of four or five drawings that show scenes for your movie. Write a caption for each drawing. Would you use animation (cartoons) or real actors for your movie? Explain.

Keys to Literature

narrator: the person telling the story

    Example: When you tell a story, you are the narrator.

myth: a story, handed down through the years, that explains how something in nature came to be

    Example: This myth tries to explain what causes the weather.

Did You Know?

The writer made up this myth, but most myths are very old. Many of them tell how the weather and the seasons came to be. In a famous Greek myth, Persephone was the goddess of spring. She lived in the underworld six months a year. Then, in the spring she visited her mother. She brought the new season with her.

Words to Know

clerk	an office worker; someone in charge of recording numbers and events
encircled	surrounded
impulse	a sudden desire to act
pyramid	a structure with a square base and four sides that meet at a point at the top
cavern	a large cave
tolerably	fairly; pretty much
neglected	ignored; not taken care of
insulting	disrespectful; hurting someone's feelings
assure	make a person certain of something; comfort
forge	a furnace or fire in which metal is heated and shaped

A Visit to the Clerk of the Weather

BY NATHANIEL HAWTHORNE, *Adapted*

READ TO FIND OUT...
Who is the clerk of
the weather?

"I don't know. I haven't spoken yet to the **clerk** of the weather," I said as a joke to my friend. He had asked me, "Do you think we shall have an early spring?"

We stood on the steps of the Mayfair Hotel. The night was not very dark, but falling snowflakes made it difficult to see. Still, I could plainly see a little old woman in a gray cloak. She was passing by at the moment and had caught my words. Her small black eyes looked at me through the mist as I spoke.

Think About It
Who is the narrator of
this story?

At the same moment, my friend shuddered, turned on his heel, and walked away. He went to warm up inside. The little old woman was by my side in an instant. When I tried to move away, her bony hand **encircled** my arm. It felt as if I were in the grasp of a skeleton.

"Let me go, madam, or by Heaven—"

"You have taken *his* name in vain often enough," she said in a hoarse whisper. "It is clear that you do not believe that he is real. Come with me. Now, don't hesitate, or I will weigh your manhood against the courage of an old woman."

"On, fool!" I exclaimed.

Predict

Where do you think
the old woman will
take the narrator?

The old woman hurried away—and I followed. I was drawn by an **impulse** that I could not resist. We moved so rapidly that streets, houses, woods, and fences seemed to be running back as we progressed. At length, I was lifted from my feet and whirled through the air. I traveled so fast that I nearly lost my breath.

The gray cloak of the old woman could be seen at some distance before me. The clouds split apart and rolled themselves on either side of her as she passed. They made a clear path for her and her follower. How far we traveled like this I cannot say. But suddenly we struck the land, and I stood upon the green grass. The sun flamed down on my head. And now, for the first time, I felt travel-worn and faint.

"I can assist you no farther," the old woman said. In a moment she had disappeared.

A little distance from where I stood was a pile of rocks. About a dozen tall, gray rocks, each several acres in height, had been thrown together in a circle. They formed a **pyramid**, with the points meeting at the top. I noticed a light smoke rising up through a small opening at the very top of this huge cone. I decided to enter this strange house. I no longer doubted that someone was living there.

I walked around the cone several times before I discovered an entrance. Several rocks had hidden it from my view. But the opening was large enough for a dozen horsemen to ride through it side-by-side. Slowly and carefully I entered the **cavern**. It was about five hundred yards all around.

Several objects drew my attention right away. Of course the living creatures were the first things I noticed. There were three huge beings in different parts of the room. And at the far side of the cavern sat a noble old man. He had long gray hair, and he was busily writing. He was the clerk of the weather.

Think About It

Tell in your own words
what the narrator sees
after the old woman leaves.

Before I spoke to anyone, I glanced around the rocky cavern. In one corner, there was a pile of red-hot thunderbolts. Against the wall hung several second-hand rainbows. They were faded and covered with dust. Next, I saw several hundred cart loads of hailstones, two large sacks of wind, and a storm that was locked in iron chains.

Then I saw that the old man knew I was there. When he had half-risen from his seat, I hurried to present myself. As I got closer, I was struck by the size of his huge body and the fierce look in his eyes. He had stuck his pen behind his ear. This pen was the top of a tall tree. Some storm had rudely torn it from its trunk. And the old man had shaved the end down to the right size for dipping in his inkwell.

He took my hand into his big palm and squeezed it. His handshake was too strong for my comfort. But his friendliness helped ease the worry in my mind. I greeted him and asked how he was doing.

"I am **tolerably** well, thank you, for an old man of three-score centuries," he replied. "From where do you come?"

"I am from Boston, sir."

"I do not recall any planet of that name," he said.

"I beg your pardon—from Earth, I should have said."

He thought for a moment. "Yes, yes, I do remember a little mud-ball in this direction"—he pointed with his arm. "But, truly I had almost forgotten it. Hum! We have **neglected** you recently. It must be looked into. We owed Mr. Jack Frost a few favors. We had to give him permission to build some ice-palaces and snow forts. But he has gone too far. He must be stopped!"

"Really, sir, if you would pay more attention to us, not only would you have my thanks, but the whole world would thank you."

He looked serious for a moment. Then he shook his head and spoke. "But, sir, I have some complaints to make with you. I have been attacked and lied about by your fellows. You probably know that there are some people on your little planet who pretend to know what I am doing. They print information that says on such

Think About It

The clerk says that certain people pretend to know what he is doing. Who are these people?

and such a day there shall be a snowstorm or thunder and lightning or a great heat wave. Some have even published **insulting** cartoons of me. And ... "

Here we were interrupted by a loud, hissing noise. It startled me and caused me to turn around.

"You must be careful. You have burned your clothes, I fear," cried my host. He was speaking to a short, fat figure, who came walking slowly toward us. He was wrapped in sheets of ice and wearing a huge wig covered with snow.

"It is nothing, your Honor," answered the figure. Its hollow voice made my blood cold. "I only walked upon the cursed coil of chain lightning. Your servant has placed it near the door. This happens each time I visit you!"

I was too busy looking at this strange visitor to notice the entrance of another guest. She placed herself right between me and the clerk of the weather before I saw her. She was a lovely, young woman, dressed in a beautifully colored gown. On her head was a green hat and on her feet were green slippers.

Think About It
Which character is wrapped up in sheets of ice and wearing a snow-covered wig?

Predict
Who do you think the lovely young woman is?

The icy dwarf moved aside as she approached. He frowned at her from under his thick eyebrows. She glanced at him and pouted like a spoiled child. She then turned to me and spoke in the sweetest voice.

"You are the stranger from Earth, I guess!"

"At your service, fair lady," I said.

"I heard of your arrival and hurried to meet you," she said. "I wish to ask about my good friends, the people of your world. My name is Spring."

"My dear lady," I said. "Your face would gladden the hearts of us all. I can tell you that your presence has been wished and prayed for by all my fellow-sufferers."

"It is too upsetting!" she cried. She threw her green hat on the ground and stomped her feet. "I suppose I am blamed for my lateness by my children of the Earth. Heaven knows, I wish to leap over your valleys and hills and stay beside your running rivers as in days of yesterday. But that ugly, evil figure holds me in his power." Here, she pointed at Jack Frost, for that's who the strange, icy figure was.

"I took him to court last year," she said. "Before the case was decided, summer arrived. But **assure** your fellows that I will not neglect them in the future. I shall be among them early. Mr. Frost must take a journey to the north to get a polar bear for his wife. She has stayed among you Earth people for so long, she now follows some of your customs. She wants a substitute for a lap-dog." She then turned away and began to talk to the clerk of the weather.

I walked about the cavern to examine its contents. A giant fellow was sweating over the fire and cooking his master's breakfast. In a moment I saw him climb a sort of rope ladder. He picked a small white cloud out of the heavens and used it as milk for the coffee.

I wandered on until I came upon a heap of rocks. Behind it sat a dozen little black fellows sitting cross-legged. They were working with all their strength to weave a thunder gust. One part of this work seemed to puzzle them the most. They had to put in the thunderbolts, which they had to handle with long pincers. Another important part was sewing on the fringe, which was made of chain lightning.

Keys to Literature

What are some of the
natural events that this
myth explains?

While I stood looking at this, a huge fellow came stumbling towards me. He asked whether I had visited the **forge**. I told him that I had not. He said that it was not operating now because there were enough

thunderbolts made for the present. But soon there might be an earthquake to fix.

I noticed that his wrist was covered with a bandage. I asked him if he had been injured there. He said that he had gotten a small scratch there. Last year he had been ordered to fire several thunderbolts upon our Earth. He did it well, until he came to the last one. He hurled it toward our world, where unfortunately it landed on the head of a certain member of Congress. But the head was so hard that the bolt bounced back to the skies and scratched his wrist.

At this moment, someone grabbed me from behind. I turned my head and saw the little old woman in the gray cloak. I was quickly hurried from the great hall. Then I was sent with as much speed as before back to the world from which I had set out on this strange and wonderful adventure.

Meet the Author

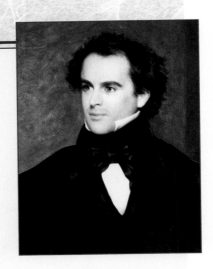

NATHANIEL HAWTHORNE *(1804–1864)*

Nathaniel Hawthorne was born in Salem, Massachusetts. He was the son of a sea captain. After his father was lost at sea, his mother kept him away from most people. Hawthorne remained shy most of his life. However, he had some good friends, including Henry Wadsworth Longfellow and Franklin Pierce, the fourteenth president of the United States.

Hawthorne is thought to be one of the greatest writers of American fiction. He wrote collections of short stories and novels. Two of his best-known novels are *The Scarlet Letter* and *The House of the Seven Gables*.

Check Your Predictions

1. Look back at the answers you gave for the Predict questions. Would you change your answers? Explain.

Understand the Story

2. Why does the old woman take the narrator to the clerk of the weather?

3. What does the cavern of the clerk of the weather look like?

4. What is the clerk's complaint about the people of Earth?

5. What kind of work does the clerk of the weather do?

Think About the Story

6. What conflict does the narrator see between Jack Frost and Spring?

7. Why does the old woman appear at the beginning and at the end of the story?

8. Why is this story called a myth?

Extend Your Response

Suppose the clerk of the weather is a guest on a TV talk show. Write four questions the talk show host might ask him. Then, write the answers the clerk of the weather might give.

Keys to Literature

sensory details: details of how something looks, sounds, smells, tastes, or feels

> Example: *His hair stood up, his mouth foamed, and his bloodshot eyes glittered.*

external conflict: a struggle that a character has with another character, with society, or with nature

> Example: In this story, Buck struggles against the men who want to control him.

Did You Know?

In *The Call of the Wild*, Buck has to survive in very cold temperatures. Buck is not a Husky, but Huskies are able to be in very cold temperatures for long periods of time. Huskies love to run and are able to pull a sled full of many things over a long distance.

Words to Know

kennels	cages for dogs
dignity	pride; self-respect
furiously	angrily
captor	someone who captures another person or animal
viciously	cruelly; evilly
savagely	fiercely; in an untamed way
grimly	in a gloomy or cold way
hatchet	a small ax with a short handle
snarled	growled angrily, showing the teeth
stagger	sway or wobble
craftiness	cleverness

from The Call of the Wild

BY JACK LONDON, *Adapted*

The Lesson

READ TO FIND OUT...
What lesson does Buck learn that he will never forget?

Buck did not read the newspapers. If he had, he would have known that trouble was brewing for strong, long-haired dogs like him. Gold had been found in the Arctic, so thousands of men were rushing north to make their fortunes. These men needed dogs, but not just any dogs. They wanted strong, heavy dogs like Buck to carry their loads. They also wanted dogs with thick, furry coats like Buck's that could withstand the cold and frost of the north country.

Buck lived in a big, sunny house in Santa Clara Valley, California. Judge Miller's place, it was called. It stood far back from the road, hidden among the bushes and poplar trees that surrounded it. A gravel driveway wound through the trees and up to the front of the house. Behind the house stretched a spacious

Keys to Literature

What **sensory details** describe Buck's house in California?

lawn that seemed to go on forever. Yet one could tell that it did not from the orchards and berry patches that grew along its border. And beyond these were the **kennels**, the great stables, the servants' cottages, and the other buildings that belonged to the Miller family.

All of this was Buck's territory. Here he was born, and here he had lived for the four years of his life. Of course, there were other dogs on the property, but they did not count. Some—like Toots, the pug, and Ysabel, the Mexican hairless—lived dull, spoiled lives inside the house. They were hardly ever seen putting their noses out of doors. Then others, like the fox terriers, spent their lives outside, but they were kept in kennels.

Buck, on the other hand, was neither a house dog nor a kennel dog. Buck ruled both worlds. And his was a grand life. He would swim with the judge's sons and take walks with the judge's daughters. At night he lay at the judge's feet as he and the judge shared the warmth of the fireplace together. He was king—that is, king over all things on Judge Miller's place, including people.

Buck's father, Elmo, was a huge Saint Bernard who had been Judge Miller's most faithful friend. Now Buck was following in his father's footsteps. At 140 pounds, he was not as large as his father. His mother, Shep, was a smaller Scotch shepherd. Still, Buck was a strong, heavy dog. His size and **dignity** gave him the right to walk like royalty around the place. Yet he never let himself become a spoiled house pet. Hunting and racing had kept the fat off and the muscles hard.

That was Buck in the fall of 1897, when gold was pulling men northward. But Buck did not know about the gold rush. Nor did he know that Manuel, the gardener, spelled danger. Manuel loved to gamble. Yet his wages were too small for such a hobby. His downfall was that he was always sure he would win. One fateful time, he did not.

Think About It

What does Buck think of the other dogs at the Miller home?

Predict

What will Manuel do to pay off his debt?

The judge and his family were gone the night of Manuel's crime. No one saw the gardener take Buck through the orchard and off into the darkness. (Buck thought he was going for a walk.) And only one man saw Buck and Manuel arrive at the railroad track. This man talked with the gardener for some time. Then money passed between the two.

"Wrap up the goods," the man said gruffly. So Manuel wrapped a thick rope around Buck's collar, which Buck allowed him to do. Buck trusted the men he knew.

"Twist the rope, and you'll choke 'em," said Manuel. But when the rope was handed to the stranger, Buck growled angrily.

Around the judge's place, such a growl was an order. But to Buck's surprise, this growl only tightened the rope further, cutting off his breath. In a rage, Buck leaped at the man. The man threw Buck to the ground, tightening the rope more. Buck fought back **furiously**. His tongue hung from his mouth. His chest panted for air. Never had he been treated this way. Never had he been so angry. Finally Buck's strength left him, and his eyes became blank. Later, when the train came, the two men threw him into a baggage car.

The next thing Buck knew, his tongue was hurting, and he was being jolted along in some kind of motion. Then the sound of the train whistle told him that he was on a train. He opened his eyes and stared like a kidnapped king. His royal eyes filled with anger as the man he spotted grabbed for his throat. But Buck was too quick for the man. His jaws bit savagely into the stranger's hand. Then he was choked again, and he blacked out.

Just then a baggage man who had heard their struggle came to check on things. "Yep, the dog has fits," said Buck's **captor**, as he hid his bloody hand

Keys to Literature

An **external conflict** is beginning between Buck and the man he was sold to. What causes this conflict?

Keys to Literature

What **sensory details** in this paragraph describe what Buck hears and feels?

Think About It

Buck's captor says he is taking Buck to the doctor for treatment against fits. Is he telling the truth? Explain.

from view. "Takin' him to 'Frisco. Dog doctor there thinks he can cure him." With that, the baggage man left Buck and the stranger alone.

Later that night Buck was taken to a saloon on the San Francisco waterfront. A meeting took place in a shed behind the saloon. There Buck's captor talked with the owner of the saloon about his trip.

"All I get is 50 for it," he grumbled. "I wouldn't do it again for a thousand in cold cash." His hand was wrapped in a bloody rag, and his pants were badly ripped. The kidnapper unwrapped his hand and looked at his injury, "If I don't get rabies from this ... "

The owner of the saloon only laughed. "If ya don't, it'll be because you were born to hang."

Dazed and in great pain, Buck tried once more to attack his enemies. Again he was thrown down and **viciously** choked. The men held him down to remove his collar and the rope. Then they threw him into a wooden cage.

Buck lay in the cage for the rest of the night, angry and ashamed. He could not understand what was happening to him. What did these strange men want with him? Why was he being kept in a cage? When he heard the door open again, Buck jumped to his feet. He thought that he was finally going to see his friend the judge again. But it was only the saloon owner looking in at him by the sickly light of a candle. Buck's throat twisted into a growl.

The next morning four men came to pick up Buck's cage. They were evil-looking men, ragged and dirty. These were more men who were bound to hurt him, Buck decided. He snarled at them through the bars of the cage. They only laughed and poked sticks at him. Buck grabbed the sticks with his teeth. But when he saw that the men wanted him to grab the sticks, he quickly lost interest and lay down quietly.

Buck's cage was then lifted into a wagon. From there he began to pass through many hands. Clerks in an office carted him around in another wagon. Then a truck carried him to a ferryboat. From the boat, he was trucked off to a train station. Finally he was placed in an express car.

For two days and nights, the express car was pulled along by a shrieking engine. The entire time Buck neither ate nor drank. Train clerks would come and go, but Buck greeted them with angry growls. The men reacted by teasing and laughing at him. They barked like dogs, flapped their arms, and howled. It was all very silly, Buck thought. It was an insult to his dignity. But he was glad about one thing—the rope was off his neck. Now he would show them. They would never get a rope around his neck again.

Buck's throat and tongue were sore and raw from lack of water. His bloodshot eyes were filled with anger. By now the judge himself would not have known Buck. The clerks were glad to unload him when the train arrived in Seattle.

Four men carefully carried his cage to a small, walled yard. There a stout man in a loose red sweater signed the driver's book. This was the man, Buck decided. He was the new enemy. Buck flung himself **savagely** against the bars. The man smiled **grimly** and picked up a club and a **hatchet**.

"You ain't going to take him out, are you?" the driver asked.

"Sure," the man answered as he pried at the bars with the hatchet. Immediately the four other men scattered. Safely on top of the wall, they waited to watch the show.

Meanwhile Buck rushed at the bars, sinking his teeth into the wood. He **snarled** as the hatchet fell on the cage. Buck wanted to get at the man in the red sweater as much as the man wanted to get at him.

Think About It

Do you think Buck's experience on the train has changed him? Explain.

Predict

What do you think will happen when Buck is taken out of his cage?

Keys to Literature

What **sensory details** describe the way Buck looks now?

"Now! You red-eyed devil," the man said as he made a large opening in the cage. Then he dropped the hatchet and took the club in his right hand.

Buck was truly a red-eyed devil by now. His hair stood up, his mouth foamed, and his bloodshot eyes glittered. He threw his 140 pounds of fury straight at the man. But in midair, Buck received a blow that jarred his teeth. He whirled over and fell to the ground. He had never been struck with a club in his life. He could not understand what was happening. With a snarl, he rose to his feet and again threw himself at the man. Again a crushing blow sent him to the ground. He was mad with rage. Again and again he charged. Each time the club smashed him down.

After one very hard blow, Buck could only **stagger** to his feet. He was too weak to attack again. Blood flowed heavily from his nose, mouth, and ears. His beautiful coat was splattered with blood and drool. But the man in the red sweater did not stop. He moved toward Buck again and leveled a frightening smash across his nose. Buck had never known pain like this before. With a lionlike roar, he hurled himself at the man again. But the man just shifted the club to his other hand and caught Buck hard below his jaw. The upward force of the blow sent Buck circling in the air. He crashed to the ground on his head and chest. One last time Buck rushed. Then the man struck a crushing blow that he had been saving for last. Buck went down, knocked cold.

"He's some dogbreaker, I'd say," said one of the men on the wall.

Slowly Buck regained his senses. But he was still too tired and hurt to move. He lay still, watching the man in the red sweater.

"Answers to the name of Buck," the man announced, as he read the note on the wooden crate. "Well, Buck,

Keys to Literature

Who is winning the **external conflict** between Buck and the men who took him? How do you know?

my boy, we've had our little meeting," he went on. "Best thing now is to let it go at that. You've learned your place, and I know mine. Be a good dog, and all will go well. Be a bad dog, and I'll beat the stuffin' out of you. Understand?"

As he spoke, the man patted Buck's bloodied head. Buck stiffened but was too hurt to move.

When the man brought food and water, Buck ate and drank eagerly. He was beaten—he knew that; but he was not broken. He had learned a lesson that he would not forget for the rest of his life. He saw that he stood no chance against a man with a club. The club, however, was only his first lesson in the rules of survival. Life would be crueler now. But he would face it bravely. He would also face it with all the **craftiness** he owned.

Predict

This story is the first chapter of the novel *The Call of the Wild*. At this point, Buck is beaten, but he is not broken. What do you think will happen to him as the story goes on?

Meet the Author

JACK LONDON *(1876–1916)*

Jack London was born in San Francisco, California. As a child, he went to school only through age 14. He loved to read, and he educated himself at public libraries. His early life was full of adventure. He was a factory worker, an oyster pirate, a sailor, a railroad hobo, and a gold prospector in the Arctic.

London is known for his exciting stories about surviving in the wilderness. People around the world love his books. They have been translated into many languages. Some of London's best-known books are *The Call of the Wild*, *White Fang*, and *The Sea-Wolf*.

Check Your Predictions

1. Look back at the answers you gave for the Predict questions. Would you change your answers? Explain.

Understand the Story

2. Why does Buck leave Judge Miller's home?

3. Where is Buck taken after he is sold?

4. Why does Buck become so angry with the men on the train?

5. Why does the man with the red sweater stop hitting Buck?

Think About the Story

6. Why do the men treat Buck the way they do?

7. What causes the external conflict between Buck and his captors?

8. Give an example of a sensory detail that describes Buck after he has been captured.

Extend Your Response

Design a book cover for this story. On the front of the book jacket, write the title and the author's name. Draw an illustration that shows what the story is about. On the back cover, write a few sentences to convince someone to read the book.

Learn More About It

THE YUKON

The Yukon is located in northwestern Canada. There are thick forests and beautiful lakes, and for most of the year, deep snow covers the ground. Summers are very short. Grizzly and black bears, moose, caribou, elk, fox, and salmon live in the Yukon.

In 1896, gold was found near the Klondike River in the Yukon. Thousands of Americans headed north, including Jack London. However, many men were not ready for the bitter cold and deep snow. In winter, they had to travel by dog sleds. Exposure to the cold could sometimes mean death.

Many gold miners were disappointed when they arrived. The gold they had hoped for had already been claimed. It was mainly the shopkeepers who made money. They charged high prices for the supplies the men needed.

Today, people travel to the Yukon for other reasons. They visit Dawson City, the town that sprung up during the Gold Rush. They also enjoy the Yukon's beautiful nature trails, lakes, and Canada's highest peak, Mount Logan.

Apply and Connect

Why would Buck be a good dog for the Yukon?

Summaries

River Man The people do not take care of their river, and the river man is forgotten. Soon, the people begin to lose their joy. The river man steals people's things so they will be forced to return to the river. When they come back to the river, they rediscover the joy it offers.

A Visit to the Clerk of the Weather An old woman takes the narrator to meet the clerk of the weather. There, he also meets Jack Frost, Spring, and others. The clerk apologizes for neglecting Earth. Spring promises to return soon. The old woman then returns the narrator to Earth.

The Call of the Wild Buck is sold and taken by men who need working dogs in the Arctic. He is treated very badly on the trip and is beaten into silence. Buck sees he has no chance against a man with a club. He learns to face whatever comes next with bravery.

insulting
generosity
glimpse
neglected
furiously

Vocabulary Review

Complete each sentence with a word from the box. Use a separate sheet of paper.

1. Thanks to Mr. Bloom's _____, the soccer team now has enough money to go to the state meet.

2. The lions fought _____ over the meat the lion trainer gave them.

3. Bree was _____ when she called Prince "ugly dog."

4. Sam _____ his plants by not watering them, and they almost died.

5. When Henry passed by the mirror, he caught a quick _____ of himself.

Chapter Quiz

Answer the following questions in one or two complete sentences. Use a separate sheet of paper.

1. **River Man** How does the river man get people to come back to the river?

2. **River Man** Why do the young man and the little girl go to the river?

3. **A Visit to the Clerk of the Weather** Why does the old woman take the narrator to the clerk of the weather?

4. **A Visit to the Clerk of the Weather** Why is Spring upset with Jack Frost?

5. **The Call of the Wild** Why does Buck finally take food and drink from the man in the red sweater?

6. **The Call of the Wild** At the end of the chapter, how does Buck decide he will face life from now on?

Critical Thinking

7. **A Visit to the Clerk of the Weather** What other title could you give this myth? Explain your choice.

8. **The Call of the Wild** What is the external conflict in this story?

Chapter Activity

A stage set has all the scenery and equipment needed to put on a play. Suppose you are creating a stage set for one of the stories in this chapter. Write a description of what you would place on the stage. Explain why you chose the things you did.

Farm by N. C. Wyeth

How does this image represent being close to the Earth?

Chapter **10** Poetry

CLOSE TO THE EARTH

Learning Objectives

- Explain what personification is.
- Identify a quatrain.
- Explain what coined words are.
- Understand the tone of a poem.
- Recognize free verse.
- Understand meter.
- Identify symbolism in a poem.

Preview Activity

Try writing a cinquain. It's easy! Write a noun that names something in nature. On the next line, write two words that describe it. On the third line, write three action words that tell about it. On the fourth line, tell how you feel about it. On the fifth line, repeat the word you wrote on the first line. You have just written a cinquain.

Poetry and Nature

A poem can be as short as two lines or as long as a book. It can have rhyme and rhythm, but it does not have to. It can be made up of one or more stanzas. The poems in this chapter have stanzas that are

quatrains: stanzas that have four lines.

free verse: stanzas that do not have a pattern.

cinquains: stanzas that have five lines.

More poems have been written about love and about nature than about any other subjects. Think about why each of the nature poems in this chapter was written. What sparked the idea?

Keys to Literature

personification: giving human characteristics to something that is not human

Example: *A Narrow Wind complains all Day*

quatrain: a stanza made up of four lines

Example: This poem has two quatrains.

Did You Know?

Emily Dickinson does some unusual things in her poems. She never gives her poems titles. Instead, the first line of a poem becomes its title. Also, she uses a capital letter for each noun in her poems, and at times, she uses dashes instead of commas or periods.

Words to Know

flake   a small, thin piece or chip

rut   a track made in the ground by wheels

debates   thinks about; tries to decide

The Sky Is Low

BY EMILY DICKINSON

The Sky is low—the Clouds are mean.
A Traveling **Flake** of Snow
Across a Barn or through a **Rut**
Debates if it will go—

5 A Narrow Wind complains all Day
How some one treated him.
Nature, like Us, is sometimes caught
Without her Diadem.

READ TO FIND OUT...
Why is the sky "low" in this poem?

Keys to Literature

The poet uses **personification** when she writes that clouds are mean. As you read, look for other examples of personification.

Keys to Literature

coined words: words that are made up

> Example: There is no such word as *mud-luscious*. The poet made up this word to mean "juicy, delicious mud."

Words to Know

luscious   juicy; delicious

lame   limping; disabled

Did You Know?

In Greek myths, Pan is the god of the woods, fields, and nature. Pan brings the seasons to humans. In this poem, a balloonman whistles and, like Pan, has feet that look like a goat's. The balloonman is a symbol of Pan.

in Just-

BY e.e. cummings

READ TO FIND OUT...
Why does the poet love spring so much?

in Just-
spring   when the world is mud-
luscious the little
lame balloonman

5   whistles   far   and wee

and eddieandbill come
running from marbles and
piracies and it's
spring

10   when the world is puddle-wonderful

the queer
old balloonman whistles
far   and   wee
and bettyandisbel come dancing

15   from hop-scotch and jump-rope and

it's
spring
and

the

20   goat-footed

balloonMan   whistles
far
and
wee

Think About It
What does *just* mean in this poem?

Springtime in Central Park by Jane Wooster Scott

Meet the Author

EMILY DICKINSON *(1830–1886)*

Emily Dickinson had a normal childhood, but by the time she was in her twenties, she hardly ever left her house. She refused to see anyone she did not know. She did write poetry, though. After she died, her relatives found 1,775 poems she had written. Only seven poems were published during her lifetime.

Dickinson created her own ways of writing. She used grammar and capital letters in an unusual way. Some of Dickinson's nature poems are "I Never Saw a Moor" and "A Narrow Fellow in the Grass."

Meet the Author

e.e. cummings *(1894–1962)*

e.e. cummings was an artist as well as a poet. For most of his life, he painted in the mornings and wrote poetry at night. cummings experimented with the way a poem looks. He made up new words and created new rules for using capitalization. He even wrote his own name without capital letters.

Two of cummings's poems are "Spring is like a perhaps hand" and "anyone lived in a pretty how town."

Understand the Poems

1. In "The Sky Is Low," what season is the poet writing about? How do you know?

2. Describe the weather in "The Sky Is Low."

3. In the poem "in Just-," how do you know that *eddieandbill* and *bettyandisbel* are children?

4. In "in Just-," why does the balloonman call the children?

Think About the Poems

5. In "The Sky Is Low," a diadem is a royal crown. What do you think it means when nature is "caught Without her Diadem"?

6. In "in Just-," which words and phrases make you think of spring?

7. "The Sky Is Low" and "in Just-" are about different kinds of days. How are the days different?

8. How does Dickinson use personification in "The Sky Is Low"?

Extend Your Response

A haiku is a Japanese poem that is also about nature. It is made up of seventeen syllables. Think of a part of nature that you like. Write your own haiku.
Line 1: five syllables followed by a comma
Line 2: seven syllables followed by a comma
Line 3: five syllables followed by a period

Keys to Literature

tone: the feeling a writer shows toward the subject of a poem or story

Example: The tone of this poem is respectful.

free verse: poetry that is not written in a regular pattern; the words do not rhyme.

Example: "Birdfoot's Grampa" is not written in a regular pattern. It has no rhyme.

Did You Know?

In spring, toads begin moving toward ponds. On their way, they can often be found on roads. Sometimes, they cross roads in large groups.

Words to Know

leaping	jumping high into the air
mist	fog or haze
accept	admit; give in to
leathery	tough like leather

$\mathcal{B}$irdfoot's Grampa

BY JOSEPH BRUCHAC

READ TO FIND OUT...
Why would someone keep stopping a car for toads?

The old man
must have stopped our car
two dozen times to climb out
and gather into his hands
5   the small toads blinded
by our lights and **leaping**,
live drops of rain.

The rain was falling,
a **mist** about his white hair
10   and I kept saying
you can't save them all,
accept it, get back in
we've got places to go.

But, **leathery** hands full
15   of wet brown life,
knee deep in the summer
roadside grass,
he just smiled and said
they have places to go to
20   *too.*

Keys to Literature

The first two stanzas of this poem have a different **tone**, or feeling, from the last stanza. At the beginning, the narrator feels annoyed with the old man. At the end, the narrator feels respect for him.

Meet the Author

JOSEPH BRUCHAC *(Born 1942)*

Joseph Bruchac lives in upstate New York. Although he is part Abenaki, part Slovak, and part English, most of his writing is about his Abenaki background. The Abenaki are Native Americans who live in southern New England. Bruchac hopes to preserve the culture, language, and music of these people.

Bruchac writes poetry, articles, stories, and novels. He also records traditional Abenaki stories and performs traditional and modern Abenaki music. He has received many honors, including the Lifetime Achievement Award from the Native Writers Circle of the Americas. He wrote the novel *The Arrow Over the Door* and his autobiography, *Bowman's Store*.

Understand the Poem

1. Who is Birdfoot?

2. Who is the old man?

3. What does the old man do when the narrator tells him to get back in the car?

4. Why does the narrator keep saying "you can't save them all"?

Think About the Poem

5. How do you know that the old man cares about nature?

6. In what way is the old man different from the narrator?

7. What is the tone of the third stanza?

8. How can you tell this poem is written in free verse?

Extend Your Response

Suppose you are Birdfoot. Write a paragraph describing your grandfather. How does he behave? What do you like about him?

Keys to Literature

meter: the rhythm, or beat, in a poem

> Example: In this poem, the meter is four beats to each line.
> *Two **roads** **diverged** in a **yellow** **wood**,*

symbolism: using something to stand for another thing

> Example: In this poem, choosing a road in the woods is a symbol of making choices in life.

Did You Know?

Although this poem is about nature, the poet said that he was not thinking about nature when he wrote it. He was thinking about a friend who had gone off to war. No matter which road his friend would take, he would be sorry he had not taken the other.

Words to Know

diverged	separated
undergrowth	small trees and bushes that grow under large trees
claim	a right

The Road Not Taken

BY ROBERT FROST

READ TO FIND OUT...
Why is a road *not* taken important?

Two roads **diverged** in a yellow wood,
And sorry I could not travel both
And be one traveler, long I stood
And looked down one as far as I could
5 To where it bent in the **undergrowth**;

Then took the other, as just as fair,
And having perhaps the better **claim**,
Because it was grassy and wanted wear;
Though as for that, the passing there
10 Had worn them really about the same,

Think About It
What does the speaker wish he could do when he has to choose between two roads in the wood?

Keys to Literature

The **meter** in this poem is four beats to each line. Read the poem aloud and listen for these beats.

And both that morning equally lay
In leaves no step had trodden black.
Oh, I kept the first for another day!
Yet knowing how way leads on to way,
15 I doubted if I should ever come back.

I shall be telling this with a sigh
Somewhere ages and ages hence:
Two roads diverged in a wood, and I—
I took the one less traveled by,
20 And that has made all the difference.

Keys to Literature

What do you think "the road less traveled" is a **symbol** of?

Meet the Author

ROBERT FROST *(1874–1963)*

Robert Frost was born in California, but he moved to New England when he was eleven. As a young man, he taught school, worked in a mill, and wrote newspaper articles. However, all he really wanted to do was write poetry.

Frost liked the rhyme and meter of poetry. He said he would just as soon play tennis without a net as write free verse. Frost won four Pulitzer Prizes for poetry in his lifetime. Two of his most famous poems are "Stopping by Woods on a Snowy Evening" and "Mending Wall."

Understand the Poem

1. In the first stanza, what does the speaker have to choose between?

2. What are the two roads in the wood like?

3. How does the speaker decide which road to take?

4. Which words and phrases tell you that the season is fall?

Think About the Poem

5. What might the speaker mean when he says that the less traveled road has made all the difference?

6. Why is the traveler sorry that he cannot travel both roads?

7. Which symbol in this poem stands for making choices in life?

8. What is the meter of this poem? Give an example from the poem.

Extend Your Response

Suppose you are walking in the same wood as the narrator. Which road would you choose? Explain why.

Chapter 10 Review

Summaries

The Sky Is Low It is a cold, wintry day. Low clouds appear in the sky. The wind is blowing, and there is snow in the air.

in Just- Spring has arrived, and it is "mud-luscious" and "puddle-wonderful." A balloonman calls children away from their games to enjoy spring.

Birdfoot's Grampa The speaker's grandfather keeps stopping his car to save toads that are blinded by his headlights. At first, the speaker is annoyed with his grandfather. Later, he appreciates his grandfather's respect for living things.

The Road Not Taken A man is walking in a woods when he comes to a fork and has to decide which road to take. He chooses the road that looks less traveled. He believes that when he thinks about his choice years later, it will have made all the difference in his life.

claim
mist
leaping
luscious
rut
diverged

Vocabulary Review

Match each word in the box with its meaning. Write the word and its matching number on a separate sheet of paper.

1. juicy; delicious
2. a right
3. jumping high in the air
4. fog
5. separated
6. a track made in the ground by wheels

Chapter Quiz

Answer the following questions in one or two complete sentences. Use a separate sheet of paper.

1. The Sky Is Low and in Just- Both poems are about nature. Which part of nature does each poem describe?

2. Birdfoot's Grampa Why does the old man move the toads?

3. The Road Not Taken Will the speaker be back in the same woods again? Explain.

Critical Thinking

4. The Sky Is Low and in Just- How does the author of each poem feel about the day? How can you tell?

5. The Sky Is Low What do you think the poet means by the last two lines of the poem?

6. in Just- Why do the children come running?

7. Birdfoot's Grampa How does the speaker feel about the old man stopping the car?

8. The Road Not Taken What do you think the title of this poem means?

Chapter Activity

Write a letter to someone you have not seen in a long time. Describe the part of the year that you like best. Use words and phrases that explain why you like this time.

Unit 4 **Review**

On a separate sheet of paper, write the letter that best completes each sentence below.

1. In "River Man," the river brings people
   A. friendship and humor.
   B. sickness and sadness.
   C. forgetfulness and sleepiness.
   D. money and luck.

2. In *The Call of the Wild,* Buck learns how to
   A. hunt for food in wild places.
   B. take charge of other sled dogs.
   C. be brave and crafty in dealing with humans.
   D. let humans think they have won.

3. In "The Sky Is Low," Emily Dickinson describes nature as
   A. boring.
   B. funny.
   C. beautiful.
   D. unpleasant.

4. In "in Just-," spring is a time when
   A. old people come running outside.
   B. children are happy to be outside jumping in puddles.
   C. people buy a lot of colorful balloons.
   D. children get their clothes dirty.

5. At the end of "Birdfoot's Grampa," the speaker
   A. accepts what his grandfather does.
   B. is angry that his grandfather will not listen to him.
   C. drives the car himself.
   D. is sad that his grandfather is getting old.

6. In "The Road Not Taken," the speaker
   A. walks down both roads.
   B. does not choose either road.
   C. turns around and goes home.
   D. chooses one road.

Making Connections
On a separate sheet of paper, write your answers to the following questions.

7. Which story in this unit has the liveliest sensory details? Give examples from the story.

8. Which poem in this unit did you like best? Write a short weather report, based on this poem. Tell how the weather may affect people in the area.

Writing an Essay
Choose one of the stories or poems in this unit. Describe the way the author presents nature. Give examples.

Unit 5 ▷ The Struggle Within

Chapter 11 ## Nonfiction

Little Things Are Big
by Jesus Colon, adapted

from **Narrative of the Life of Frederick Douglass**
by Frederick Douglass, adapted

Chapter 12 ## Short Stories

Amigo Brothers
by Piri Thomas, adapted

Ambush
by Tim O'Brien

Ribbons
by Laurence Yep, adapted

Chapter 13 ## Poetry

Ballad of Birmingham
by Dudley Randall

Taught Me Purple
by Evelyn Tooley Hunt

Simple-song
by Marge Piercy

Ghosts by Diana Ong (Born 1940)

Struggles are as different as people themselves. What kinds of struggles do people experience?

Chapter 11 / Nonfiction
THE STRUGGLE WITHIN

Learning Objectives

- Define nonfiction writing.
- Explain what an essay is.
- Recognize an autobiography.
- Understand what a paradox is.
- Explain internal and external conflict.
- Identify an analogy.

Preview Activity

Think about conflicts you have read about, heard of, or faced yourself. Fold a sheet of paper in half. Label one side Internal Conflicts. Label the other side External Conflicts. Write three examples of each type of conflict.

Nonfiction and Conflict

Nonfiction is about real people and real events. Two types of nonfiction are

essay: a short piece of writing that expresses the writer's personal ideas about a subject.

autobiography: the story of a person's life written by that person.

The nonfiction selections in this chapter are about people who struggle with themselves. They must overcome internal conflicts in order to deal with their problems.

Keys to Literature

paradox: a statement that seems impossible but that may actually be true

> Example: The title, "Little Things Are Big," is a paradox. A small decision can be part of a very big problem.

internal conflict: the conflict a person has within himself or herself when trying to make a decision

> Example: In this essay, the author struggles between wanting to help a woman and being afraid to.

Did You Know?

The setting of this essay is the New York City subway system. Most subway trains run along tracks in tunnels below the ground. The trains run all day and night. Parts of some subways are actually above ground.

Words to Know

subway	a train that runs underground
platform	a raised area where people wait for a train
steep	slanting sharply; sloping
courtesy	good manners; kindness
prejudiced	disliking people because they belong to a different group from one's own
explode	blow up
racism	the belief that one race is better than another

Little Things Are Big

BY JESUS COLON, *Adapted*

It was very late. It was the night before Memorial Day. She came into the **subway** at the 34th Street Pennsylvania Station. I am still trying to remember how she was able to get on the train. She had so much to deal with. She was holding a baby on her right arm. She had a travel bag in her left hand. There were two children, a boy and a girl about three and five years old, walking behind her. She was a nice looking white lady in her early twenties.

READ TO FIND OUT...

Is there ever a good reason not to help someone in need?

Keys to Literature

The title of this selection is a **paradox**. Big and little are opposites. How can things be big and little at the same time?

Subway by Patricia Mollica

At Nevins Street, in Brooklyn, we saw her getting ready to get off at the next station. The next station was Atlantic Avenue. I had to get off at that station, too. I knew it was going to be hard for her to get off with a baby, two small children, and a medium-sized travel bag.

And here I was, ready to get off, too. I had nothing to carry. I did not even have a book. I almost always carry a book. Without a book, I feel like I don't have all my clothes on. But that night I had nothing.

The train came in to the Atlantic station. Some white man got up from his seat and helped her out. He put the children on the long, empty **platform**. There were only two adults on the platform some time after midnight on the night before Memorial Day.

Predict

Will the author help the woman with the children?

I could see the long, **steep** steps going down to the street. Should I offer to help her, as the white man had done? Should I take the girl and the boy by their hands and lead them down the long steps?

Puerto Ricans are known for their **courtesy**. And here I was—a Puerto Rican—with people who needed help. It was past midnight. A white lady, a baby, and two white children needed help getting down the stairs.

Keys to Literature

What makes the conflict in this essay an **internal conflict**?

But how could I go up to this woman? I am an African American man and a Puerto Rican. This white lady might be **prejudiced** against African Americans. How would she feel about an African American coming up to her in an empty subway station late at night?

What would she say? How would she react? Perhaps she was coming to the city from a small town with her children and a travel bag. Would she say: Yes, of course, you can help me. Or would she think I was just trying to get too friendly with her? Or would she think something worse than that? What would I do if she screamed when I walked up to her?

Could I be wrong about her? Every day, so many bad things are written in the papers about African Americans and Puerto Ricans. For a long, long minute, I could not decide what to do. Inside me were the manners that every Puerto Rican passes on from father to son. These manners were struggling inside me. If I went to her, the situation could **explode**. The prejudices people learn could suddenly burst out. These are the prejudices that keep people apart.

It was a long minute. Then I walked by her as though I had seen nothing. I acted as though I did not care that she needed help. I was like a rude animal walking on two legs. I moved away from her on the long platform. I was almost running. I left the children and the travel bag and her with the baby on her arm. I reached the steps and ran down them two at a time. When I came out on the street, the cold air slapped my face.

Think About It

What does the author mean when he says the situation could explode?

Think About It

What does the author decide to do?

Entrance to Subway by Mark Rothko

This is what **racism** and prejudice can do to people and to a nation! This is what happens when these false walls keep us apart from each other.

Dear lady, if you were not prejudiced, I failed you. I know there is one chance in a million that you will read what I have written here. I will take that chance, anyway. If you were not prejudiced, I failed you, lady. I failed your children. I failed myself.

I buried my courtesy early on the morning of Memorial Day. But I am making a promise to myself. If something like this ever happens to me again, I am going to offer to help.

Then I will have my courtesy with me again.

Think About It

Why does the author write directly to the woman here?

Meet the Author

JESUS COLON (1901–1974)

Jesus Colon was born in Cayey, Puerto Rico. When he was seventeen years old, he hid aboard a ship and traveled to New York. Colon had left Puerto Rico to find work and a better life. While he tried to support himself in New York, he became aware of the poor working conditions that other immigrant workers faced.

Colon wrote about the racism he experienced as a black Puerto Rican. He also wrote about the struggles of poor immigrants in New York. His writings include essays, newspaper articles, stories, and autobiographical essays. His book of essays is called *A Puerto Rican in New York, and Other Sketches.*

Check Your Predictions

1. Look back at the answer you gave for the Predict question. Would you change your answer? Explain.

Understand the Story

2. Why does the author want to help the woman?

3. Why does the author decide not to help the woman?

4. Whom does the author say he has failed?

5. The next time something like this happens to the author, what does he say he will do?

Think About the Story

6. What does the author mean when he writes, "This is what racism and prejudice can do"? Explain.

7. What is the author's internal conflict in this essay?

8. Why do you think this essay is called "Little Things Are Big"?

Extend Your Response

Suppose the author sent his essay to the woman. How do you think she would react to it? What do you think she would say in response? Write a letter from the woman to the author that describes her feelings. Be sure to include a heading, the body, and a closing in your letter.

Keys to Literature

analogy: comparing something unknown with something you already know

> Example: Douglass compares a ship to an angel because they are both free to "fly" around the world.

external conflict: a struggle that a person has with another person, with society, or with nature

> Example: A physical fight is an external conflict.

Words to Know

reputation	what most people think about a person
discipline	punishment; correction
brute	a beast; a wild animal
plantation	a large piece of land where crops are grown by workers who live there
fast	held tight; fastened
hopper	a grain bin
curry	clean an animal's coat with a currycomb or brush
assurance	confidence
determination	having your mind set on accomplishing something

from Narrative of the Life of Frederick Douglass

BY FREDERICK DOUGLASS, *Adapted*

READ TO FIND OUT...
How does a horrible experience help someone grow and change?

My master and myself had quite a number of differences. He found me unfit for his purpose.... One of my greatest faults was to let his horse run away. It would go down to his father-in-law's farm, which was about five miles from St. Michael's. I would then have to go after it.

I had a reason for this kind of carelessness, or carefulness. The reason was that I could always get something to eat when I went there. Master William Hamilton, my master's father-in-law, always gave his slaves enough to eat. I never left there hungry, no matter how fast I had to return.

Predict

What will happen to Douglass when he goes to live with Mr. Covey?

Master Thomas finally said that he couldn't take it any longer. I had lived with him for nine months. During that time he had given me a number of whippings, all to no good purpose. He was set to hurt or, as he said, to break my spirit. For this purpose, he loaned me for one year to a man named Edward Covey.

Mr. Covey was a poor man, a farm-renter. He rented the place upon which he lived and all the field hands who worked on the farm. Mr. Covey had gotten a very high **reputation** for breaking young slaves. This reputation was of great value to him. It let him get his farm tilled at much less cost than he could have had it done without such a reputation. Some slave holders thought it wasn't much of a loss to allow Mr. Covey to train their slaves for one year. He could hire young help easily because of his reputation.

Mr. Covey was a professor of religion. He was a member and a class-leader in the Methodist church. All of this added weight to his reputation as a "slave-breaker." I was aware of all these facts. I had been told about them by a young man who'd lived there. Still, I made the change gladly. This way I was sure of getting enough to eat. This was not an easy task for a hungry man.

Think About It

Why were young enslaved men sent to Mr. Covey?

I went to live with Mr. Covey on January 1, 1833. For the first time in my life, I was now a field hand.... My first six months with Mr. Covey were the worst time of my life as a slave. We were worked in all kinds of weather. It was never too hot or too cold. It could never rain, blow, hail, or snow too hard for us to work in the field.

I was somewhat hard to manage when I first went there. But a few months of this **discipline** tamed me. Mr. Covey succeeded in breaking me. I was broken in body, soul, and spirit. My ability to bounce back from things was crushed. My mind became weak. My desire to read disappeared. The dark night of slavery closed in upon me. See a man turned into a **brute**.

Sunday was my only time to relax. I spent this day in a sort of beast-like state, between sleep and wake, under some large tree. At times I would rise up. A flash of energy and freedom would race through my soul. That feeling flickered for a moment and then vanished. I sank down again, mourning over my terrible condition. I sometimes thought of taking my life and that of Covey. But I was prevented by a combination of hope and fear. Now my sufferings on that **plantation** seem like a dream rather than a reality.

Our house stood within several yards of Chesapeake Bay. I have often, in the stillness of a summer's Sunday, stood all alone upon the banks of that noble bay. I've looked upon the waters with a sad heart and a tearful

Think About It

Is Mr. Covey successful in "breaking" Douglass? Explain.

▶ Southern plantation owners bought enslaved people to work on their property and to grow crops in their fields.

eye. I have traced the countless number of sails moving off to the mighty ocean. The sight of these sails always affected me powerfully. My thoughts would force me to speak. With no audience but God, I would pour out my soul's complaint. In my rude way, I would speak to the great number of moving ships.

"You are loosed from your **moorings** and are free. I am **fast** in my chains and am a slave! You move happily before the gentle breeze. And I sadly before the bloody whip! You are freedom's angels that fly around the world. I am bound in bands of iron! O, that I were free! O, that I were on one of your bold decks and under your protecting wing!

"Alas! Between me and you the muddy waters roll. Go on, go on. O, that I could also go! Could I but swim! If I could fly! O, why was I born a man of whom to make a brute! O, God, save me! God, deliver me! Let me be free! Is there any God? Why am I a slave?

"I will run away. I will not stand it. Only think of it—100 miles straight north, and I am free! Try it? Yes! I will take to the water. And when I get to the head of the bay, I will turn my canoe loose. Then I will walk straight through Delaware and into Pennsylvania. When I get there, I shall not be required to have a pass. I can travel without being bothered.

"Let the first opportunity offer, and I am off. Meanwhile, I will try to be strong. I am not the only slave in the world. Why should I worry? I can take as much as any of them. It may be that my misery in slavery will only increase my happiness when I get free. There is a better day coming."

This I used to think. And this I used to say to myself. I was driven almost to madness at one moment. Then at the next, I accepted my terrible condition.

I have already said how terrible my condition was during my first six months with Mr. Covey. Then events

Keys to Literature

Here, Douglass uses an **analogy** to compare his life to a ship on an ocean. The ship is free and is like an angel that flies around the world.

▶ The *100 miles straight north* would take him to Pennsylvania, a free state.

caused a change in the way he treated me. You have seen how a man was made a slave. You shall see how a slave was made a man.

It was one of the hottest days of the month of August 1833. Bill Smith, William Hughes, a slave named Eli, and myself were busy fanning wheat. The work was simple. It required strength rather than brains. Yet to someone not used to such work, it was very hard. At about three o'clock that day, I broke down. I was gripped with a violent headache. I felt very dizzy. I was shaking in every part of my body.

Knowing what was coming, I gathered my nerves. I thought it wouldn't help to stop working. I stood for as long as I could stagger to the **hopper** with grain. When I couldn't stand it any longer, I fell. I felt as if I was being held down by a great weight. Of course, the fan stopped. Every one had his own work to do. No one could do someone else's work and have his own go on, too.

Mr. Covey was at the house, about 100 yards from where we were fanning. He heard the fan stop. He left right away and came to the spot where we were. He quickly asked what was the matter. Bill said that I was sick. There was no one to bring the wheat to the fan.

By this time, I had crawled away under the side of the fence that surrounded the yard. I was hoping to find relief by getting out of the sun. Mr. Covey asked where I was. One of the field hands told him. He came over to me and looked at me awhile. Then he asked me what was the matter. I told him as well as I could. I had barely enough strength to speak.

He then gave me a savage kick in the side. He told me to get up. I tried to do so but fell back down. He gave me another kick and again told me to rise. I again tried and this time succeeded in getting to my feet. I stooped to get to the tub with which I was feeding the fan. As I did, I again staggered and fell.

Predict

What will happen to change the way Mr. Covey treats Douglass?

▶ *Fanning wheat* is a way of separating the parts of the wheat that can be made into flour from the parts that cannot.

Predict

What will Mr. Covey do when he sees how sick Douglass is?

I lay down in this position. Then Mr. Covey took up the hickory stick that Hughes had been using to strike off the wheat. Mr. Covey used it to give me a heavy blow upon the head. It made a large wound, and the blood ran freely. Then he told me again to get up.

I made no effort to do so. I had made up my mind to let him do his worst. In a short time after receiving this blow, my head felt better. Mr. Covey had now left me to my fate....

I spent the next day mostly in the woods. I had two choices. I could go home and be whipped to death. Or I could stay in the woods and be starved to death. That night I met up with Sandy Jenkins, a slave I knew. He had a free wife who lived about four miles from Mr. Covey's farm. Because it was Saturday, he was on his way to see her.

▶ Douglass runs away at this time.

I told Sandy what happened. He very kindly invited me to go home with him. I did, and we talked this whole matter over. I got his advice as to what course was best for me to take. He told me, seriously, that I must go back to Covey. However, he said that before I went, I must go with him to another part of the woods. There we would find a certain *root*, which he wanted me to carry *always on my right side*. If I did, he said it would make it impossible for Mr. Covey, or any other white man, to whip me. Sandy said he had carried it for years. Since he'd done so, he'd never been hit.

At first, I turned down the idea. I thought that the simple carrying of this *root* would not do what he said it would do. I did not want to take it. But Sandy told me it was necessary. He said it could do no harm, even if it did no good.

To please him, I finally took the *root*. Then according to his direction, I carried it upon my right side. It was Sunday morning. I started for home right away. When I entered the yard gate, Mr. Covey came out. He was on his way to a meeting. He spoke to me very kindly. He

Think About It

Does Sandy offer Douglass good advice? Explain.

told me to drive the pigs from a lot nearby. Then he walked toward the church.

Now this conduct of Mr. Covey really made me stop and think. Perhaps there was something in the *root* that Sandy had given me. I half believed the *root* was something more than I at first had taken it to be.

All went well until Monday morning. On this morning, the power of the *root* was fully tested. It was long before daylight. I was called to go and rub, **curry**, and feed the horses. I obeyed and was glad to obey.

While I was throwing down some blades from the loft, Mr. Covey entered the stable. He had a long rope with him. I was half out of the loft. Mr. Covey caught hold of my legs and began tying me up. I gave a sudden spring. As I did so, I was brought sprawling to the stable floor.

Mr. Covey now seemed to think he had me. He thought he could do what he pleased. But at this moment, I made up my mind to fight. I grabbed Covey hard by the throat. As I did so, I rose. He held on to me, and I to him.

My holding back was so unexpected, that Covey seemed startled. He shook like a leaf. This gave me **assurance**, and I held him.... He asked me if I planned on continuing to hold back. I told him I did, no matter what. I told him he had used me and beat me for six months. I was determined not to be used that way any longer.

With that, he tried to drag me to a stick that was lying just outside the stable door. He meant to knock me down. Just as he was leaning over to get the stick, I grabbed him by the collar. I brought him suddenly to the ground.

By this time Bill came. Covey called upon him for help. Bill wanted to know what he could do. Covey said, "Take hold of him!" Bill said his master had hired him out to work and not to help whip me. So he left Covey and myself to fight our own battle.

We were at it for nearly two hours. Covey finally let me go. He was rapidly puffing and blowing. He said that if I had not resisted, he wouldn't have whipped me half as much. The truth was that he had not whipped me at all. I thought he had gotten entirely the worst end of the fight. He had drawn no blood from me, but I had from him.

I spent six months more with Mr. Covey. In that time, he never laid a finger upon me in anger. He'd sometimes say he didn't want to get hold of me again.

Predict

Who will win the conflict? What makes you think so?

"No, you need not," I thought. "For you will come off worse than before."

This battle with Mr. Covey was the turning-point in my career as a slave. It gave me a new **determination** to be free. I felt as I never felt before. It was a glorious rebirth, from the tomb of slavery, to the heaven of freedom.

I now promised myself something. For however long I remained a slave in form, the day had passed forever when I could be a slave in fact. I also let a fact be known about me. Whichever white man expected to succeed in whipping, must also succeed in killing me.

From this time, I was never again what might be called fairly whipped. I remained a slave for four years longer. And I had several fights. But I was never whipped.

Meet the Author

FREDERICK DOUGLASS (1818–1895)

Frederick Douglass was born into slavery near Tuckahoe, Maryland. Until he was a teenager, he worked as a servant in his master's house. There, he learned to read and write. Douglass escaped to freedom in 1838, when he was 20 years old. He moved to New York, where he fought against slavery for the rest of his life.

Douglass was a brilliant speaker and gave many speeches in the North about the evils of slavery. In 1845, Douglass published his autobiography, *Narrative of the Life of Frederick Douglass*. In 1847, he published an antislavery newspaper called the *North Star*. He also organized black soldiers during the Civil War and held several positions in the U.S. government.

Check Your Predictions

1. Look back at the answers you gave for the Predict questions. Would you change your answers? Explain.

Understand the Story

2. Why does Douglass often let Mr. Thomas's horse run away?

3. Why does Mr. Thomas send Douglass to Mr. Covey?

4. Who wins the fight? How does Mr. Covey treat Douglass after the fight?

Think About the Story

5. What kind of person is Mr. Covey? Give examples from the story.

6. What kind of person is Douglass? Give examples from the story.

7. How is the external conflict between Mr. Covey and Douglass resolved?

8. Douglass makes an analogy between his determination and being reborn. How are these two ideas similar?

Extend Your Response

Most book covers contain blurbs, or short reviews, about the books. Write a three-sentence blurb about *Narrative of the Life of Frederick Douglass*. Be sure to include your opinion of the book.

Learn More About It

SLAVERY ON PLANTATIONS

During the 1700s and 1800s, large plantation owners wanted cheap labor to work in the fields. They used enslaved people from Africa to raise and harvest the crops. These people were very important to the economy of the South.

Some African Americans worked in plantation houses. The women were cooks, maids, and child-care workers. The men were carpenters, blacksmiths, and painters.

However, most enslaved people worked long, hard days in the fields. An overseer directed them and kept a close watch over them. Anyone who did not work hard was punished.

Enslaved workers who disobeyed orders could be whipped or sold. People who tried to run away were often beaten or whipped, and sometimes they were killed.

Apply and Connect

Why does Frederick Douglass return to Mr. Covey even though he knows he might be whipped to death?

Two Cotton Pickers by William A. Walker

Summaries

Little Things Are Big Jesus Colon sees a white woman with her children struggling on a subway train. He wants to help her, but he thinks she might be afraid of him because he is not white. He decides not to. Later, he is sorry that he let racism get in the way of helping someone in need.

Narrative of the Life of Frederick Douglass As a young man, Douglass is sent to Mr. Covey to be "broken." Douglass is beaten even when he is very sick. He decides to run away but soon returns. He fights back the next time Mr. Covey tries to beat him. He promises himself that he will never again allow himself to be whipped.

courtesy
reputation
discipline
prejudiced
assurance
steep

Vocabulary Review

Match each word in the box with its meaning. Write the word and its matching number on a separate sheet of paper.

1. slanting sharply
2. disliking people because they belong to a different group
3. what most people think about someone
4. confidence
5. good manners
6. punishment

Chapter Quiz

Answer the following questions in one or two complete sentences. Use a separate sheet of paper.

1. **Little Things Are Big** Why does the woman on the subway need help?

2. **Little Things Are Big** According to the writer, what are Puerto Rican people known for?

3. **Little Things Are Big** What does the writer do at the end of the essay?

4. **Narrative of the Life of Frederick Douglass** How does Mr. Thomas treat Douglass?

5. **Narrative of the Life of Frederick Douglass** How does Mr. Covey treat Douglass?

6. **Narrative of the Life of Frederick Douglass** What does Douglass learn from his stay at Mr. Covey's?

Critical Thinking

7. **Little Things Are Big** What is the paradox in this essay?

8. **Narrative of the Life of Frederick Douglass** What is the internal conflict within Douglass?

Chapter Activity

Compare Jesus Colon and Frederick Douglass. Draw two overlapping circles. Write Colon in one of the outer circles and Douglass in the other outer circle. Write Both People in the middle section. Think of ways they are different from each other. Write your ideas in the outer circles. Think of how they are alike. Write those ideas in the overlapping part.

Faces in Closet by Daniel DeNapoli

This image shows a man in a room full of masks. Why do people wear different masks in life?

Chapter 12 · Short Stories

THE STRUGGLE WITHIN

Learning Objectives

- Explain what colloquial language is.
- Identify the omniscient point of view.
- Recognize sensory details in a short story.
- Recognize realism as a style of writing.
- Identify the turning point of a short story.
- Recognize foreshadowing to predict events.

Preview Activity

Think of a time when you had to make a choice. What happened? How did you arrive at your decision? Write a journal entry to record your answers. You may wish to share your journal entry with a classmate.

Short Stories and the Struggle Within

A short story is a type of fiction. Stories can be written from different points of view.

first-person point of view: A story character tells the story, using *I* to refer to himself or herself.

third-person point of view: A narrator tells the story, using *he* and *she* to refer to the characters.

omniscient point of view: The narrator knows what all the characters do, say, and feel.

In a short story about a "struggle within," the character's conflict is within himself or herself. The character has a choice to make. You can decide for yourself whether the characters in this chapter make the right decisions.

Keys to Literature

colloquial language: everyday language people use when talking to friends

> Example: "*Let's stop a while, bro. I think we both got something to say to each other.*"

omniscient point of view: when the narrator knows what all the story characters do, say, and feel; An omniscient narrator uses *he, she*, and *they* to refer to the characters.

> Example: In this story, the narrator knows what both Antonio and Felix do, say, and feel.

Did You Know?

Boxing is a sport in which two athletes wear padded gloves and fight each other in a raised area called a ring. The winner is the one who wins the most points or who knocks out his or her opponent. When someone is knocked out, he or she is unable to get up before a count of ten.

Words to Know

lightweight	a weight class for boxers who weigh between 127 and 135 pounds
bouts	fights, or matches, in boxing
slugger	hitter
division	a group at a certain weight or age level
draw	a tie; when the fighters have equal points at the end of a match
sparring	boxing for practice without throwing blows
amigo	"friend" in Spanish
champion	a winner of a match or a series of matches
challenger	in boxing, the one who fights the champion
referee	a person who judges a match or a game

Amigo Brothers

BY PIRI THOMAS, *Adapted*

Antonio Cruz and Felix Varga were both seventeen years old. They were such close friends that they felt like brothers. They had known each other since they were children. They had grown up on the lower east side of Manhattan in the same apartment building.

Antonio was thin and had light skin. Felix was short and had a heavier, dark body. Antonio's hair was always falling over his eyes. Felix wore his dark hair in an Afro.

Both boys had a dream. Each wanted to be the **lightweight** champion of the world. Every chance they had, the boys worked out.

Before the sun came up, they would go running along East River Drive. They wore sweat shirts, short towels around their necks, and handkerchiefs around their foreheads.

READ TO FIND OUT...
What happens when best friends want the same thing, but only one of them can have it?

Predict

Antonio and Felix both dream of becoming the lightweight champion. How will this dream affect their friendship?

Keys to Literature

The author uses **colloquial language** to describe the kids in this story. What does "dreamed positive" mean?

While some kids were into negative stuff on the street, Antonio and Felix were positive. They slept, ate, rapped, and dreamed positive. The boys had a bigger collection of *Fight* magazines than anyone. They had a scrapbook of torn tickets from every boxing match they had ever been to. They could answer any question about a fighter.

Both boys had fought many **bouts** for their community. They had won medals—gold, silver, and bronze. Each boy had his own fighting style, too. Antonio's thin body and long arms and legs made him the better boxer. Felix's short body, with its heavy muscles, made him the better **slugger**. When the boys practiced with each other, it had always been a tough fight.

Predict

Who will win the fight? Why?

Now a big day was coming. The boys would fight each other in the **division** finals for the Boy's Club. The fight was August seventh, two weeks away.

The boys still ran together along East River Drive. But even when they were joking with each other, they could feel a wall going up between them.

One morning, they met as usual for their workout. They fooled around with a few punches in the air, slapped skin, and then ran along the edge of the dirty East River.

After they had run a mile or so, Felix said, "Let's stop a while, bro. I think we both got something to say to each other."

Think About It

At this point in the story, which is the bigger conflict: the external conflict between the boys or the internal conflict inside each boy? Explain.

Antonio nodded. They couldn't act as though nothing unusual was going on. Not when two buddies were going to be competing with each other in a few short days.

Antonio said, "It's about our fight, right?"

"Yeah, right," Felix said.

"Ever since I found out it was going to be you against me, I've been thinking about it," Antonio said.

"I've been awake at night. I've been pulling punches on you, trying not to hurt you."

"Same here," Felix said. "I mean, we are both good fighters, and we both want to win. But only one of us can win. There ain't gonna be no **draw** in this fight."

Antonio nodded. "Yeah. We both know that in the ring, the best man wins. Friend or no friend. Brother or no brother."

"Let's promise something right here," Felix said. "When we get into the ring, it's gonna be like we never met. We gotta be like two strangers who want the same thing—and only one can have it. See what I mean?"

Antonio smiled. "*Si*, (Yes) I know. No pulling punches. We go all the way."

"Yeah, that's right," Felix said, "and listen, don't you think it's a good idea if we don't see each other until the day of the fight? I'm going to stay with my Aunt Lucy in the Bronx. I can use Gleason's gym for working out. My manager says he's got some **sparring** partners who fight like you."

Antonio said, "Watch yourself, Felix. I hear there's some pretty heavy dudes up in the Bronx. Be careful, okay?"

"Okay," Felix said. "You watch yourself, too."

The **amigo** brothers were not ashamed to hug each other tightly.

The days before the fight passed much too slowly. The boys kept out of each other's way.

The night before the big fight, Antonio went up to the roof of his building. He tried not to think of Felix. He thought he had prepared his mind pretty well for the fight. But he wouldn't really know until he got in the ring. He wanted to knock out Felix quickly, so his friend would not get hurt.

Keys to Literature

What is an example of **colloquial language** in this paragraph?

Keys to Literature

What does the **colloquial language** "some pretty heavy dudes" mean?

Up in the South Bronx, Felix went to a movie. He wanted to stop thinking about hitting Antonio's face with his fists. The movie was *The Champion* with Kirk Douglas.

In the movie, the **champion** was getting beat up. His face was being pounded into raw, wet hamburger. His eyes were cut and bleeding. One eye was swollen. The other eye was almost swollen shut. He was saved only by the sound of the bell.

▶ As Felix watches the movie, he begins to imagine that he and Antonio are in the movie. He sees himself as the champion. He sees Antonio as the fighter who is challenging his championship title.

Felix became the champion, and Antonio became the **challenger**.

The champion was bent over. His nose was broken and bloody. The challenger thought he had the champ beat. He hit the champ with a left. The champ came back with a right that exploded into the challenger's brains.

Instead of the face on the movie screen, Felix saw Antonio's face. Felix saw himself in the ring. He blasted Antonio against the ropes. The challenger fell slowly to the ground. He was a broken, bloody mess.

Think About It

How does the movie help Felix get ready for the fight?

Felix had found how to get himself ready for the fight. It was Felix the Champion vs. Antonio the Challenger.

Antonio was still out on the roof, worrying about the upcoming fight. He wondered what the fight would do to his friendship with Felix. He started having doubts. He cut out the negative thinking real quickly by doing some fancy fighting steps. He filled the night air with fast punches. Felix would not be his *amigo* brother tomorrow. He would just be another fighter to beat. Like Felix, Antonio hoped to win by knocking his friend out in the first round.

Think About It

An internal conflict is a struggle a character has within himself or herself. What is Antonio's internal conflict?

All over the neighborhood, people were interested in the fight. There were posters for the fight on the walls of stores. Lots of people bet on the fight. They bet everything from a can of soda to real money on the fighter they thought would win.

The fight was in Tompkins Square Park. That morning, the park was as busy as a beehive. Workers set up the ring, the seats, and the guest speakers' stand. The fights began shortly after noon. But people started coming into the park much earlier.

Community leaders got up to speak. Great boxers who had fought years ago also spoke.

At last it was time for the main event. Felix stepped into one corner as Antonio stepped into the opposite corner. The crowd roared. Antonio and Felix bowed to each other and raised their arms in the air.

The **referee** told the fighters, "No low hits. No punching on the back of the head. Let's have a clean fight."

BONG! BONG! ROUND ONE. Felix wasted no time. He came quickly up to Antonio with a left punch. Antonio slipped away from the punch. He hit Felix with one-two-three left punches. This series of punches snapped Felix's head back. Felix felt a shock go through his body. He knew now that Antonio was going to fight his hardest, friend or no friend.

Bong! It was the end of the round. Felix walked back to his corner. His ear was still ringing from Antonio's punches.

Antonio danced back to his corner. Burns from Felix's gloves had made angry red marks on his ribs.

Bong! Bong! Round two. Felix rushed out of his corner like a bull. He gave Antonio a hard right punch to his head.

Antonio hit back with quick lefts and rights, giving Felix some painful blows.

Felix rushed at Antonio. He made a move with his right fist, then hit Antonio with his left. But Antonio ducked the blow and hit Felix on the chin. Lights exploded in Felix's head.

Think About It

A simile is a comparison of two things, using the word *as* or *like*. What is the busy park being compared to?

Predict

What will happen in the next round?

Keys to Literature

How does the **omniscient point of view** make the boxing match seem more real?

The crowd went wild as Felix's legs wobbled. He fought off Antonio's punches. Then he came back with a strong right punch that taught Antonio a lesson.

Antonio came back with a left hook. He got Felix in the eye. The pain was a haze in front of Felix's face. He swung out. He couldn't really see Antonio. But the roar of the crowd told him he had knocked Antonio down. Antonio got up, ducked, and threw a right punch that dropped Felix on his back.

Felix got up as fast as he could. His head was in a fog. The bell rang. It was the end of the round.

In the other corner, Antonio was doing what all fighters do when they are hurt. They sit and smile at everyone.

Bong! Round three—the last round. Up to now, the boys had fought an even fight. But everyone knew there would be no draw. This round was it.

This time it was Antonio who came out fast from his corner. Antonio's fists came fast and hard. Felix was pounded against the ropes.

The crowd loved it. So far the two boys had fought with *mucho corazón* (a lot of heart).

Both boys punched away. Felix's left eye was tightly closed. Blood poured from Antonio's nose. They fought toe-to-toe.

The crowd was quiet now. The sound of the boys' punches could be heard around the park. The referee could not believe how hard they were fighting each other.

Bong! Bong! Bong! The bell rang but Felix and Antonio didn't even hear it. They kept on punching. They were out of control.

Finally, the referee pulled Felix and Antonio apart. Cold water was poured over the boys.

Think About It

Why does the narrator remind you that there will be no draw?

Think About It

Why do Antonio and Felix keep fighting even after the bell rings?

Think About It

Why doesn't the narrator tell who wins the match?

The boys looked around. Then they ran toward each other. The crowd cried out. It looked like the boys were going to try to kill each other! But the fear of the crowd changed to cheers. The two *amigos* met and hugged.

No matter who won, they knew they would always be champions with each other.

The announcer got up to speak. He said, "Ladies and Gentlemen. The winner is …"

He turned to point to the winner. But suddenly he saw that he was alone in the ring. The two champions had already walked away, arm in arm.

Meet the Author

PIRI THOMAS *(Born 1928)*

Piri (Juan Pedro) Thomas was born in New York City. His mother was Puerto Rican, and his father was Cuban. Many people considered him African American. As a child, he struggled with who he was. This struggle is the theme of most of his stories.

As a young man, Thomas was sent to prison for attempted robbery. While he was there, he worked on his writing. When he came out of prison, he decided to become a writer as well as a positive role model for children and recovering drug addicts. His novels, short stories, poems, and essays are often based on his life in Spanish Harlem. His best-known work is his autobiography, *Down These Mean Streets: Stories from El Barrio.*

Check Your Predictions

1. Look back at the answers you gave for the Predict questions. Would you change your answers? Explain.

Understand the Story

2. What dream do Antonio and Felix both have?

3. What is the conflict between Antonio and Felix?

4. What do the boys promise each other before the fight?

5. How do the boys prove that they are amigo brothers?

Think About the Story

6. Why don't the boys stay to find out who won the fight?

7. Why do you think the author uses colloquial language in this story?

8. Why do you think the author uses the omniscient point of view rather than the first-person point of view?

Extend Your Response

What would you do for your best friend? What would you expect your best friend to do for you? Write a letter to this person, explaining your thoughts about friendship.

Keys to Literature

sensory details: details that show how something looks, sounds, smells, tastes, or feels

> Example: *I tried to swallow whatever was rising from my stomach, which tasted like lemonade, something fruity and sour.*

realism: a style of writing in which people and events are presented the way they actually are in life

> Example: *I was afraid of him—afraid of something—and as he passed me on the trail I threw a grenade ...*

Did You Know?

The Vietnam War is the setting of this story. About 2.7 million Americans served in this war. One of them was the author, Tim O'Brien. He saw many terrible things in Vietnam. He continues to write about the war in stories like this one.

Words to Know

slender	thin
grenade	a small bomb that can be thrown by hand
ambush	a surprise attack from a hidden place
platoon	a unit in the army
groping	searching blindly
repellent	something that keeps insects away, like a spray
stooped	hunched over; bent forward and downward
muzzle	the front end of the barrel of a gun
ponder	think about carefully
morality	rules of right and wrong
gape	stare in surprise with mouth open
dwell on	think about all the time

Ambush

BY TIM O'BRIEN

READ TO FIND OUT...
How does the narrator feel, knowing that he has killed someone?

When she was nine, my daughter Kathleen asked if I had ever killed anyone. She knew about the war; she knew I'd been a soldier. "You keep writing these war stories," she said, "so I guess you must've killed somebody." It was a difficult moment, but I did what seemed right, which was to say, "Of course not," and then to take her onto my lap and hold her for a while. Someday, I hope, she'll ask again. But here I want to pretend she's a grown-up. I want to tell her exactly what happened, or what I remember happening, and then I want to say to her that as a little girl she was absolutely right. This is why I keep writing war stories:

Think About It
Why does the narrator hope his daughter will someday ask him again if he killed anyone?

He was a short, **slender** young man of about twenty. I was afraid of him—afraid of something—and as he passed me on the trail I threw a **grenade** that exploded at his feet and killed him.

Or to go back:

Shortly after midnight we moved into the **ambush** site outside My Khe. The whole **platoon** was there, spread out in the dense brush along the trail, and for five hours nothing at all happened. We were working in two-man teams—one man on guard while the other slept, switching off every two hours—and I remember it was still dark when Kiowa shook me awake for the final watch. The night was foggy and hot. For the first few moments I felt lost, not sure about directions, **groping** for my helmet and weapon. I reached out and found three grenades and lined them up in front of me; the pins had already been straightened for quick throwing. And then for maybe half an hour I kneeled there and waited. Very gradually, in tiny slivers, dawn began to break through the fog, and from my position in the brush I could see ten or fifteen meters up the trail. The mosquitoes were fierce. I remember slapping at them, wondering if I should wake up Kiowa and ask for some **repellent**, then thinking it was a bad idea, then looking up and seeing the young man come out of the fog. He wore black clothing and rubber sandals and a gray ammunition belt. His shoulders were slightly **stooped**, his head cocked to the side as if listening for something. He seemed at ease. He carried his weapon in one hand, **muzzle** down, moving without any hurry up the center of the trail. There was no sound at all—none that I can remember. In a way, it seemed, he was part of the morning fog, or my own imagination, but there was also the reality of what was happening in my stomach. I had already pulled the pin on a grenade. I had come up to a crouch. It was entirely automatic. I did not hate the young man; I did

Think About It

Why does the narrator prepare grenades if nothing has happened all night?

Keys to Literature

This part of the story has many **sensory details**. Find a sensory detail that describes how something looks.

not see him as the enemy; I did not **ponder** issues of **morality** or politics or military duty. I crouched and kept my head low. I tried to swallow whatever was rising from my stomach, which tasted like lemonade, something fruity and sour. I was terrified. There were no thoughts about killing. The grenade was to make him go away—just evaporate—and I leaned back and felt my mind go empty and then felt it fill up again. I had already thrown the grenade before telling myself to throw it. The brush was thick and I had to lob it high, not aiming, and I remember the grenade seeming to freeze above me for an instant, as if a camera had clicked, and I remember ducking down and holding my breath and seeing little wisps of fog rise from the earth. The grenade bounced once and rolled across the trail. I did not hear it, but there must've been a sound, because the young man dropped his weapon and began to run, just two or three quick steps, then he hesitated, swiveling to his right, and he glanced down at the grenade and tried to cover his head but never did. It occurred to me then that he was about to die. I wanted to warn him. The grenade made a popping noise—not soft but not loud either—not what I'd expected—and there was a puff of dust and smoke—a small white puff—and the young man seemed to jerk upward as if pulled by invisible wires. He fell on his back. His rubber sandals had been blown off. There was no wind. He lay at the center of the trail, his right leg bent beneath him, his one eye shut, his other eye a huge star-shaped hole.

It was not a matter of live or die. There was no real peril. Almost certainly the young man would have passed by. And it will always be that way.

Later, I remember, Kiowa tried to tell me that the man would've died anyway. He told me that it was a good kill, that I was a soldier and this was a war, that I

Think About It

The narrator wants to warn the young man. What might the other soldiers say if they knew?

Keys to Literature

Realism is a style of writing in which people and events are described exactly as they are in real life. Find examples that show the horrors of war.

should shape up and stop staring and ask myself what the dead man would've done if things were reversed.

None of it mattered. The words seemed far too complicated. All I could do was **gape** at the fact of the young man's body.

Even now I haven't finished sorting it out. Sometimes I forgive myself, other times I don't. In the ordinary hours of life I try not to **dwell on** it, but now and then, when I'm reading a newspaper or just sitting alone in a room, I'll look up and see the young man coming out of the morning fog. I'll watch him walk toward me, his shoulders slightly stooped, his head cocked to the side, and he'll pass within a few yards of me and suddenly smile at some secret thought and then continue up the trail to where it bends back into the fog.

Predict

Will Kiowa's words help the narrator forget this event?

Meet the Author

TIM O'BRIEN *(Born 1946)*

Tim O'Brien was born in Austin, Minnesota. He went to college at the beginning of the Vietnam War. Although he was against the war, he reported for military service when he was drafted and was sent to Vietnam. He served in Vietnam as an infantry foot soldier between 1969 and 1970.

After Vietnam, O'Brien attended Harvard Graduate School. He then worked as a newspaper reporter for the *Washington Post* but left to write about his experiences in Vietnam. His novel *Going After Cacciato* is about a soldier who decides to run away from the Vietnam War. The novel won a National Book Award in 1979. O'Brien continues to write about Vietnam.

Check Your Predictions

1. Look back at the answer you gave for the Predict question. Would you change your answer? Explain.

Understand the Story

2. Why did the narrator throw the grenade?

3. What was the young man doing that proves he was not a threat to the platoon?

4. Years later, how is what the narrator imagines different from what happened?

Think About the Story

5. Why does the narrator write war stories?

6. Do you think the narrator did the right thing when he lied to his daughter? Explain.

7. Write one sensory detail from "Ambush" to describe what happened. Tell how this sensory detail makes the story powerful.

8. Why do you think realism is a good style for a war story?

Extend Your Response

Suppose that you are a newspaper reporter. Your assignment is to interview a veteran—someone who has fought in a war. Write three questions that you would ask.

Learn More About It

THE VIETNAM WAR

Between 1960 and 1973, the United States was involved in a war to stop communism in Vietnam. The United States was afraid that the Communists would take over not only Vietnam but other countries in the area, too.

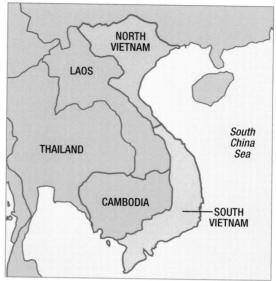

At first, the United States sent advisers to help the South Vietnamese government. Later, it sent supplies and fighting troops. The United States realized that fighting the Viet Cong would not be easy. The Viet Cong were the Communist Vietnamese troops in South Vietnam. Many Americans at home protested. They felt that the Vietnam War was a mistake and that Americans should not be fighting in it.

Finally, President Nixon announced a plan called Vietnamization. The plan was to turn over the fighting of the Vietnamese War to the South Vietnamese. A peace agreement in 1973 ended the role of the United States in Vietnam.

Apply and Connect

In "Ambush," which side was the narrator fighting for?

Keys to Literature

foreshadowing: hints about what might happen later in a story

> Example: Stacy's grandmother's strong reaction to Stacy's toe shoes gives the reader a hint that there will be a conflict later.

turning point: the event in a story that leads to a solution to the problem

> Example: In this story, the turning point is when Stacy finds out her grandmother's secret.

Words to Know

ballet	a kind of dance, made up of graceful turns and jumps
drool	let liquid run out of the mouth, as a baby does
stumped	walked in a stiff way with heavy feet
belongings	personal items, often packed in luggage
exotic	unfamiliar, as if from another country
fluttered	moved like flapping wings
alien	strange; coming from another place
calloused	hardened with thick skin
assumed	thought something was true
tainted	damaged, ruined, or spoiled
spine	the part of a book where the pages are bound together

Ribbons

BY LAURENCE YEP, *Adapted*

READ TO FIND OUT...
How can a pair of shoes affect a relationship?

The sunlight swept over the broad grassy square, across the street, and onto our living-room rug. In that bright, warm rectangle of light, I practiced my **ballet**. Ian, my little brother, giggled and ran around me while I did my exercises.

A car stopped outside, and Ian rushed to the window. "She's here! She's here!" he shouted excitedly. "Paw-paw's here!" *Paw-paw* is Chinese for grandmother—for "mother's mother."

I squeezed in beside Ian so I could look out the window, too. Dad's head was just disappearing as he leaned into the trunk of the car. A pile of luggage and cardboard boxes wrapped in rope sat by the curb. "Is that all Grandmother's?" I said. I didn't see how it would fit into my old bedroom.

Mom laughed behind me. "We're lucky she had to leave her furniture behind in Hong Kong." Mom had been trying to get her mother to come to San Francisco for years. Grandmother had finally agreed, but only because the British were going to return the city to the Chinese Communists in 1997. Because Grandmother's airfare and legal expenses had been so high, there wasn't enough money for Madame Oblomov's ballet school. I'd had to stop my daily ballet lessons.

Predict

What is the problem, or conflict, in this story?

The rear car door opened, and a pair of carved black canes poked out like six-shooters. "Wait, Paw-paw," Dad said, and slammed the trunk shut. He looked sweaty and tired.

Grandmother, however, was already using her canes to get to her feet. "I'm not helpless," she insisted to Dad.

Ian was relieved. "She speaks English," he said.

"She worked for a British family for years," Mom explained.

Turning, Ian ran towards the stairs. "I've got the door," he cried. Mom and I caught up with him at the front door and made him wait on the porch. "You don't want to knock her over," I said. For weeks, Mom had been preparing us for just this moment. Ian was supposed to wait, but in his excitement he began bowing to Grandmother as she struggled up the outside staircase.

Predict

What might have happened to the grandmother's feet?

Grandmother was a small woman in a padded silk jacket and black pants. Her hair was pulled back behind her head. On her small feet she wore a pair of cotton slippers shaped like boots, with furred tops that hid her ankles.

"What's wrong with her feet?" I whispered to Mom.

"They've always been that way. And don't mention it," she said. "She's ashamed of them."

I was instantly curious. "But what happened to them?"

"Wise grandchildren wouldn't ask," Mom warned.

Mom bowed formally as Grandmother reached the porch. "I'm so glad you're here," she said.

Grandmother gazed past us to the stairway leading up to our second-floor apartment. "Why do you have to have so many steps?" she said.

Mom sounded just like a child. "I'm sorry, Mother," she said.

Dad tried to change the subject. "That's Stacy, and this little monster is Ian."

"*Joe sun, Paw-paw,*" I said. "Good morning, Grandmother." It was afternoon, but that was the only Chinese I knew, and I had been practicing it.

Mother had taught us a proper Chinese greeting for the last two months. I thought Grandmother also deserved an American-style bear hug. However, when I tried to put my arms around her and kiss her, she stiffened in surprise. "Nice children don't **drool** on people," she snapped at me.

To Ian, anything worth doing was worth repeating, so he bowed again. "*Joe sun, Paw-paw.*"

Grandmother brightened in an instant. "He has your eyes," she said to Mom.

Mom bent and lifted Ian into her arms. "Let me show you our apartment. You'll be in Stacy's room."

Grandmother didn't even thank me. Instead, she **stumped** up the stairs after Mom, trying to get a smile from Ian, who was staring at her from over Mom's shoulder.

Keys to Literature

An example of **foreshadowing** is when Stacy first sees her grandmother's feet, and no one will answer questions about them.

▶ In China, people bow to show respect.

Grandmother's climb was long, slow, and difficult. *Thump, thump, thump.* Her canes struck the boards as she slowly climbed the steps. It sounded like the slow, steady beat of a heart.

Mom had told us her mother's story often enough. When Mom's father died, Grandmother had strapped my mother to her back and walked across China to Hong Kong to escape the Communists who had taken over her country. I had always thought her journey was heroic, but it seemed even braver when I realized how wobbly she was on her feet.

I was going to follow Grandmother, but Dad waved me down to the sidewalk. "I need you to watch your grandmother's things until I finish bringing them up," he said. He took a suitcase in either hand and set off, catching up with Grandmother at the foot of the first staircase.

While I waited for him to come back, I looked at Grandmother's pile of **belongings**. The boxes, laced with tight cords, were covered with words in Chinese and English. I could almost smell their **exotic** scent, and in my imagination I pictured sunlit waters lapping at beautiful docks. Hong Kong was probably as exotic to me as America was to Grandmother. Almost without thinking, I began to dance.

Dad came back out, his face red from climbing the stairs. "I wish I had half your energy," he said. Crouching, he used the cords to lift a box in each hand.

I pirouetted, and the world spun round and round. Madame Oblomov said that I should still practice every day. I had waited for this day, not only for Grandmother's sake but for my own. "Now that Grandmother's here, can I begin my ballet lessons again?" I asked.

Dad turned toward the house. "We'll see, honey."

Disappointment made me protest. "But you said I had to give up the lessons so we could bring her from Hong Kong," I said.

"Well, she's here."

Think About It

How would you feel if you had to give something up for one of your relatives?

Dad hesitated and then set the boxes down. "Try to understand, honey. We've got to set your grandmother up in her own apartment. That's going to take even more money. Don't you want your room back?"

Poor Dad. He looked tired and worried. I should have shut up, but I loved ballet almost as much as I loved him. "Madame put me in the fifth division already. If I'm gone much longer, she might make me start over again with the beginners."

"It'll be soon. I promise." He looked guilty as he picked up the boxes and struggled toward the stairs.

Dad had taken away the one hope that had kept me going during my time away from Madame. Suddenly I felt lost, and the following weeks only made me more confused. Mom started laying down all sorts of new rules. First, we couldn't run around or make noise because Grandmother had to rest. Then we couldn't watch our favorite TV shows because Grandmother couldn't understand them. Instead, we had to watch Westerns on one of the cable stations because it was easier for her to figure out who was the good guy and who was the bad one.

Worst of all, Ian got all of her attention—and her candy and anything else she could bribe him with. It finally got to me on a warm Sunday afternoon a month after she had arrived. I'd just returned home from a long walk in the park with some friends. I was looking forward to something cool and sweet, when I found her giving Ian an ice cream bar I'd bought for myself. "But that was *my* ice cream bar," I complained as he gulped it down.

"Big sisters need to share with little brothers," Grandmother said, and she patted him on the head to encourage him to go on eating.

When I complained to Mom about how Grandmother was spoiling Ian, she only sighed. "He's a boy, Stacy. Back in China, boys are everything."

Think About It

What aren't Stacy and her brother allowed to do after their grandmother arrives?

It wasn't until I saw Grandmother and Ian together the next day that I thought I really understood why she treated him so much better. She was sitting on a kitchen chair with her head bent over next to his. She had taught Ian enough Chinese so that they could hold short, simple conversations. With their faces so close, I could see how much alike they were.

Ian and I both have the same brown eyes, but his hair is black, while mine is brown, like Dad's. In fact, everything about Ian looks more Chinese. Except for the shape of my eyes, I look as white as Dad. And yet, people sometimes stare at me as if I were a freak. I've always told myself that it's because they never learned manners, but it was really hard to have my own grandmother make me feel that way.

Even so, I kept telling myself: Grandmother is a hero. She saved my mother. She'll like me just as much as she likes Ian once she gets to know me. And, I thought in a flash, the best way to know a person is to know what she loves. For me, that was the ballet.

Predict

How will Stacy's grandmother feel about Stacy's love for ballet?

Ever since Grandmother had arrived, I'd been practicing my ballet alone in the room I now shared with Ian. Now I got out the special box that held my satin toe shoes. I had been so proud when Madame said I was ready to use them. As I lifted them out, the satin ribbons **fluttered** down around my wrists. I slipped one of the shoes onto my foot, but when I tried to tie the ribbons around my ankles, the ribbons came off in my hands.

I could have asked Mom to help me reattach them, but then I remembered that at one time Grandmother had supported her family by being a seamstress.

Grandmother was sitting in the big chair in the living room. She stared uneasily out the window as if she were gazing not upon the broad, green lawn of the square, but upon an **alien** desert.

"Paw-paw," I said, "can you help me?"

Think About It

How might you feel if you moved to a new country and did not understand the customs?

Predict

What will Stacy do now that her grandmother tries to take away her ribbons?

Grandmother gave a start when she turned around and saw the ribbons dangling from my hand. Then she looked down at my bare feet, which were **calloused** from three years of daily lessons. When she looked back at the satin ribbons, it was with a hate and disgust that I had never seen before. "Give those to me." She held out her hand.

I clutched the ribbons tightly against my stomach. "Why?"

"They'll ruin your feet." She lunged toward me and tried to snatch them away.

Angry and confused, I took a few steps back and showed her the shoe. "No, they're for dancing!"

All Grandmother could see, though, was the ribbons. She managed to struggle to her feet without the canes and almost fell forward on her face. Somehow, she caught her balance. Arms reaching out, she stumbled after me. "Lies!" she said.

"It's the truth!" I backed away so fast that I bumped into Mom as she came running from the kitchen.

Mom immediately **assumed** it was my fault. "Stop yelling at your grandmother!" she said.

By this point, I was in tears. "She's taken everything else. Now she wants my toe-shoe ribbons."

Grandmother panted as she leaned on Mom. "How could you do that to your own daughter?"

"It's not like you think," Mom tried to explain.

However, Grandmother was too upset to listen. "Take them away!"

Mom helped Grandmother back to her easy chair. "You don't understand," Mom said.

All Grandmother did was stare at the ribbons as she sat back down in the chair. "Take them away. Burn them. Bury them."

Mom sighed. "Yes, Mother."

Think About It

Do you think Stacy's mother's advice about letting her grandmother "cool off" is good? Explain.

As Mom came over to me, I stared at her in amazement. "Aren't you going to stand up for me?"

But she acted as if she wanted to break any ties between us. "Can't you see how worked up Paw-paw is?" she whispered. "She won't listen to reason. Give her some time. Let her cool off." She worked the ribbons away from my fingers. Then she also took the shoe.

For the rest of the day, Grandmother just turned away every time Mom and I tried to raise the subject. It was as if she didn't want to even think about satin ribbons.

That evening, after the dozenth attempt, I finally said to Mom, "She's so weird. What's so bad about satin ribbons?"

"She connects them with something awful that happened to her," Mom said.

That puzzled me even more. "What was that?"

She shook her head. "I'm sorry. She made me promise never to talk about it to anyone."

Think About It

Is Stacy right to ignore her grandmother? Explain.

The next morning, I decided that if Grandmother was going to be mean to me, then I would be mean to her. I began to ignore her. When she entered a room I was in, I would turn around and leave.

For the rest of the day, things got more and more tense. Then I happened to go into the bathroom early that evening. The door wasn't locked, so I thought it was empty, but Grandmother was sitting fully clothed on the edge of the bathtub. Her slacks were rolled up to her knees and she had her feet soaking in a pan of water.

"Don't you know how to knock?" she snapped, and dropped a towel over her feet.

However, she wasn't quick enough, because I saw her bare feet for the first time. Her feet were like taffy that someone had stretched out and twisted. Each foot bent downward in a way that feet were not meant to, and her toes stuck out at odd angles, more like lumps than toes. I didn't think she had all ten of them, either.

"What happened to your feet?" I whispered in shock.

Looking ashamed, Grandmother flapped a hand in the air for me to go. "None of your business. Now get out."

She must have said something to Mom, though, because that night Mom came in and sat on my bed. Ian was outside playing with Grandmother. "Your grandmother's very upset, Stacy," Mom said.

"I didn't mean to look," I said. "It was horrible." Even when I closed my eyes, I could see her twisted feet.

I opened my eyes when I felt Mom's hand on my shoulder. "She was so ashamed of them that she didn't even like me to see them," she said.

"What happened to them?" I wondered.

Mom's forehead frowned as if she wasn't sure how to explain things. "There was a time back in China when people thought women's feet had to be shaped a certain way to look beautiful. When a girl was about five, her mother would gradually bend her toes under the sole of her foot."

"Ugh!" Just thinking about it made my own feet ache. "Her own mother did that to her?"

Mom smiled sadly. "Her mother and father thought it would make their little girl pretty so she could marry a rich man. They were still doing it in some of the back areas of China long after it was outlawed in the rest of the country."

I shook my head. "There's nothing lovely about those feet."

"I know. But they were usually wrapped in silk ribbons." Mom brushed some of the hair from my eyes. "Because they were a symbol of the old days, Paw-paw undid the ribbons as soon as we were free in Hong Kong—even though they kept back the pain."

I was even more puzzled now. "How did the ribbons do that?"

Think About It

What happened to Stacy's grandmother's feet in China?

Keys to Literature

This is the **turning point** in this story because Stacy finds out what happened to her grandmother's feet.

Think About It

What does Stacy mean by "I rubbed my own foot in sympathy"?

Predict

How will Stacy show her grandmother that *her* ribbons are different?

Mom began to brush my hair with quick, light strokes. "The ribbons kept the blood from flowing freely and bringing more feeling to her feet. Once the ribbons were gone, her feet ached. They probably still do."

I rubbed my own foot in sympathy. "But she doesn't complain."

"That's how tough she is," Mom said.

Finally the truth dawned on me. "And she thought my toe-shoe ribbons were like her old ones."

Mom lowered the brush and nodded. "And she didn't want you to go through the same pain she had."

I guess Grandmother loved me in her own way. When she came into the bedroom with Ian later that evening, I didn't leave. However, she tried to ignore me—as if I had become **tainted** by her secret.

When Ian demanded a story, I sighed. "All right. But only one."

Naturally, Ian chose the fattest story he could, which was my old collection of fairy tales by Hans Christian Andersen. Years of reading had cracked the **spine** so that the book fell open in his hands to the story that had been my favorite when I was small. It was the original story of "The Little Mermaid"—not the cartoon. The picture in the tale showed the mermaid posed like a ballerina in the middle of the throne room.

"This one," Ian said, and pointed to the picture of the Little Mermaid.

When Grandmother and Ian sat down on my bed, I began to read. However, when I got to the part where the Little Mermaid could walk on land, I stopped.

Ian was impatient. "Come on, read," he ordered, patting the page.

"After that," I went on, "each step hurt her as if she were walking on a knife." I couldn't help looking up at Grandmother.

This time she was the one to pat the page. "Go on. Tell me more about the mermaid."

So I went on reading to the very end, where the Little Mermaid changes into sea foam. "That's a dumb ending," Ian said. "Who wants to be pollution?"

"Sea foam isn't pollution. It's just bubbles," I explained. "The important thing was that she wanted to walk even though it hurt."

"I would rather have gone on swimming," Ian insisted.

"But maybe she wanted to see new places and people by going on the land," Grandmother said softly. "If she had kept her tail, the land people would have thought she was odd. They might even have made fun of her."

When she glanced at her own feet, I thought she might be talking about herself—so I seized my chance. "My satin ribbons aren't like your old silk ones. I use them to tie my toe shoes on when I dance." Setting the book down, I got out my other shoe. "Look."

Grandmother fingered the ribbons and then pointed at my bare feet. "But you already have calluses there."

I began to dance before grandmother could stop me. After a minute, I struck a pose on half-toe. "See? I can move fine."

She took my hand and patted it clumsily. I think it was the first time she had showed me any sign of love. "When I saw those ribbons, I didn't want you feeling pain like I do."

I covered her hands with mine. "I just wanted to show you what I love best—dancing."

"And I love my children," she said. I could hear the pain in her voice. "And my grandchildren. I don't want anything bad to happen to you."

Predict

How will Stacy's grandmother react to Stacy's dancing?

Think About It

How do Stacy and her grandmother feel about each other now?

Suddenly I felt as if there were an invisible ribbon binding us, tougher than silk and satin, stronger even than steel; and it joined her to Mom and Mom to me.

I wanted to hug her so badly that I just did. Though she was stiff at first, she gradually softened in my arms.

"Let me have my ribbons and my shoes," I said in a low voice. "Let me dance."

"Yes, yes," she whispered fiercely.

I felt something on my cheek and realized she was crying, and then I began crying, too.

"So much to learn," she said, and began hugging me back. "So much to learn."

Think About It

What does the grandmother mean when she says, "so much to learn"?

Meet the Author

LAURENCE YEP *(Born 1948)*

Laurence Yep was born in San Francisco, California. While he was growing up, he was troubled by who he was. He did not feel he had a culture of his own. Yep was born Chinese American, but he spoke only English. He often felt like an outsider.

A lot of Yep's writing is about teenagers and their problems with their identity. His characters often feel like they do not belong, too. His most famous books are *Dragonwings* and *Rainbow People*. They each have won many awards. His most recent books are about Chinese mythology.

Check Your Predictions

1. Look back at the answers you gave for the Predict questions. Would you change your answers? Explain.

Understand the Story

2. Why does Stacy have to stop her ballet lessons?

3. How does Stacy's grandmother treat her brother?

4. How does Stacy's grandmother treat her?

5. What happened to Stacy's grandmother's feet?

Think About the Story

6. What is one event that foreshadows the conflict between Stacy and her grandmother?

7. How does the conflict between Stacy and her grandmother create a problem for Stacy's mother?

8. What is the turning point in the story?

Extend Your Response

Is "Ribbons" a good title for this story?
Write a paragraph to explain your ideas.

Summaries

Amigo Brothers Two best friends dream of becoming the lightweight champion. However, they must fight each other first. The boys agree they will not hold back during the match, but they worry about hurting each other and hurting their friendship. After the fight, the boys hug each other. They leave together before finding out who won.

Ambush The narrator's young daughter asks if he killed anyone in the Vietnam War. He says, "No." The truth is that during the war, he tossed a grenade at a young man, killing him. Although he knows he did his job as a soldier, he still feels guilty. He says that is why he writes war stories. He hopes his daughter will ask him again when she is older and will understand what he did.

Ribbons Stacy's grandmother comes from Hong Kong to live with the family. However, she acts cold toward Stacy. The grandmother gets upset when she sees Stacy's ribbons. Stacy finds out that her grandmother's feet were bound with ribbons when she was a child in China. When Stacy explains that her ribbons are different, she and her grandmother understand each other.

draw
morality
belongings
alien
tainted

Vocabulary Review

Complete each sentence with a word from the box. Use a separate sheet of paper.

1. The food was _____ and had to be thrown away.

2. Deciding whether or not to help her friend tested Sidney's _____.

3. Each person in the contest had the same number of points, so the contest was a _____.

4. Sharing was an _____ idea to the two-year-old.

5. Before the family moved away, they packed all of their _____.

Chapter Quiz

Answer the following questions in one or two complete sentences. Use a separate sheet of paper.

1. **Amigo Brothers** What title are both Felix and Antonio competing for?

2. **Amigo Brothers** Why does Felix decide to leave his neighborhood for awhile?

3. **Ambush** What was the young man doing when the narrator threw the grenade?

4. **Ambush** Why does the narrator hope that his daughter will ask him again if he killed anyone during the war?

5. **Ribbons** What two things does Stacy have to give up for her grandmother, even though they are important to her?

6. **Ribbons** What sensory details create a picture of Stacy's grandmother's feet? Give an example from the story.

Critical Thinking

7. **Ambush** How would this story be different if it were written from the omniscient point of view?

8. **Ribbons** Why is foreshadowing an important tool in this story?

Chapter Activity

Write a conversation between a character in "Amigo Brothers" and the narrator in "Ambush." Have the characters tell each other what important lesson they learned.

This image could be of a person who is struggling with an internal conflict. Is this how you picture Struggle? Explain.

Weeper by Diana Ong

Chapter 13 / Poetry

THE STRUGGLE WITHIN

Learning Objectives

- Understand what irony is.
- Recognize a quatrain.
- Explain denotation and connotation.
- Recognize a metaphor.

Preview Activity

Think of a movie you have seen in which the character struggles with himself or herself. What picture comes to mind? Write down four words that describe this picture. Next, write four sentences that use these words. Arrange the sentences to create a short poem.

Poetry and Conflict

Each word and phrase in a poem carries a lot of meaning. Below are some ways that poems express meaning:

metaphor: a comparison of two things that does not use the word *as* or *like*.

irony: a result that is the opposite of what is expected.

denotation: the actual meaning of a word.

connotation: a feeling that is suggested by a word.

Poems often express struggles. Sometimes, there is no resolution to the conflict. The poems in this chapter show different kinds of struggles.

Keys to Literature

quatrain: a stanza made up of four lines

Example: The poem on the opposite page has eight quatrains.

irony: a result that is the opposite of what is expected

Example: In this poem, danger comes where it is least expected.

Did You Know?

This poem is based on a real event. On September 15, 1963, a bomb was thrown into a church in Birmingham, Alabama. Four African American girls died.

Words to Know

fierce	violent; strong
choir	a singing group
drawn	pulled on
sacred	holy, religious
explosion	a blast from a bomb
clawed	dug into with fingernails

Ballad of Birmingham

BY DUDLEY RANDALL

"Mother, dear, may I go downtown
instead of out to play,
and march the streets of Birmingham
in a freedom march today?"

5   "No, baby, no, you may not go,
for the dogs are **fierce** and wild,
and clubs and hoses, guns and jails
ain't good for a little child."

"But, mother, I won't go alone.
10 Other children will go with me,
and march the streets of Birmingham
to make our country free."

"No, baby, no, you may not go,
for I fear those guns will fire.
15 But you may go to church instead,
and sing in the children's **choir**."

READ TO FIND OUT…
Why would a mother be afraid to let her child go to a freedom march?

Keys to Literature

This ballad is made up of stanzas called **quatrains**. How many quatrains are there in the entire poem?

▶ The first half of the poem is written in dialogue. The mother and daughter are having a conversation.

Mourners at the funeral of a young girl who was killed at the bombing of the Sixteenth Street Baptist Church in Birmingham, Alabama, on September 15, 1963.

▶ The second half of the poem is from the point of view of a third-person narrator.

She has combed and brushed her nightdark hair,
and bathed rose petal sweet,
and **drawn** white gloves on her small brown hands,
20 and white shoes on her feet.

The mother smiled to know her child
was in the **sacred** place,
but that smile was the last smile
to come upon her face.

25 For when she heard the **explosion**,
her eyes grew wet and wild.
She raced through the streets of Birmingham
calling for her child.

She **clawed** through bits of glass and brick,
30 then lifted out a shoe.
"O, here's the shoe my baby wore,
but, baby, where are you?"

Keys to Literature

Irony is the opposite result from what you might expect. What happens at the church?

Meet the Author

DUDLEY RANDALL *(1914–2000)*

Dudley Randall was born in Washington, D.C., and as a young boy, he moved to Detroit, Michigan. When he was only thirteen years old, he published his first poem. It appeared in the *Detroit Free Press*.

After college, Randall worked as a librarian. He also translated many Russian poems into English. Randall is best known as a poet and as the founder of his own magazine, called *Broadside Press*. In his magazine, Randall published his own poems as well as the poems of other African American poets. After the 1967 race riots in Detroit, Randall published *Cities Burning*.

Understand the Poem

1. What happens to the child at the church?

2. In Line 21, why does the mother smile?

3. In Line 25, why does the mother fear that her daughter is in danger?

4. In Line 29, why does the mother claw through the glass and brick?

Think About the Poem

5. There were many terrible events during the fight for civil rights in the 1960s. Why would the poet choose the bombing of a Birmingham church to write about?

6. What do Lines 11 and 12 mean?

7. What is the irony in this poem?

8. How are the first four quatrains of the poem different from the last four?

Extend Your Response

Write a sentence that summarizes each stanza of the poem. Then, use the sentences you wrote to create a paragraph that summarizes what happens in the poem.

Keys to Literature

connotation: an idea or feeling suggested by a word

>   Example: The connotation of *purple* is "royalty."

denotation: the actual meaning of a word

>   Example: The denotation, or actual meaning, of *purple* is "a color that is a mixture of red and blue."

Did You Know?

The ideas in this poem were used by Alice Walker to write her novel *The Color Purple*. The novel explores how African American women struggled for dignity and self-respect. *The Color Purple* was made into a movie.

Words to Know

tenement	an apartment building that is rundown
orbit	an area that a person stays in
molding	trim on a wall or ceiling
lack	absence; need

Taught Me Purple

BY EVELYN TOOLEY HUNT

My mother taught me purple
Although she never wore it.
Wash-gray was her circle,
The **tenement** her **orbit**.

5   My mother taught me golden
And held me up to see it,
Above the broken **molding**,
Beyond the filthy street.

My mother reached for beauty
10 And for its **lack** she died,
Who knew so much of duty
She could not teach me pride.

Somewhere in America by Robert Brackman

Meet the Author

EVELYN TOOLEY HUNT *(1904–1997)*

Evelyn Tooley Hunt was born in Hamburg, New York. She graduated from William Smith College in the 1920s, but she did not publish her first collection of poems until 1961. Hunt is best known for writing Japanese poetry called haiku in an American style. She used the name Tao-Li when she published haiku.

Hunt's poems describe her respect for different cultures. She is the author of several collections of poems, including *Look Again Adam, Toad Song, The Haiku of Tao-Li,* and *Dancer in the Wind*.

Understand the Poem

1. Where do the mother and daughter live?

2. What does the mother know a lot about?

3. According to the daughter, what two things were missing in the mother's life when she died?

4. Find three words or phrases in the poem that show that the mother and child are poor.

Think About the Poem

5. What does the daughter mean when she says "wash-gray" was her mother's circle?

6. What does *purple* mean in this poem?

7. In Line 5, what does the phrase *taught me golden* mean?

8. Why didn't the mother teach her daughter pride?

Extend Your Response

Write a poem about what colors mean to you. Choose two colors. Write a sentence for each color that explains what connotations each color has for you.

Keys to Literature

metaphor: a comparison of two things that does not use the word *like* or *as*.

Example: *your thoughts are my brothers and sisters*

Words to Know

communicate	talk; make your thoughts and feelings known
sealed	closed
clumsy	awkward
outlive	last longer than someone or something else

Simple-song

BY MARGE PIERCY

When we are going toward someone we say
you are just like me
your thoughts are my brothers and sisters
word matches word
5   how easy to be together.

When we are leaving someone we say
how strange you are
we cannot **communicate**
we can never agree
10 how hard, hard and weary to be together.

READ TO FIND OUT...
What happens to people
when they fall in and out
of love?

Keys to Literature

The **metaphor** "your
thoughts are my brothers
and sisters" means that
two people's thoughts
are very close.

Memories of Childhood by Helene Brandt

Think About It

The first stanza is about falling in love. What is the second stanza about?

We are not different nor alike
but each strange in his leather bodies
sealed in skin and reaching out **clumsy** hands
and loving is an act
15 that cannot **outlive**
the open hand
the open eye
the door in the chest standing open.

Meet the Author

MARGE PIERCY *(Born 1936)*

Marge Piercy was born in Detroit, Michigan. She began writing poems at fifteen, and as a young writer, she supported herself by working many part-time jobs. She was a secretary, a switchboard operator, and a store clerk.

Piercy's writing is often about the way people are connected to each other. She says, "We are taught to think of ourselves as separate beings, but we are part of a people, part of a history, part of each other." Piercy's first poetry collection is called *Breaking Camp*. Her first novel, *Going Down Fast*, was published in 1969.

Understand the Poem

1. According to the speaker, when do people say, "you are just like me"?

2. When do people say, "how strange you are"?

3. What is one reason that couples break up?

4. According to the poem, what is necessary for love to work?

Think About the Poem

5. What point does Stanza 1 make? Stanza 2? Stanza 3?

6. The metaphor in the first stanza compares the thoughts of people in love to "brothers and sisters." Make up a metaphor that compares the thoughts of people who have fallen out of love.

7. Reread the last stanza. What does "sealed in skin" and "reaching out clumsy hands" mean?

8. Do you think this poem is just about love? Is it also about friendship?

Extend Your Response

What is important to you in a friendship? How should you go about keeping it? Write a list of your views.

Summaries

Ballad of Birmingham A girl asks her mother if she can go to a freedom march. Her mother says that it is not safe to go. Instead, the mother sends her daughter to church. The church is bombed that day, and the girl is killed in the explosion.

Taught Me Purple A mother wants her daughter to learn self-respect. Even though there is ugliness all around them, the mother teaches her daughter dignity and beauty.

Simple-song At the beginning of a relationship, everything is easy. At the end of a relationship, being together and talking to each other is very hard. People try to reach toward others. For love to last, people have to be open with each other.

Vocabulary Review

For each sentence below, write *true* if the underlined word is used correctly. If it is not used correctly, change the underlined word to make the sentence true. Use a separate sheet of paper.

1. Working hard for a long time can make you <u>weary</u>.
2. A church is considered a <u>sacred</u> place.
3. The girl wanted to dance in the <u>choir</u>.
4. Ali felt <u>shame</u> in winning first place in the basketball league.
5. A <u>lack</u> of water makes it hard for a plant to grow.

Chapter Quiz

Answer the following questions in one or two complete sentences. Use a separate sheet of paper.

1. Ballad of Birmingham How does the mother try to protect her child?

2. Ballad of Birmingham What happens to the child in the church?

3. Taught Me Purple What two colors does the mother teach her daughter? What do they stand for?

4. Taught Me Purple What is the one thing the mother cannot teach her child?

5. Simple-song What do people who are breaking up have a hard time doing?

6. Simple-song According to the speaker, what must remain open in order for love to last?

Critical Thinking

7. Taught Me Purple What is the conflict in this poem?

8. Simple-song In line 12, what is the connotation of the word *leather*?

Chapter Activity

Think about a conflict between two people. Draw a comic strip about the conflict between them. What would they say to each other?

Unit 5 **Review**

On a separate sheet of paper, write the letter that best completes each sentence below.

1. In "Narrative of the Life of Frederick Douglass," Mr. Covey stops whipping Douglass because

   A. Douglass gives up.
   B. Douglass fights back.
   C. Mr. Covey feels guilty.
   D. Douglass runs away.

2. In "Little Things Are Big," the author wants to

   A. stop riding the subway.
   B. leave the train before the woman does.
   C. act like he does not care.
   D. show courtesy.

3. In "Amigo Brothers," a conflict exists because

   A. Felix does not want to be friends anymore.
   B. two friends fight each other.
   C. Antonio wins the boxing match.
   D. Felix is a better boxer.

4. In "Ribbons," Stacy's parents must pay for

   A. Chinese classes for Ian.
   B. new ballet shoes and ribbons.
   C. airfare and expenses for Stacy's grandmother.
   D. airplane tickets to Hong Kong for the family.

5. The conflicts in "Ballad of Birmingham" and "Taught Me Purple" are both about

   A. children who want to attend freedom marches.
   B. families that are poor.
   C. mothers who want a good life for their children.
   D. children who die doing something dangerous.

Making Connections

On a separate sheet of paper, write your answers to the following questions.

6. Which poem in this unit did you find the most powerful? Explain. Give examples.

7. Each selection in this unit contains a conflict. Which conflict interested you most? Explain.

Writing an Essay
Choose one selection from the unit and rewrite the ending. If the selection is a poem, change the last stanza. If the selection is fiction or nonfiction, change the last paragraph.

Unit 6 > Close to the Heart

Chapter 14 Memoirs

from Childtimes
*by Eloise Greenfield and
Lessie Jones Little*

The Medicine Bag
*by Virginia Driving Hawk Sneve,
adapted*

Chapter 15 Poetry

Mother to Son
by Langston Hughes

Lament
by Edna St. Vincent Millay

To My Dear and Loving Husband
by Anne Bradstreet

Housecleaning
by Nikki Giovanni

Passing into Womanhood by Howard Terpning

What feelings do you think the painter was trying to show?

Chapter 14 / Memoirs

CLOSE TO THE HEART

Learning Objectives

- Explain what a memoir is.
- Recognize the first-person point of view.
- Identify dialect.
- Recognize character clues.
- Identify the conflict in a story.

Preview Activity

Think of the people who are close to your heart. They might be family members, friends, teachers, or guardians. Make a list of three people and tell a friend why you feel each person is special to you.

Memoirs and Things Close to the Heart

A memoir tells about an event in a person's life or a certain period of a person's life. In a memoir,

- the writer tells about his or her *own* life.
- the characters are often family members or close friends.
- the writer tells about real experiences.
- the setting is a real time and place.

Memoirs are often very personal and tell about people, places, and events that are important to the writer.

Keys to Literature

first-person point of view: a narrator tells the story, using *I* to refer to himself or herself

Example: *I don't know why Mama ever sewed for me.*

dialect: the form of a language that is spoken by people living in a certain place

Example: *One night, ... me and my brother John was coming 'cross that field over yonder.*

Words to Know

lopsided	uneven
joint	a place where two bones are joined
mantel	a shelf over a fireplace
commence	start; begin
challenging	daring someone to a contest
stroke	a sudden illness that is caused when a blood vessel in the brain is blocked or broken
descendants	children and grandchildren
procession	people moving forward one after another

from Childtimes

BY ELOISE GREENFIELD AND LESSIE JONES LITTLE

Mama Sewing

READ TO FIND OUT...
What are *childtimes*?

I don't know why Mama ever sewed for me. She sewed for other people, made beautiful dresses and suits and blouses, and got paid for doing it. But I don't know why she sewed for me. I was so mean.

It was all right in the days when she had to make my dresses a little longer in the front than in the back to make up for the way I stood, with my legs pushed back and my stomach stuck out. I was little then, and I trusted Mama. But when I got older, I worried.

Mama would turn the dress on the wrong side and slide it over my head, being careful not to let the pins stick me. She'd kneel on the floor with her pin cushion, fitting the dress on me, and I'd look down at that dress, at that **lopsided**, raw-edged, half-basted, half-pinned *thing*—and know that it was never going to look like anything. So I'd pout while Mama frowned and sighed and kept on pinning.

Keys to Literature

This paragraph is written from the **first-person point of view**. What does the narrator tell you about herself here?

Sometimes she would sew all night, and in the morning I'd have a perfectly beautiful dress, just right for the school program or the party. I'd put it on, and I'd be so ashamed of the way I had acted. I'd be too ashamed to say I was sorry.

But Mama knew.

Pa

Keys to Literature

The narrator uses **dialect**. He uses the phrase *ain't doing nothing*, which means "is not doing anything."

▶ Pa is the narrator's grandfather. Her father is called "Daddy."

"Leave the children alone," he used to tell mamas and daddies. "They ain't doing nothing."

Pa was a sharecropper. He worked in the fields, farming the land for the white man who owned it, and got paid in a share of the crops he raised. Along with that, he had almost always had some kind of little business going, even when Daddy was a boy—a meat market, an icehouse, a cleaner's, a grocery store.

Long before I was born, Pa had been a member of the Marcus Garvey group that used to meet in Parmele on Sunday afternoons. It was one of thousands of branches of the United Negro Improvement Association headed by Marcus Garvey. They met to talk about the beauty and strength of blackness, and to plan the return of black people to Africa.

I didn't think my grandfather was afraid of anything except the frogs that came out of the mud-filled ditches at night and flopped across the yard, and he knew plenty of names to call them. The thumb on his right hand looked like a little baldheaded man. The top **joint** had been cut off in a farm accident, and he had put it in a jar of preserving liquid that stayed on the front-room **mantel**. I never got tired of looking at it.

Children hung around Pa, nieces and nephews and neighbors, listening to his stories, giggling at his jokes. Some nights there would be just us—Wilbur, Gerald, and me, with our grandfather—sitting on the porch

Think About It

Here, the narrator tells you more about her grandfather. What details and character clues tell you what he is like?

where the only light was that of the stars and the nearest house was a long way down the road. He'd tell scary stories, and get really tickled when we got scared. He swore his ghost stories were true.

"One night," he'd say, "me and my brother John was coming 'cross that field over yonder." He'd make his arm tremble and point toward the woods across the highway. "And we **commence** to hearing this strange sound. Ummmmm-*umph*! Ummmmm-*umph*! And we looked up and saw this ... this *haint*!"

He'd twist his face and narrow his eyes in horror as he stared out into the darkness, and I could just feel all those haints hovering behind us, daring us to turn around and run for the door.

Sometimes Pa would stop right in the middle of a story.

"Then what happened, Pa?" one of us would ask.

"Oh, I left after that," he'd say, and he'd laugh. Then we'd laugh, small nervous laughs, wanting to believe that it had all been just a joke.

Every year when it was time for us to leave, a sudden change would come over Pa. One minute he'd be **challenging** Daddy to a foot race that never took place, and the next minute he was weak and sick, trying to get us to stay. He didn't think he would live to see us the following summer, he'd say. At breakfast he'd begin the blessing with, "Lord, I sure do thank You for allowing me to see my family one last time before You call me home," and he'd pray a long, sad prayer that brought tears to our eyes.

Predict

Is Pa really sick?

But finally, when nothing worked, Pa would give up and help Daddy load the car with suitcases and with sacks of fresh corn and peanuts. There'd be hugs and kisses and more tears, and then we'd drive away, leaving him and Granny standing on the side of the road, waving, waving, waving, getting smaller and smaller, until they blended into one and disappeared.

Pa never liked to leave home. Granny came to visit us a few times over the years, but Pa always made an excuse. He couldn't get away right then, he had too much work to do, or something. One year, though, he had to come. He'd had a **stroke**, and Mama and Daddy brought him to Washington to take care of him. The stroke had damaged his body and his mind, so that he didn't understand much of what was going on around him, but he knew he wasn't where he wanted to be. Mama would take him for a walk and he'd ask people on the street, "Which way is Parmele?"

Think About It

Why did Pa come to Washington, even though he did not want to?

My grandfather never got back to Parmele. He lived in Washington for eighteen months, and then, in 1951, at the age of seventy-eight, he died.

Martha Ann Barnes Ridley

I called my great-grandmother Mama Ridley, because that's what Mama called her. Actually, though, I don't think I ever really called her anything, except in my mind. I guess I must have talked to her sometimes, but I don't remember those times. I just remember that she was the small lady who lived in a bed, upstairs in Grandma's house.

Mama Ridley had fallen and broken her hip, and she never got out of bed again. She couldn't turn herself over, Grandpa had to do it, and she was in pain much of the time. But Mama told me that Mama Ridley loved her great-grandchildren. Whenever we got dressed up to go out, she'd say, "Let the children come in here before you go, so I can see what they got on." But nothing of her voice comes back to me. I can only see her lying there.

I was eight years old when Mama Ridley died. I wish so much that I had known her better. Hearing Mama and Grandma talk about her makes me know how much I missed.

Family

Family. All this running through my mind....

Saturday Sunday mornings Daddy making pancakes big as the plate Daddy making fat hamburgers leftover stuffed with rice green peas enough for everybody. Hot nights leave our hot one room sleep till midnight pillows blankets grass bed beside the river. Lincoln Park evenings Mama other mothers bench-talk children playing.

Give Mama her lesson take my piano lesson teach Mama. Downtown Wilbur Gerald Eloise wait in the car have fun get mad have fun get mad. Go for a ride park car New York Avenue hill dark watch trains wave

Think About It

In this part of the story, sentences run together without much punctuation. Why does the writer do this?

passengers sitting in lighted window squares sliding by. Gerald tell us the movie tell us show us be the gangster be the good guy be the funny guy tell us show us. Look out the window wait wait snow stopping Daddy going to make snow ice cream ready to eat without freezing.

Vedie little sister turning somersaults we laugh. Vera baby sister fat baby laughing we laugh. Play games I'm thinking of a word I'm thinking of a word that starts with *S* guess give a clue it's blue. Radio hear-see squeaking door ghosts scary music. Parade take turns on Daddy's shoulder watch the floats watch the firemen march watch the horns watch the sound of the bass drum.

Easter Monday picnic zoo dyed eggs lionhouse popcorn polar bear picnic. Merry-go-round Mama

Think About It

What activities does the narrator remember enjoying with Vedie and Vera?

laughing. Sparrow's Beach sun water-splashing sandy legs Mama laughing. Mama laughing....

All this running through my mind now, running through my mind now.

Family.

Well—our stories are told. Grandma's, Mama's, and mine. It's been good, stopping for a while to catch up to the past. It has filled me with both a great sadness and a great joy. Sadness to look back at suffering, joy to feel the unbreakable threads of strength.

Now, it's time for us to look forward again, to see where it is that we're going. Maybe years from now, our **descendants** will want to stop and tell the story of their time and their place in this **procession** of children.

A childtime is a mighty thing.

Meet the Author

ELOISE GREENFIELD *(Born 1929)*

Eloise Greenfield was born in Parmele, North Carolina. She wrote *Childtimes* with her mother, Lessie Jones Little. The story tells of three generations of Greenfield's family. It is told from three different points of view—Greenfield's, her mother's, and her grandmother's. The part you have just read is told from Greenfield's point of view.

Greenfield lives in Washington, D.C., where she grew up. She has written many books for children and young adults. Her hope is that young people will love words as much as she does. Greenfield has won many awards for her writing. She has worked with other writers to publish African American literature. She wrote "Harriet Tubman" and *Rosa Parks*.

Check Your Predictions

1. Look back at the answer you gave for the Predict question. Would you change your answer? Explain.

Understand the Story

2. Why was the narrator mean to Mama?

3. Even though Pa was a sharecropper, what other small businesses did he have?

4. What activities did the narrator do with her family?

Think About the Story

5. How do you know that the family members got along well?

6. What does the narrator mean when she says, "A childtime is a mighty thing"?

7. From which point of view is this memoir written? Explain.

8. Why does the author use dialect when Pa speaks?

Extend Your Response

Write about your own childtimes. Describe what you were like as a child. Then, tell about an event, experience, or person that you remember very well.

Learn More About It

AUTOBIOGRAPHIES AND MEMOIRS

An autobiography is the story of a person's life that is written by the person. It is told from the first-person point of view. The writer uses words like *I* or *me* to refer to himself or herself. A memoir tells about an event or a part of a person's life.

Some autobiographies and memoirs are written by well-known people, such as Helen Keller, Frederick Douglass, Abraham Lincoln, and Rosa Parks. Their stories often include important events in history. Other autobiographies and memoirs are written by ordinary people or are about everyday events. The authors of *Childtimes* wrote about ordinary moments that meant a great deal to them.

People in every field write autobiographies and memoirs, from sports figures to presidents, and from movie stars to astronauts. Autobiographies and memoirs let readers experience real life through another person's eyes, in different times in history, and in different countries of the world.

Marian Anderson by Laura Wheeler Waring

This painting shows the singer Marian Anderson. Her autobiography is called My Lord, What a Morning.

Apply and Connect

If you were to write an autobiography or a memoir, what everyday moments would you include? Which people in your life would you include?

Keys to Literature

character clues: the thoughts, actions, and words in a story that help you understand what a character is like

> Example: In this memoir, Grandpa's actions show his bravery and pride.

conflict: problems in a story that need to be solved

> Example: The narrator is both proud and ashamed of his grandfather.

Did You Know?

The Sioux are a proud nation of Native Americans. They were forced onto reservations after gold was discovered on their land. In 1890, U.S. soldiers fought the Sioux at Wounded Knee, South Dakota. Hundreds of Sioux were killed. In this story, Grandpa is a Sioux who lives on a reservation.

Words to Know

impressed	made someone think highly of something
exaggerated	made something seem better or worse than it really was
authentic	genuine; real
stately	appearing important and worthy of respect
muttered	said softly
trembling	shaking
reluctantly	not wanting to do something; unwillingly
patiently	calmly dealing with something
seldom	not often; rarely
protection	a guard against harm or danger

The Medicine Bag

VIRGINIA DRIVING HAWK SNEVE, *Adapted*

READ TO FIND OUT...
What is inside Grandpa's medicine bag?

My kid sister Cheryl and I liked to brag about our grandpa, Joe Iron Shell. He was a Sioux Indian. Our friends had always lived in the city. They only knew about Indians from movies and TV. They were **impressed** by our stories. Maybe we **exaggerated** and made Grandpa and the reservation seem wonderful. But when we came back to Iowa after visiting Grandpa, we always had some exciting story to *tell*.

We always had some **authentic** Sioux article to show our friends. One year Cheryl had new moccasins that Grandpa had made. On another visit Grandpa gave me a drum. It was small, flat, and round and was made from cow skin. On the drum was a painting of a warrior riding a horse. Grandpa taught me a real Sioux chant to sing while I beat the drum with a stick. The stick was covered with leather and had a feather on the end. Man, my friends thought that was great.

Predict

Who will the characters in this story be?

Think About It

What do the narrator's friends think is great?

We never showed our friends a picture of Grandpa. Not that we were ashamed of him. But we knew the great stories we told didn't go with the real thing. Our friends would have laughed if they'd seen a picture of Grandpa. He wasn't tall and **stately** like Indians on TV. His hair wasn't in braids. It hung in gray strings on his neck. And he was old. He was our great-grandfather. He lived all by himself on the Rosebud Reservation in South Dakota. He didn't live in a teepee, but in a shack made out of logs and tar-paper. So when Grandpa came to visit us, I was so ashamed and embarrassed I wanted to die.

There are a lot of yapping poodles and other fancy little dogs in our neighborhood. Most of the time you'll hear them barking one at a time from their yard. But that day it sounded as if a whole pack of them was barking together in one spot.

I got up and walked to the curb to see what all the fuss was about. About a block away, someone was walking down the middle of the street. Around this person a crowd of little kids were yelling and dogs were yapping and growling.

I watched the group as it slowly came closer. At the center of all the kids and dogs was a man wearing a tall black hat. He'd slow down now and then to look at something in his hand. Then he'd look at the houses on both sides of the street. All of a sudden I knew who the man was. I felt hot and cold at the same time. I whispered, "Oh, no! It's Grandpa!"

I stood on the curb. I wanted to run and hide, but I couldn't move. Then I got mad when I saw how the yapping dogs were growling and nipping at the old man's baggy pants leg. He poked at them in a tired way with his cane. "Stupid dogs," I said. I ran to help Grandpa.

I kicked and yelled at the dogs to drive them away. They put their tails between their legs and ran in all directions. The kids ran to the curb where they watched me and the old man.

"Grandpa," I said. My voice cracked and made me feel dumb. I bent to pick up his beat-up suitcase, which was tied shut with a rope. But he put the suitcase right down in the street and shook my hand.

"*Hau. Tazoka*, Grandchild," he said in Sioux.

The whole neighborhood was watching. All I could do was stand there and shake the old man's hand. I saw how his gray hair hung down from his big black hat. The hat had a tired-looking feather in it. His suit was wrinkled. It hung like a sack on his body. As he shook my hand, his coat fell open. He was wearing a bright red shiny shirt. His tie was a string tie with beads on it. His clothes wouldn't look strange on the reservation, but they sure did here. I wanted to sink right into the street.

"Hi," I **muttered** with my head down. When I felt his bony hand **trembling**, I tried to pull my hand away. I looked at his face and saw how tired he was. I felt like crying. I couldn't think of anything to say. I picked up Grandpa's suitcase and took his arm. I led him up the driveway to our house.

Mom was standing on the steps. I don't know how long she'd been watching us. Her hand was over her mouth. She looked as if she couldn't believe what she saw. Then she ran to us.

She went to hug Grandpa, then stopped herself. I remembered that the Sioux didn't do things like that. It would have embarrassed Grandpa.

"*Hau*, Marie," Grandpa said as he took Mom's hand. She smiled and took his other arm.

We helped him up the steps. Just then the door opened with a bang. Cheryl came running out of the house. She was all smiles. It was clear that she was glad to see Grandpa. I was ashamed of how I felt.

Cheryl gave a happy yell. She said, "Grandpa! You came to see us!"

Grandpa smiled. Mom and I let go of him as he held out his arms to my ten-year-old sister. She was still young enough to be hugged.

"*Wicincala*, little girl," he said, and then he fell over. He had passed out. Mom and I carried him into her sewing room. We had a spare bed in there.

We put Grandpa on the bed. Mom stood there, patting his shoulder. She didn't seem to know what to do.

I said, "Shouldn't we call the doctor, Mom?"

"Yes," she said with a sigh. "You get Grandpa into bed, Martin."

I **reluctantly** moved to the bed. Grandpa wouldn't have wanted Mom to take his clothes off. But I didn't want to, either. He was so skinny that his coat slipped

Keys to Literature

Cheryl is happy to see Grandpa. How do her feelings make the narrator's **conflict** even greater?

off easily. When I untied his tie and opened his shirt collar, I felt a small leather bag. It hung from a leather string around his neck. His old cowboy boots were tight. It seemed to hurt him a little as I jerked them off.

I put the boots on the floor and saw why they fit so tightly. Each one was stuffed with money. I looked at the money and started to ask about it, but Grandpa's eyes were closed again.

Mom came back with some water. She said, "The doctor thinks Grandpa is worn out from the heat." She wiped Grandpa's face with a washcloth. Then she gave a big sigh. "Oh, *hinh*, Martin," she said. "How do you think he got here?"

We found out after the doctor left. Grandpa was sitting up in bed. He was angry because Mom was trying to feed him soup.

Dad had come home from work just as the doctor was leaving. "Grandpa," he said, "tonight you let Marie feed you." He gently pushed Grandpa back against the pillows. Dad went on, "You're not really sick. The doctor said you just got too tired and hot after your long trip."

Grandpa took it easy then. Between sips of soup, he told us about his trip. After our visit to see him, he thought that he would like to see where his only living descendants lived and what our home was like. Also, he felt lonely after we left.

I knew everyone felt as badly as I did, and Mom felt the worst. Mom was the only family Grandpa had left. Even after Mom married Dad, who's a white man and teaches college in our city, and even after Cheryl and I were born, Mom made sure that every summer we spent a week with Grandpa.

I never thought that Grandpa would feel lonely after our visits. And none of us noticed how old and weak he had become. But Grandpa knew how old he was

Predict

What is the small leather bag Grandpa is wearing?

Think About It

Who are Grandpa's descendants?

getting, and so he came to us. He had ridden buses for two and a half days. When he came to the city, he was tired and stiff from sitting so long. He had set out, walking, to find us.

Grandpa had stopped to rest on the steps of some building downtown. A policeman found him. Grandpa said that the cop was a good man. The cop had taken Grandpa to the bus stop. He'd waited with Grandpa until the bus came and then told the bus driver to let Grandpa out at Bell View Drive. After Grandpa got off the bus, he started walking again. But when he walked on the sidewalk, he couldn't see the house numbers on the other side of the street. So he walked in the middle of the street. That's when all the little kids and dogs followed him.

I knew everybody felt as badly as I did. Yet, I was proud of Grandpa. After all, he was eighty-six years old, and he had never been away from the reservation. But he was brave enough to take a long trip alone.

Grandpa asked Mom, "You found the money in my boots?"

Mom said, "Martin did. Grandpa, you shouldn't have carried so much money. What if someone had stolen it from you?"

Grandpa laughed. He said, "I would have known if anyone tried to take the boots off my feet. I've saved the money for a long time. It's a hundred dollars—for my funeral. But you take it now. Use it to buy food while I'm here. I don't want my visit to be hard for you."

Dad said, "You don't need to do that, Grandpa. It's good to have you here with us. I'm only sorry we didn't think of bringing you home with us this summer. You wouldn't have had to make such a long, hard trip."

This made Grandpa happy. He said, "Thank you. But do not feel bad that you didn't bring me with you. I would not have come then. It was not time." The way he said it, no one could argue with him. To Grandpa and the Sioux, a thing would be done when it was the right time to do it. That's the way it was.

Grandpa went on, looking at me. He said, "Also, I have come because soon it will be time to give Martin the medicine bag."

This is a beaded Sioux medicine bag.

Think About It

Why will Grandpa give the medicine bag to Martin, the narrator, instead of to Martin's father?

We all knew what that meant—Grandpa thought he was going to die. When a man in the family died, the medicine bag, along with its story, was passed on to the oldest male child.

Grandpa kept looking at me. He said, "Even though the boy has a white man's name, the medicine bag will be his."

I didn't know what to say. I had the same hot and cold feeling that I had when I first saw Grandpa in the street. The medicine bag was the dirty leather bag I had found around his neck. I thought, "I could never wear such a thing." I almost said it out loud. I thought of having my friends see it in gym class or at the swimming pool. I thought of the smart things they would say. But I knew I would have to take the medicine bag. I swallowed hard and took a step toward the bed.

But Grandpa was tired. He said, "Not now, Martin. It is not the time. Now I will sleep."

So that's how Grandpa came to be with us for two months. My friends kept asking to come to see him. I kept making up reasons why they couldn't. I told myself that I didn't want them laughing at Grandpa. But it really wasn't Grandpa I was afraid they'd laugh at.

Cheryl was happy to bring her friends to see Grandpa. Every day after school, she'd bring home a group of kids. There would be a group of giggling girls or little boys with their eyes wide with wonder. Grandpa would sit on the patio, and they'd crowd around him.

Grandpa would smile in his gentle way. He would **patiently** answer all their questions. He'd tell them stories of brave warriors, ghosts, and animals. The kids listened without a sound. Those little guys thought Grandpa was great.

Finally, my friends came over. This was because nothing I said had stopped them. Hank, who was supposed to be my best friend, said: "We're going to see the great Indian of Bell View Drive. My brother has seen him three times, so he ought to be well enough to see us."

When we got to my house, Grandpa was sitting on the patio. He had on his red shirt. But today he also wore a leather vest decorated with beads. Instead of his cowboy boots, he wore moccasins with beads. Of course, he had his old black hat on—he was **seldom** without it. But his hat had been brushed. The white feather in it looked bright and proud. His silver hair lay over his shirt collar.

I stared at him. So did my friends. I heard one of my friends say in a low voice, "Wow!"

Grandpa looked up. When his eyes met mine, they looked as if they were laughing. He nodded to me, and my face got all hot. Grandpa had known all along I was afraid he would embarrass me in front of my friends.

"*Hau, hoksilas*, boys," he said and held out his hand.

My friends shook his hand one by one as I told Grandpa their names. They were so polite that I almost

Predict

What will Hank think of Grandpa?

Keys to Literature

What **character clues** show that Grandpa is a wise man?

These moccasins were made by Sioux a hundred years ago.

laughed. They said, "How, there, Grandpa," and even, "How-do-you-do, Sir?"

I said, "You guys want some lemonade or something?" No one said anything. They were listening to Grandpa. He was telling them how he'd killed the deer his vest was made from.

Grandpa did most of the talking while my friends were there. I was so proud of him. I couldn't believe how quiet and polite my friends were. Mom had to tell them to leave when it was time for supper. As they left, they shook Grandpa's hand. They said to me, "Martin, he's really great!"

"Yeah, man! Don't blame you for keeping him to yourself."

Think About It

How do Martin's friends behave? How does that make Martin feel?

This is a Sioux vest. It was made around 1910.

"Can we come back?"

But after they left, Mom said, "No more visitors for a while, Martin. Grandpa won't say so, but his strength hasn't come back. He likes having people visit, but it makes him tired."

That evening, before he went to sleep, Grandpa called me to his room. He said, "Tomorrow, when you come home, it will be time to give you the medicine bag."

I felt a hard squeeze where my heart is supposed to be. I was scared, but I said, "OK, Grandpa."

All night I had strange dreams about thunder and lightning on a high hill. From far away, I heard the slow beat of a drum. When I woke up in the morning, I felt as if I hadn't slept at all. School seemed like it would never end. When it finally did end, I ran home.

Grandpa was in his room, sitting on the bed. The shades were down, and the place was dark and cool. I sat on the floor in front of Grandpa, but he didn't even look at me. It seemed like a long time before he spoke.

At last, Grandpa said, "I sent your mother and sister away. What you will hear today is only for a man's ears. What you will be given is only for a man's hands." Then he was silent. I felt a cold wave down my back.

Grandpa began, "Soon after my father became a man, he made a vision quest to find a spirit guide for his life. You don't know how it was back then. That is when the great Sioux of the Teton mountains were made to stay on a reservation. The Sioux had a great need for *Wakantanka*, the Great Spirit, to guide them. But too many of the young men were full of hate. They had no hope. They thought it was no good to look for a vision. Why should they, when the best part of their life was gone—when there was nothing for them but the reservation, which they hated? But my father kept to the old ways.

"My father got ready for his quest with a sweat bath, to make himself clean inside and out. Then he

Think About It
Why is Martin scared to be given the medicine bag?

▶ A *vision quest* is a journey made by a Sioux boy when he turns twelve. The boy looks for a spirit that will guide and protect him for the rest of his life. The spirit may appear in a dream.

went alone to a high hill, without food, to pray. After three days he was given his sacred dream. In the dream he looked a long time, and then he found the white man's iron.

"My father did not understand this vision of finding iron. This belonged to the white people and at that time they were the enemy.

"He came down from the hill to wash himself in the stream below. There, he found a place where a camp had been. At the place where a fire had been built, there was a broken iron kettle. The broken kettle was like a shell. This was a sign that meant his dream was true.

"My father took a piece of the iron for his medicine bag. He had made the bag from elk skin years before, to use for his vision quest.

"My father went back to his village. He told his dream to the wise old men of the tribe. They gave him the name *Iron Shell*. But they, too, did not understand my father's dream. My father, now Iron Shell, kept the piece of iron with him at all times. He believed that it gave him **protection** from the evil things that went on in those sad days.

"Then a terrible thing happened to Iron Shell. Soldiers took him and several other young men away from their homes. The young men were sent far away to a white man's school. Iron Shell was angry and lonely. He missed his parents and the young girl he had just married.

"At first, Iron Shell would not try to learn. He would not let the teacher try to change him. One day it was his turn to work in the school's blacksmith shop. As he walked into the shop, he knew his medicine had brought him there. Now he would learn and work with the white man's iron.

"Iron Shell became a blacksmith. That was his work when he came back to the reservation. All his life he kept

Think About It

After the vision quest, what name is Grandpa's father given? Why?

the medicine bag with him, and never let it go. When he was old, and I was a man, he gave it to me. This was because no one made the vision quest anymore."

Grandpa stopped talking. Then he covered his face with his hands. I stared at him. I couldn't believe what I saw. Grandpa's shoulders were shaking with quiet sobs. I looked away until he began to speak again.

He said, "I kept the bag until my son, your mother's father, was a man and had to leave us. He had to fight in the war across the ocean. I gave him the bag. I felt it would keep him safe when he was fighting. But he did not take it with him. He was afraid that he would lose it. He died in a far-off place."

Again Grandpa was still. I felt his sadness around me.

Grandpa cleared his throat. He said, "My son had only a daughter—your mother. It is not right for her to know these things."

He opened his shirt, pulled out the leather bag, and lifted it over his head. He held the bag in his hand. He turned it over and over as if he wanted to remember forever how it looked.

Grandpa opened the bag and took out two things that were inside. He said, "In the bag is the broken piece of the iron kettle, a small rock from the hill of the vision quest, and a piece of the sacred sage." He held the bag upside down and dust—what was left of the sage—fell out.

Grandpa said, "After the bag is yours, you must put a piece of sage inside. Never open the bag again until you pass it on to your son." Grandpa put back the small stone and the piece of iron. Then he tied the bag.

Somehow I knew it was time to stand up. Grandpa slowly got up from the bed. He stood in front of me and held the bag before my face. I closed my eyes. I waited for him to put the bag over my head.

Think About It
What does Grandpa think was the cause of his son's death?

▶ Sage is an herb. It is used in cooking. Some people think that sage has the power to make them pure and clean.

Grandpa said, "No, you do not need to wear it." He put the soft leather bag in my hand. He closed my other hand over it. He said, "It would not be right to wear it. In this time and place no one will understand. Put it away in a safe place until you are on the reservation again. Wear it then, when you put in a new piece of the sacred sage."

Grandpa turned and sat again on the bed. He leaned his head against the pillow in a tired way. He said, "Go. I will sleep now."

I said, "Thank you, Grandpa," in a soft voice. I left with the bag in my hands.

That night Mom and Dad took Grandpa to the hospital. Two weeks later, I stood alone on the land of the reservation. I put the sacred sage in my medicine bag.

Meet the Author

VIRGINIA DRIVING HAWK SNEVE (Born 1933)

Virginia Driving Hawk Sneve is a member of the Rosebud Sioux nation. She was raised on a reservation in South Dakota. In addition to being a writer, Sneve has been an English teacher and a school counselor.

Sneve's novels and short stories have won many awards. She uses her understanding of Sioux customs in her writing. She says she wants to give young people a true picture of Native American life. Some of her books include *Jimmy Yellow Hawk*, *When Thunders Spoke*, and *Betrayed*.

Check Your Predictions

1. Look back at the answers you gave for the Predict questions. Would you change your answers? Explain.

Understand the Story

2. Why does Grandpa come to see the family?

3. What do Martin's and Cheryl's friends think of Grandpa?

4. What is inside Grandpa's medicine bag?

Think About the Story

5. What is Martin's conflict in this story?

6. Why does the author use Sioux words in the story?

7. How do you know that Grandpa has died?

8. What character clues show that Grandpa is proud to be Sioux?

Extend Your Response

What would you put in your own medicine bag? Describe the bag and its contents. Tell why you would include each object.

Summaries

from **Childtimes** The narrator offers character sketches of members of her family—her mother, her grandfather, her father, her great-grandmother, and her sisters. She remembers the many happy times they had together when she was a child.

The Medicine Bag Martin's Native American great-grandfather comes for a visit. Martin is proud but also embarrassed by him. Grandpa has always lived on a reservation and follows Sioux customs. Now he is old and weak. Before he dies, he gives Martin his medicine bag.

impressed
descendants
commence
authentic
procession
exaggerated

Vocabulary Review

Match each word in the box with its meaning. Write the word and its matching number on a separate sheet of paper.

1. genuine
2. family members
3. people moving forward in a line
4. made someone think highly of something
5. made something seem better or worse than it really was
6. start

Chapter Quiz

Answer the following questions in one or two complete sentences. Use a separate sheet of paper.

1. Childtimes At the end of the memoir, how does the narrator feel about remembering the past?

2. Childtimes How does Pa react when his family is about to leave Parmele?

3. Childtimes From what point of view is the story written?

4. The Medicine Bag How does Martin feel when he first sees Grandpa walking down the street?

5. The Medicine Bag Compare how Cheryl and Martin feel about Grandpa's visit.

6. The Medicine Bag Why does Grandpa tell Martin about the vision quest?

Critical Thinking

7. Childtimes Which family member do you find most interesting? Explain.

8. The Medicine Bag Why is the medicine bag so important to Grandpa?

Chapter Activity

In both "Childtimes" and "The Medicine Bag," the narrators tell about male characters who are important to them. Write the first paragraph of a memoir about a man who has been important to you. Your memoir could begin, "I remember _____. He always _____."

Circle of Love by Michael Escoffery

How has the artist created a heart shape in the painting?

Chapter 15 / Poetry

CLOSE TO THE HEART

Learning Objectives

- Explain what a metaphor is.
- Recognize dialect.
- Understand free verse.
- Identify repetition in a poem.
- Analyze rhyme and rhythm in a poem.
- Identify slang.

Preview Activity

Think about a favorite song that deals with something close to the heart. What emotions does the song express? What words in the song express those emotions? What other words might express the same emotions?

Poetry and Things Close to the Heart

A poem is made up of separate lines. Each line has its own importance. Some of the poems in this chapter have

- **rhythm**, or beat, like a song.
- words that **rhyme**, or have the same ending sound.
- language that forms a **sharp picture** in your mind.
- **repetition** of words and sentences to create a mood.

Poems about things that are close to the heart express strong emotions and feelings. The poems in this chapter are about love, life, and death.

Keys to Literature

metaphor: a comparison of two things that does not use the word *like* or *as*

   Example: The sun was a golden plate.

dialect: the form of a language that is spoken by people living in a certain place

   Example: *I'se still climbin'...*

Did You Know?

"Mother to Son" has no pattern of rhythm, and the words at the end of lines do not rhyme. The poem does not have stanzas either. The poem works because it is built around a comparison.

Words to Know

crystal	clear glass or stone that is expensive
splinters	thin, sharp pieces of wood that can stick into your hands or feet

Mother to Son

BY LANGSTON HUGHES

READ TO FIND OUT...

What is the most
important thing the
speaker tells her son?

Keys to Literature

The poet uses a
metaphor. What does
he compare life with?

Well, son, I'll tell you:
Life for me ain't been no **crystal** stair.
It's had tacks in it,
And **splinters**,
5   And boards torn up,
And places with no carpet on the floor—
Bare.
But all the time
I'se been a-climbin' on,
10 And reachin' landin's,
And turnin' corners,
And sometimes goin' in the dark
Where there ain't been no light.
So boy, don't you turn back.
15 Don't you set down on the steps
'Cause you finds it's kinder hard.
Don't you fall now—
For I'se still goin', honey,
I'se still climbin',
20 And life for me ain't been no crystal stair.

Meet the Author

LANGSTON HUGHES *(1902–1967)*

Langston Hughes was born in Missouri. As an adult, he moved to Harlem, in New York City. There, he and other African American writers became part of a movement called the Harlem Renaissance. This group of people produced a great number of poems, short stories, plays, and essays.

Hughes not only wrote poems and short stories, but he also wrote scripts for plays and movies. His writing was about African Americans who tried to keep their dreams alive. Two of his poems are "Harlem" and "The Weary Blues."

Understand the Poem

1. Who is the speaker in this poem?

2. In Lines 3 and 4, the speaker says her life has had tacks and splinters in it. What does she mean?

3. In Line 15, what does the speaker mean when she tells her son not to sit down on the steps?

4. Which line in this poem is repeated? Why?

Think About the Poem

5. The speaker says she is still climbing the stairs. What keeps her going?

6. How do you feel about the speaker in this poem? Why?

7. Why does the speaker compare her life to climbing stairs?

8. How does the use of dialect make the speaker seem real?

Extend Your Response

Create your own metaphors. Begin by thinking of two people you know. What would you compare their lives to? You can start each metaphor with "_____'s life was _____."

Examples: Dad's life was a stormy season.
My cousin's life has not been a bowl of cherries.

Keys to Literature

repetition: words or sentences used over and over to create a feeling or mood

   Example: In this poem, *Life must go on* is repeated.

Did You Know?

Poets have always written laments about the death of people they loved or admired. One of the great American laments was written by Walt Whitman about the death of Abraham Lincoln. The poem is called "When Lilacs Last in the Dooryard Bloom'd." This lament is about a husband and father.

Words to Know

lament   a poem or song that expresses great sadness over a death

*L*ament

BY EDNA ST. VINCENT MILLAY

READ TO FIND OUT...
What makes this poem
so sad?

Listen, children:
Your father is dead.
From his old coats
I'll make you little jackets;
5 I'll make you little trousers
From his old pants.
There'll be in his pockets
Things he used to put there,
Keys and pennies
10 Covered with tobacco;
Dan shall have the pennies
To save in his bank;
Anne shall have the keys
To make a pretty noise with.
15 Life must go on,
And the dead be forgotten;
Life must go on,
Though good men die;
Anne, eat your breakfast;
20 Dan, take your medicine;
Life must go on;
I forget just why.

Think About It
Who is speaking?

Keys to Literature

How many times does
the speaker say that "Life
must go on"? Why does
she **repeat** this?

The Prairie Is My Garden by Harvey Dunn

Meet the Author

EDNA ST. VINCENT MILLAY *(1892–1950)*

Edna St. Vincent Millay was born in Rockland, Maine. She began writing poetry when she was a child, and in high school she was the editor-in-chief of her school magazine. Millay entered a poetry contest and won a scholarship to college. Her first book of poetry came out the year she graduated.

Millay wrote about personal subjects, such as love, sadness, death, and nature. She gave readings of her poetry and became quite famous. Two of her poems are "First Fig" and "The Ballad of the Harp-Weaver."

Understand the Poem

1. What does the mother say she will make from the father's old coats?

2. What is Dan supposed to do with the pennies from his father's pockets?

3. What is Anne supposed to do with the keys from her father's pockets?

4. About how old are the children? Explain.

5. What line is repeated?

Think About the Poem

6. What will the mother's life be like now that her husband is dead? Explain.

7. What does "Life must go on" mean in this poem?

8. Why does the mother say in the last line that she forgets why life must go on?

Extend Your Response

Write a paragraph to explain why you think people write laments.

Keys to Literature

rhyme: words that sound alike

> Example: *We* and *thee*; *man* and *can*

rhythm: a sound pattern of stressed syllables, or beats, in a poem

> Example: In this line, every other syllable is strong.
> If **ever** two were **one**, then **sure**ly **we**.

Words to Know

quench	stop or put out
ought	nothing
recompense	reward
manifold	many ways
persevere	continue on

To My Dear and Loving Husband

BY ANNE BRADSTREET

READ TO FIND OUT...
Does the writer think that love ends with death?

If ever two were one, then surely we.
If ever man were lov'd by wife, then thee;
If ever wife was happy in a man,
Compare with me ye women if you can.
5 I prize thy love more than whole mines of gold,
Or all the riches that the East doth hold.
My love is such that rivers cannot **quench**,
Nor **ought** but love from thee, give **recompense**.
Thy love is such I can no way repay,
10 The heavens reward thee **manifold**, I pray.
Then while we live, in love let's so **persevere**,
That when we live no more, we may live ever.

Keys to Literature

In poems, rhyming words come at the ends of lines. Which words in this poem **rhyme**?

This poem has a **rhythm**, or beat. Try reading the poem aloud. Listen for the rhythm.

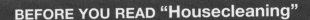

Keys to Literature

slang: very informal language

Example: *Dug* is slang for "liked."

Did You Know?

Some poems do not have capital letters or punctuation. This makes the poem feel informal, or as if someone is just talking.

Words to Know

straightening	organizing; putting things in order; making things neat
cabinets	cupboards
unfortunately	without luck; unhappily

*H*ousecleaning

BY NIKKI GIOVANNI

i always liked housecleaning
even as a child
i dug **straightening**
the **cabinets**
5 putting new paper on
the shelves
washing the refrigerator
inside out
and **unfortunately** this habit has
10 carried over and i find
i must remove you
from my life

READ TO FIND OUT...

What kind of
housecleaning is
going on in this poem?

Keys to Literature

What does the speaker
mean by the **slang** phrase,
I dug straightening?

Coffee Break. Artist unknown

Meet the Author

ANNE BRADSTREET *(1612–1672)*

Anne Bradstreet was born in England. She and her family were Puritans who came to America to worship freely. Puritan women were usually not educated. She is one of only a few women writers of the 1600s in America.

Bradstreet's poetry tells about her personal experiences of raising her family in a new and difficult world. She writes about the people she loves and about Puritan values.

Meet the Author

NIKKI GIOVANNI *(Born 1943)*

Nikki Giovanni's real name is Yolande Cornelia Giovanni. She was born in Knoxville, Tennessee. She grew up in Cincinnati, Ohio, but returned to Knoxville every summer to visit her grandparents.

During the 1960s, Giovanni became a part of the civil rights movement. Her early poetry shows strong feelings about equal rights for all Americans. Later, she wrote poetry about her own life. She said, "I care more about what *is* said than about *how* it is said." She has been an important supporter of African Americans. Some of Giovanni's poems are "Spin a Soft Black Song," "Ego-Tripping," and "Vacation Time."

Understand the Poems

1. How does the speaker in "To My Dear and Loving Husband" feel about her husband?

2. What kind of cleaning does the speaker in "Housecleaning" do in Lines 11 and 12?

3. In "To My Dear and Loving Husband," what is very important to the speaker?

4. How does the speaker in "Housecleaning" feel about the person in her life?

Think About the Poems

5. What is the main feeling expressed by each poem?

6. The last lines of "Housecleaning" are probably meant to be a surprise. Explain why.

7. Which of the two poems has rhyme and rhythm?

8. Which of the two poems has slang? Give an example.

Extend Your Response

Reread "To My Dear and Loving Husband." Then, rewrite the poem using everyday language.

Summaries

Mother to Son The speaker tells her son that going through life is like climbing stairs. Even though her life is hard, she keeps trying to do her best. Her son must also keep trying to succeed.

Lament A mother tells her two children that their father is dead but that life must go on. They must continue with everyday life.

To My Dear and Loving Husband A woman tells her husband how much she loves him. She values his love more than anything else. She wants their love to continue always—even after they die.

Housecleaning The speaker says she has always enjoyed cleaning and straightening. Then, she tells someone that she is going to remove him or her from her life.

persevere

splinters

cabinets

unfortunately

quench

Vocabulary Review

Complete each sentence with a word from the box. Use a separate sheet of paper.

1. I got _____ in my fingers when I lifted the wooden board.

2. Even though training for the track meet was hard, he decided to _____.

3. I wanted to keep the puppy, but, _____, the owner wanted it back.

4. Drinking a lot of water will help _____ your thirst.

5. Dana put the clean dishes away in the kitchen _____.

Chapter Quiz

Answer the following questions in one or two complete sentences. Use a separate sheet of paper.

1. **Mother to Son** What does the speaker say her life has *not* been like?

2. **Lament** A lament is a poem of sadness. What happened to the woman's husband?

3. **To My Dear and Loving Husband** What is the main feeling this poem expresses?

4. **To My Dear and Loving Husband** How much does the speaker say she prizes her husband's love?

5. **Housecleaning** What has the speaker liked to do since childhood?

Critical Thinking

6. Why do poets in this chapter repeat words and phrases? Give an example.

7. In both "Mother to Son" and "Lament," a mother gives advice. What lesson do they both teach?

Chapter Activity

Choose a poem from this chapter, and decide whom the poet is speaking to. Write a letter to that person. Tell him or her what the poet's message is.

Unit 6 Review

On a separate sheet of paper, write the letter that best completes the sentence below.

1. In "Childtimes," when Mama sews clothes for the narrator, the narrator feels
   A. happy.
   B. embarrassed.
   C. tired.
   D. scared.

2. In "The Medicine Bag," Grandpa gives Martin the medicine bag because
   A. it is too heavy for him to carry.
   B. Martin says he wants it as soon as possible.
   C. it must be passed down in the family.
   D. Grandpa thinks someone may steal it.

3. In "Mother to Son," the speaker says her life has been
   A. a crystal stair.
   B. difficult.
   C. like a soft carpet.
   D. like falling down.

4. In "Lament," who has died? The speaker's
   A. husband.
   B. father.
   C. son.
   D. brother.

5. In "To My Dear and Loving Husband," the speaker expresses
   A. sadness over a death.
   B. joy at the birth of a child.
   C. deep love.
   D. a wish to be alone.

6. In "Housecleaning," the poet wants to get rid of
   A. kitchen cabinets.
   B. shelves.
   C. someone in her life.
   D. her childhood.

Making Connections

On a separate sheet of paper, write your answers to the following questions.

7. Did you prefer the poetry or the stories in this unit? Explain.

8. Which story or poem had the most realistic details? Give examples.

Writing an Essay

Who or what is "close to your heart"? Describe this person, place, or thing. Explain why he, she, or it is so dear to you.

Chapter 16 ## Autobiography

Escape!
by James W. C. Pennington,
adapted

At Last I Kill a Buffalo
by Luther Standing Bear, adapted

Chapter 17 ## Short Stories

The Secret Life of Walter Mitty
by James Thurber, adapted

The Invalid's Story
by Mark Twain, adapted

His Hair Flows Like a River by T. C. Cannon

How does this painting create a sense of boldness and daring?

Chapter 16 Autobiography

DANGER AND ADVENTURE

Learning Objectives

- Recognize the atmosphere of a story.
- Explain what a narrative is.
- Identify a character's internal conflict.
- Understand a story's theme.

Preview Activity

Think of an adventure that you have had. How would you make it interesting and exciting for others to read? What kinds of conflicts did you experience? Where would you begin the exciting part of your story? Write down your ideas. Share them with a friend.

Autobiography and Danger and Adventure

An autobiography is a true story of a person's life, written by that person. A complete autobiography usually tells about the person's whole life, using many events. Autobiographical writing has

- a main character who is the author.
- a first-person point of view.
- real settings and events.
- characters who are real people.

Danger and adventure are important parts of some autobiographies. This kind of event is sometimes the turning point in the writer's life.

Keys to Literature

atmosphere: the general mood of a piece of literature

Example: Words like *unusual silence* help create an atmosphere of suspense and danger.

narrative: a story; a report of what has happened

Example: "Escape!" is a narrative of what happened when James Pennington headed to the North.

Did You Know?

African Americans who were escaping slavery often used the North Star to determine the right direction to travel. The North Star always appears in the same position in the sky. By looking at its position, they could tell which direction was north.

Words to Know

quarter	an area; a section
nourishment	food to keep you healthy and alive; something that provides good health, growth, and development
desperate	in terrible need; almost hopeless
tollgate	a place where you pay to travel on a road or cross a bridge
crisis	a time of great danger; a turning point at which a major change takes place
blacksmith	a person who shapes hot metal, such as iron, into horseshoes, pots, or other objects
resistance	fighting back
captors	people who catch someone
fugitive	someone who is running away from people who are looking for him or her

$\mathcal{E}$scape!

BY JAMES W. C. PENNINGTON, *Adapted*

READ TO FIND OUT...

What is the greatest danger the author faces as he tries to escape?

It was now two o'clock. I stepped into the slave **quarter**. There was an unusual silence. The house looked poor. The only piece of food I could see was a bit of corn bread. It weighed about a half-pound. I placed it in my pocket. I took a last look at the house and at a few small children who were playing at the door.

I crossed the barnyard and in a few moments reached a small cave. Near the cave's mouth was a pile of stones into which I had placed my clothes. From here, I had to go through thick and heavy woods to town, where my brother lived.

This town was six miles away. It was now near three o'clock. My goals were not to be seen on the road and to get to the town before dark. I was well known in town. If anyone were to have seen me, I would have once again been chased.

Keys to Literature

What details create an **atmosphere** of danger and suspense?

The first six miles, I traveled very slowly. During this walk, a difficult question was bothering me: Shall I visit my brother as I pass through town and show him what I've done? My brother was older than me, and we were very close. I always asked him for advice.

I entered the town about dark. I decided not to show myself to my brother. I passed through the town without being seen. Darkness hid me, a lonely wanderer from home and friends. My only guide was the *North Star*. By this star, I knew that I would go north. But at what point I should reach Pennsylvania, or when and where I should find a friend, I did not know....

The night was warm for the time of year. It passed quietly, and I was very tired. Then about three o'clock in the morning, I began to feel cold.

At this moment, I began to feel gloomy. The thought of being completely poor was more than I could bear. My heart began to melt. How will I survive with just a piece of dry corn bread? What **nourishment** is there in it to warm the nerves of one already chilled to the heart?

While these thoughts were on my mind, the day dawned. I was in the middle of an open field. I hid among a pile of corn stalks, a few hundred yards from the road.

Here I spent my first day. The day was an unhappy one. My hiding place was very dangerous. I had to sit in an uncomfortable position the whole day. I had no chance to rest. Besides this, my small piece of bread did not give me the nourishment that I so badly needed.

I was relieved when night came again. By this time, not a crumb of my bread was left. I was hungry and began to feel **desperate**....

Think About It

As the narrator travels north, the setting changes. Where is he now?

At the dawn of the third day, I continued my travel. I had found my way to a public road during the night. Very early in the morning, I came to a **tollgate** where I only saw one person. It was a boy about 12 years old. I asked him where the road led. He said it led to Baltimore. I asked him how far it was. He said it was 18 miles.

That information shocked me. My master lived 80 miles from Baltimore. I was now 62 miles from home. That distance in the right direction would have placed me several miles across the Mason-Dixon line. But I was still in the state of Maryland....

By the time I had walked a mile on this road, it was about nine o'clock. I came upon a young man with a load of hay. He drew up his horses and spoke to me in a very kind tone. The following conversation took place between us:

"Are you traveling far, my friend?"

"I am on my way to Philadelphia."

"Are you free?"

"Yes, sir."

"I suppose, then, you have free papers?"

"No, sir, I have no papers."

"Well, my friend, you should not travel on this road. You will be caught before you have gone three miles. There are men living on this road who are always on the lookout for your people. It is rare that one who tries to pass by day escapes them."

He then very kindly gave me some advice. He told me to turn off the road at a certain point. He said I should find my way to a certain house where I would be met by an old gentleman. That man would tell me whether I should stay until night or go on....

Predict

What might happen when the narrator meets another traveler?

Think About It

Why does the narrator lie about being a free man?

I went on for about a mile more. I had gone about five miles from the tollgate that I mentioned earlier. It was now about ten o'clock in the morning. My strength was nearly gone because I had not eaten very much food. But my mind was greatly excited. I thought very little about my *need* for food.

Normally, I would have been glad to see the tavern I came upon. But as things stood, I thought it was a dangerous place to pass, much less to stop at. I passed it as quietly and quickly as possible. Then from a lot across the road, I heard a serious voice cry, "Halloo!"

Think About It

Why was the tavern a dangerous place for the narrator?

I turned my face to the left, from where the voice came. I noticed it was from a man who was digging potatoes. I answered him politely. Then the following conversation took place:

"Who do *you* belong to?"

"I am free, sir."

"Have you got papers?"

"No, sir."

"Well, you must stop here."

By this time, he had made his way into the road and climbed on top of a fence that separated us.

"My business is onward, sir," I said. "I do not wish to stop."

"I will see then if you don't stop, you black rascal."

He was now in the middle of the road. He began to come quickly after me.

I saw that a **crisis** was at hand. I had no weapons of any kind, not even a pocketknife. I asked myself, shall I surrender without a struggle? The answer was, "No."

Think About It

The narrator has a conversation with himself. What plan does he make?

What will you do? Continue to walk. If he runs after you, run. Get him as far from the house as you can. Then turn suddenly and strike him on the knee with a stone. At least that will keep him from chasing you.

This was a desperate plan. But I could not think of another one. My skill as a **blacksmith** had given me good aim. I felt quite sure that I only needed to get a stone in my hand. If I had time to throw it, I would not miss his knee.

He began to take short breaths. He was mad because I did not stop. And I was angry at being chased by a man to whom I had not done the least harm. I had just begun to look for a stone to grasp. Then he made a tiger-like leap at me. We started running.

At this moment, he yelled out, "Jake Shouster!" At the next moment, the door of a small house to the left was opened. Out jumped a shoemaker with a knife in his hand. He sprang forward and grabbed me by the collar. Then the other man grabbed my arms from behind. I was now in the grasp of two men, both of whom were larger than me. One of them was armed with a dangerous weapon.

Standing in the door of the shoemaker's shop was a third man. In the potato lot I had passed, there was still a fourth man. My heart melted away. I sunk without **resistance** into the hands of my **captors**. They dragged me right away into the tavern that was near.

"Come now, this matter may easily be settled without you going to jail. Who do you belong to, and where did you come from?"...

I decided to insist that I was free. This was not good enough for them since I could not prove it. They tied my hands. Then we set out to a local official who lived about a half a mile away.

When we got to his house, he was not at home. It was a disappointment to the others, but to me it was a relief. However, I soon learned they planned on going to another official in the neighborhood. About 20 minutes later, we stood before his door. But he was not home, either.

Keys to Literature

What details in this paragraph add to the **atmosphere** of danger?

Think About It

What would the narrator need in order to prove that he was free?

By this time, it had gotten to be one or two o'clock. My captors began to feel restless at the loss of time. We were about a mile and a quarter from the tavern. As we set out on our return, they held a meeting.

They knew it would be difficult for me to climb over fences with my hands tied. So they untied me. "Now John," one of the men said. John was the name they had given me. "If you have run away from anyone, it would be much better for you to tell us!"

I continued to say that I was free. However, I knew that my situation was very serious. We were still just a short distance from my home. The knowledge of my being a runaway might catch up with me at any moment....

We got to the tavern at three o'clock. They asked me again to tell the truth. I saw that my attempt to escape only strengthened their feeling that I was a **fugitive**.

I said, "If you don't put me in jail, I will tell you where I am from." They promised.

"Well," I said, "a few weeks ago, I was sold from the eastern shore to a slave-trader. He had a large gang, and he set out for Georgia with us. When he got to a town in Virginia, he became sick. Then he died of smallpox. Several of his gang also died of it. The people in the town became worried. They did not wish the gang to remain among them. No one claimed us or wished to have anything to do with us. I left the rest and thought I would go somewhere and get work."

When I said this, they seemed to believe my story. At the same time, however, I noticed that some of the men began to panic. They were frightened by the idea that I was one of a smallpox gang. Several of those who had gathered near me moved away....

I was now left alone with the first man I saw in the morning. In a serious manner, he made this offer to me: "John, I have a brother living in Risterstown, four

Predict

What will happen if the men discover that the narrator is lying?

Think About It

Why does the narrator want his captors to think he has been exposed to smallpox?

miles away. He keeps a tavern. I think you had better go and live with him until we see what will turn up. He wants someone to take care of his horses." I agreed to this at once. "Well, take something to eat," he said, "and I will go with you."

I knew it wouldn't do me any good to go into that town. There were prisons, posters, newspapers, and travelers there. My intention was to start with him, but not to enter town alive....

The narrator escapes again before he gets to Risterstown. He keeps going north to freedom.

Think About It

If you were the narrator, would you continue to travel on the road? Explain.

After several hours, I found my way back to the road. But traveling quickly was not possible. All I could do was keep my legs moving, which I did with great difficulty.

Near the end of the night, I suffered greatly from the cold. There was a heavy frost. I expected at every moment to fall on the road and die. I came to a cornfield covered with Indian corn. I went into this field and ate an ear of corn. I thought I would rest a little in the cornfield before starting out again. But I was so weary that I soon fell asleep.

When I awoke, the sun was shining around. I got up in alarm. But it was too late to think of finding any other shelter. So I settled down and hid myself as best as I could from the daylight.

After I recovered a little from my fright, I began again to eat my corn. Grain by grain, I worked away at it. When my jaws grew tired, I rested. Then I started again fresh. Nearly the whole morning had gone by before I was finished....

Think About It

How does the narrator get his strength back?

I got my strength back. I felt that I was at least safe from starving to death. So, I set out more quickly than I had since Sunday and Monday night. I had a feeling, too, that I must be near free soil. I hadn't the least idea where I should find a home or friend. Still, my spirits were so high, that I took the whole road to myself. I ran, hopped, skipped, jumped, and talked to myself....

This joyful mood only lasted an hour or two. Then a gloom came over me with these questions: But where are you going? What are you going to do? What will you do with freedom without your father, mother, sisters, and brothers? What will you say when you are asked where you are born? You know nothing of the world.

These questions made me think about the great difficulties I still had to face.

Think About It
Why does the narrator feel joyful, and then quickly feel gloomy again?

Saturday morning came. My strength still seemed fresh. Yet, I began to feel a hunger that was worse than I had felt before. I decided, at all risk, to continue my travel by daylight. I would ask the first person I met for information....

I continued my flight on the public road. A little after the sun rose, I came in sight of another tollgate. For a moment, all the events that happened at the tollgate on Wednesday morning came back to me. I stopped. But, then I decided that I would try again.

Think About It
Why would a tollgate be dangerous for the narrator?

I arrived at the gate. I found it attended by an old woman. I asked her if I was in Pennsylvania. She said I was. Then I asked her if she knew where I could find work. She said she did not. But she told me to go to W. W., a Quaker, who lived about three miles from her. She said he would be interested in me. She gave me directions to get there. I thanked her and wished her a good morning.

In about half an hour, I stood shaking at the door of W. W. I knocked. The door opened upon a well-spread table. The sight of it increased my hunger about seven times. I did not dare to enter. I said that I'd been sent to him to find work.

"Well, come in and take thy breakfast and get warm," he said. "We will talk about it. Thee must be cold without any coat."

"Come in and take thy breakfast and get warm."

The words were spoken by a stranger. But they were spoken with such kindness that they made a great impression on me. They made me believe that I had found a friend and a home....

To this day, those words remind me of what I was at that time. My condition was as terrible as that of any human being could be. I had only four pieces of clothing. I was a starving fugitive, without home or friends. There was a reward offered for me in the public papers. I was being chased by cruel manhunters.

I had no claim upon the man to whose door I went. Had he turned me away, I would surely have died. No, he took me in and gave me his food. He even shared with me his own clothes. I had never before received such treatment at the hands of any white man.

▶ The Quakers believed enslavement was wrong. Many Quakers were part of the Underground Railroad and helped people escape to free states in the North.

Keys to Literature

This **narrative** is only part of the story of the narrator's escape. To find out more, read the *Fugitive Blacksmith*, his autobiography.

Meet the Author

JAMES W. C. PENNINGTON *(1807–1870)*

James Pennington was born into enslavement in Maryland. When he was about 20 years old, he escaped to freedom in Pennsylvania. There, a Quaker taught him how to read and write. Pennington later worked as a schoolteacher. He joined with others who fought against enslavement.

Pennington wrote his autobiography, *The Fugitive Blacksmith*, which tells about his journey from Maryland to Pennsylvania. He also wrote a book called *A Text Book of the Origin and History of the Colored People*.

AFTER YOU READ "Escape!"

Check Your Predictions

1. Look back at the answers you gave for the Predict questions. Would you change your answers? Explain.

Understand the Story

2. Where is the narrator trying to go? Why?

3. What makes the narrator feel so frantic and hopeless?

4. Who in this story is helpful to the narrator?

5. Why does the narrator decide not to go into Risterstown?

Think About the Story

6. Why might the narrator not trust the man who offers to go with him to Risterstown?

7. What is the atmosphere of this story?

8. What makes "Escape!" a narrative?

Extend Your Response

Make up a list of rules for the narrator that will keep him from being captured on his way north. Write your rules.

Learn More About It

THE MASON-DIXON LINE

The Mason-Dixon Line is an imaginary line on a map. It runs mainly from east to west. Pennsylvania is north of this border. West Virginia and Maryland are south of it. Then the line turns south and separates Delaware from Maryland.

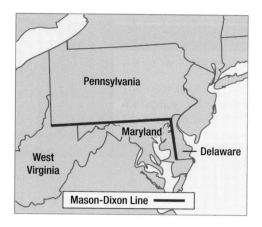

In the 1700s, the American colonies of Maryland and Pennsylvania were arguing over a piece of land. Both colonies said the land belonged to them. They decided to settle their argument scientifically.

They hired two surveyors—Charles Mason and Jeremiah Dixon. They measured the size, shape, and boundaries of the whole area. When they were done, they set up big stones to mark the borderline between the two colonies.

During the Civil War, the Mason-Dixon Line became a rough dividing line between the North and the South. In fact, some people believe that the terms *Dixie* and *Dixieland* come from the name *Mason-Dixon Line*. These words refer to the South.

Apply and Connect

Why does the narrator in "Escape!" try to get north of the Mason-Dixon Line?

Keys to Literature

theme: the main idea of a story, novel, play, or poem

> Example: The theme of this story is the importance of telling the truth.

internal conflict: the struggle a person has within himself or herself when trying to make a decision

> Example: In this memoir, the narrator must decide whether exaggerating an accomplishment is more important than telling the truth.

Words to Know

sufficient	enough; as much as is needed
preceding	coming just before
commodity	something that can be traded or sold
justified	showed to be right
gratification	a feeling of pride or thankfulness
tackle	begin to or try to do something difficult
gait	way of walking or running
marksmanship	aim; accuracy in shooting
temptation	thinking about doing something wrong
resolved	decided
regretted	felt sorry or guilty for something
customary	usual; normally done
exploits	brave or daring actions

At Last I Kill a Buffalo

BY LUTHER STANDING BEAR, *Adapted*

At last the day came when my father allowed me to go on a buffalo hunt with him. What a proud boy I was!

Ever since I could remember my father had been teaching me the things that I should know and preparing me to be a good hunter. I had learned to make bows and to string them and to make arrows and tip them with feathers. I knew how to ride my pony no matter how fast he would go, and I felt that I was brave and did not fear danger. All these things I had learned for just this day when father would allow me to go with him on a buffalo hunt. It was the event for which every

READ TO FIND OUT...

How does the narrator decide whether or not to lie to his father?

Keys to Literature

Sometimes, a title gives clues to the **theme**, or main idea, of a story. One of the themes of this story is the importance to a Sioux boy of killing his first buffalo.

The Buffalo Hunt by Charles Marion Russell

Sioux boy eagerly waited. To ride side by side with the best hunters of the tribe, to hear the terrible noise of the great herds as they ran, and then to help to bring home the kill was the most thrilling day of any Indian boy's life. The only other event that could equal it would be the day I went for the first time on the warpath to meet the enemy and protect my tribe.

On the following early morning, we were to start, so the evening was spent in preparation. Although the tipis were full of activity, there was no noise nor confusion outside. Always the evening before a buffalo hunt and when everyone was usually in his tipi, an old man went around the circle of tipis calling, "I-ni-la, I-ni-la," not loudly, but so everyone could hear. The old man was saying, "Keep quiet. Keep quiet." We all knew that the scouts had come in and reported buffalo near and that we must all keep the camp in stillness. It was not necessary for the old man to go into each tipi and explain to the men that tomorrow there would be a big hunt, as the buffalo were coming. He did not order the men to prepare their weapons and neither did he order the mothers to keep children from crying. The one word, "I-ni-la," was **sufficient** to bring quiet to the whole camp. That night there would be no calling or shouting from tipi to tipi, and no child would cry aloud. Even the horses and dogs obeyed the command for quiet, and all night not a horse neighed and not a dog barked. The very presence of quiet was everywhere. Such is the orderliness of a Sioux camp that men, women, children, and animals seem to have a common understanding and sympathy. It is no mystery, but natural that the Indian and his animals understand each other very well both with words and without words. There are words, however, that the Indian uses that are understood by both his horses and dogs. When on a hunt, if one of the warriors speaks the word "A-a-ah" rather quickly and sharply, every man,

Sioux Village, Lake Calhoun, near Fort Snelling, 1835–1836 by George Catlin

horse, and dog will stop instantly and listen. Not a move will be made by an animal until the men move or speak further. As long as the hunters listen, the animals will listen also.

The night **preceding** a buffalo hunt was always an exciting night, even though it was quiet in camp. There would be much talk in the tipis around the fires. There would be sharpening of arrows and of knives. New bowstrings would be made and quivers would be filled with arrows.

It was in the fall of the year and the evenings were cool as father and I sat by the fire and talked over the hunt. I was only eight years of age, and I know that father did not expect me to get a buffalo at all, but only to try perhaps for a small calf should I be able to

Think About It

How does the narrator show that the horses and dogs understand what to do?

get close enough to one. Nevertheless, I was greatly excited as I sat and watched father working in his easy, firm way.

I was wearing my buffalo-skin robe, the hair next to my body. Mother had made me a rawhide belt and this, wrapped around my waist, held my blanket on when I threw it off my shoulders. In the early morning I would wear it, for it would be cold. When it came time to shoot, I should not want my blanket, but the belt would hold it in place.

You can picture me, I think, as I sat in the glow of the campfire, my little brown body bare to the waist watching and listening intently to my father. My hair hung down my back, and I wore moccasins and breechcloth of buckskin. To my belt was fastened a rawhide holster for my knife, for when I was eight years of age we had plenty of knives. I was proud to own a knife, and this night I remember I kept it on all night. Neither did I lay aside my bow, but went to sleep with it in my hand, thinking, I suppose, to be all the nearer ready in the morning when the start was made.

Father sharpened my steel points for me and also sharpened my knife. The whetstone was a long stone that was kept in a buckskin bag, and sometimes this stone went all over the camp; every tipi did not have one, so we shared this **commodity** with one another. I had as I remember about ten arrows, so when father was through sharpening them I put them in my rawhide quiver. I had a rawhide quirt, too, which I would wear fastened to my waist. As father worked, he knew I was watching him closely and listening whenever he spoke. By the time all preparations had been made, he had told me just how I was to act when I started out in the morning with the hunters.

We went to bed, my father hoping that tomorrow would be successful for him so that he could bring home some nice meat for the family and a hide for my mother to tan. I went to bed, but could not go to sleep at once, so filled was I with the wonderment and excitement of it all. The next day was to be a test for me. I was to prove to my father whether he was or was not **justified** in his pride in me. What would be the result of my training? Would I be brave if I faced danger and would father be proud of me? I did not know it that night that I was to be tried for the strength of my manhood and my honesty in this hunt. Something happened that day which I remember above all things. It was a test of my real character, and I am proud to say that I did not find myself weak, but made a decision that has been all these years a **gratification** to me.

The next morning the hunters were catching their horses about daybreak. I arose with my father and went out and caught my pony. I wanted to do whatever he did and show him that he did not have to tell me what to do. We brought our animals to the tipi and got our bows and arrows and mounted. From all over the village came the hunters. Most of them were leading their running horses. These running horses were eager for the hunt and came prancing, their ears straight up and their tails waving in the air. We were joined with perhaps a hundred or more riders, some of whom carried bows and arrows and some armed with guns.

The buffalo were reported to be about five or six miles away as we should count distance now. At that time, we did not measure distance in miles. One camping distance was about ten miles, and these buffalo were said to be about one-half camping distance away.

Think About It

How are the father's thoughts about the hunt different from the son's?

Predict

What will happen to test the narrator's character?

Some of the horses were to be left at a stopping place just before the herd was reached. These horses were pack animals that were taken along to carry extra blankets or weapons. They were trained to remain there until the hunters came for them. Though they were neither hobbled nor tied, they stood still during the shooting and noise of the chase.

My pony was a black one and a good runner. I felt very important as I rode along with the hunters and my father, the chief. I kept as close to him as I could.

Two men had been chosen to scout or to lead the party. These two men were, in a sense, policemen whose work it was to keep order. They carried large sticks of ash wood, something like a policeman's billy, though longer. They rode ahead of the party while the rest of us kept in a group close together. The leaders went ahead until they sighted the herd of grazing buffalo. Then they stopped and waited for the rest of us to ride up. We all rode slowly toward the herd, which on sight of us had come together, although they had been scattered here and there over the plain. When they saw us, they all ran close together as if at the command of a leader. We continued riding slowly toward the herd until one of the leaders shouted, "Ho-ka-he!" which means "Ready, Go!" At that command, every man started for the herd. I had been listening, too, and the minute the hunters started, I started also.

Away I went, my little pony putting all he had into the race. It was not long before I lost sight of father, but I kept going just the same. I threw my blanket back and the chill of the autumn morning struck my body, but I did not mind. On I went. It was wonderful to race over the ground with all these horsemen about me. There was no shouting, no noise of any kind except the pounding of the horses' hooves. The herd was now

Think About It

What new thing does the narrator tell you about his father?

Predict

As the hunters start toward the herd of buffalo, what will happen?

running and had raised a cloud of dust. I felt no fear until we had entered this cloud of dust, and I could see nothing about me—only hear the sound of hooves. Where was father? Where was I going? On I rode through the cloud, for I knew I must keep going.

Then all at once I realized that I was in the midst of the buffalo, their dark bodies rushing all about me and their great heads moving up and down to the sound of their hooves beating upon the earth. Then it was that fear overcame me, and I leaned close down upon my little pony's body and clutched him tightly. I can never tell you how I felt toward my pony at that moment. All thought of shooting had left my mind. I was seized by blank fear. In a moment or so, however, my senses became clearer, and I could distinguish other sounds beside the clatter of hooves. I could hear a shot now and then, and I could see the buffalo beginning to break up into small bunches. I could not see my father nor any of my companions yet, but my fear was vanishing and I was safe. I let my pony run. The buffalo looked too large for me to **tackle**, anyway, so I just kept going. The buffalo became more and more scattered. Pretty soon I saw a young calf that looked about my size. I remembered now what father had told me the night before as we sat about the fire. Those instructions were important for me now to follow.

I was still back of the calf, being unable to get alongside of him. I was eager to get a shot, yet afraid to try, as I was still very nervous. While my pony was making all speed to come alongside, I chanced a shot and to my surprise my arrow landed. My second arrow glanced along the back of the animal and sped on between the horns, making only a slight wound. My third arrow hit a spot that made the running beast slow up in his **gait**. I shot a fourth arrow, and though

Think About It

The narrator's feelings change quickly here from excitement to fear. What causes this change?

The Buffalo Hunter by Seth Eastman

it, too, landed, it was not a fatal wound. It seemed to me that it was taking a lot of shots, and I was not proud of my **marksmanship**. I was glad, however, to see the animal going slower, and I knew that one more shot would make me a hunter. My horse seemed to know his own importance. His two ears stood straight forward, and it was not necessary for me to urge him to get closer to the buffalo. I was soon by the side of the buffalo and one more shot brought the chase to a close. I jumped from my pony, and as I stood by my fallen game, I looked all around wishing that the world could see. But I was alone. In my determination to stay by until I had won my buffalo, I had not noticed that I was far from everyone else. No admiring friends were about, and as far as I could see I was on the plain alone. The herd of buffalo had completely disappeared. As for Father, much as I wished for him, he was out of sight, and I had no idea where he was.

I stood and looked at the animal on the ground. I was happy. Everyone must know that I, Ota K'te, had killed a buffalo. But it looked as if no one knew where I was, so no one was coming my way. I must then take something from this animal to show that I had killed it. I took all the arrows one by one from the body. As I took them out, it occurred to me that I had used five arrows. If I had been a skillful hunter, one arrow would have been sufficient, but I had used five. Here it was that **temptation** came to me. Why could I not take out two of the arrows and throw them away? No one would know, and then I should be more greatly admired and praised as a hunter. As it was, I knew that I should be praised by my father and mother, but I wanted more. And so I was tempted to lie.

I was planning this as I took out my skinning knife that father had sharpened for me the night before. I skinned one side of the animal, but when it came to turning it over, I was too small. I was wondering what to do when I heard my father's voice calling, "To-ki-i-la-la-hu-wo. Where are you?" I quickly jumped on my pony and rode to the top of a little hill nearby. Father saw me and came to me at once. He was so pleased to see me and glad to know that I was safe. I knew that I could never lie to my father. He was too fond of me, and I too proud of him. He had always told me to tell the truth. He wanted me to be an honest man, so I **resolved** then to tell the truth even if it took from me a little glory. He rode up to me with a glad expression on his face, expecting me to go back with him to his kill. As he came up, I said as calmly as I could, "Father, I have killed a buffalo." His smile changed to surprise, and he asked me where my buffalo was. I pointed to it, and we rode over to where it lay, partly skinned.

Predict

Will the narrator lie about how many arrows he used?

Keys to Literature

After the narrator has an **internal conflict**, why does he decide to tell his father the truth?

Father set to work to skin it for me. I had watched him do this many times and knew perfectly well how to do it myself, but I could not turn the animal over. There was a way to turn the head of the animal so that the body would be balanced on the back while being skinned. Father did this for me, while I helped all I could. When the hide was off, father put it on the pony's back with the hair side next to the pony. On this, he arranged the meat so it would balance. Then he covered the meat carefully with the rest of the hide, so no dust would reach it while we traveled home. I rode home on top of the load.

I showed my father the arrows that I had used and just where the animal had been hit. He was very pleased and praised me over and over again. I felt more glad than ever that I had told the truth, and I have never **regretted** it. I am more proud now that I told the truth than I am of killing the buffalo.

We rode to where my father had killed a buffalo. There we stopped and prepared it for taking home. It was late afternoon when we got back to camp. No king ever rode in state who was more proud than I that day as I came into the village sitting high up on my load of buffalo meat. Mother had now two hunters in the family, and I knew how she was going to make a fuss over me. It is not **customary** for Indian men to brag about their **exploits**, and I had been taught that bragging was not nice. So I was very quiet, although I was bursting with pride. Always when arriving home I would run out to play for I loved to be with the other boys, but this day I lingered about close to the tipi so I could hear the nice things that were said about me. It was soon all over camp that Ota K'te had killed a buffalo.

Think About It

How does the narrator feel as he rides back into his village?

My father was so proud that he gave away a fine horse. He called an old man to our tipi to cry out the news to the rest of the people in camp. The old man stood at the door of our tipi and sang a song of praise to my father. The horse had been led up, and I stood holding it by a rope. The old man who was singing called the other old man who was to receive the horse as a present. He accepted the horse by coming up to me, holding out his hands to me, and saying, "Ha-ye," which means "Thank you." The old man went away very grateful for the horse.

That ended my first and last buffalo hunt. It lives only in my memory, for the days of the buffalo are over.

Think About It

What details of Sioux life and customs do you learn from this paragraph?

Sioux Encamped on the Upper Missouri, Dressing Buffalo Meat by George Catlin

Meet the Author

LUTHER STANDING BEAR *(1868–1939)*

Luther Standing Bear was born on a reservation in South Dakota. He was educated at the Carlisle Indian School, a boarding school in Pennsylvania. As an adult, he was a teacher and an actor in movies such as *The Santa Fe Trail*. He also toured with the Buffalo Bill Wild West Show.

Standing Bear gave speeches to help improve the treatment of Native Americans. He also became a writer. Some of his books are *My People, the Sioux*; *Land of the Spotted Eagle*; and an autobiography, *My Indian Boyhood*.

Check Your Predictions

1. Look back at the answers you gave for the Predict questions. Would you change your answers? Explain.

Understand the Story

2. What does the narrator need to learn in order to be ready for a buffalo hunt?

3. What are the pack horses used for?

4. What does the narrator almost lie about?

Think About the Story

5. How does the buffalo hunt create an internal conflict for the narrator?

6. Why is the narrator more proud of telling the truth than of killing his first buffalo?

7. What does "the days of the buffalo are over" mean?

8. What is the main theme of this story?

Extend Your Response

Write a short scene for a movie based on the buffalo hunt. Make a list of characters. Tell where the setting of the scene will be. Then, create your scene using characters, actions, and dialogue.

Chapter 16 ▷ Review

Summaries

Escape! The narrator describes his escape to a free state. He uses the North Star as his guide. Many times, he is almost captured or is very hungry. Finally, he finds food, safety, and freedom in the home of a Quaker.

At Last I Kill a Buffalo The narrator describes his first buffalo hunt. He tells how his Sioux village prepares for the hunt and what the hunt is like. When he realizes that he has used five arrows to kill his first buffalo, he is tempted to lie to his father. In the end, he decides to tell the truth. His parents are very proud of him.

| temptation |
| resolved |
| crisis |
| justified |
| desperate |

Vocabulary Review

Complete each sentence with a word from the box. Use a separate sheet of paper.

1. Joe felt a great _____ to eat that second piece of cake.

2. When our only quarterback was removed from the football game, it was a _____ for our team.

3. Adam and Tammy _____ never to watch that program again.

4. I was so tired, I was _____ to go to sleep.

5. Because she had won her medal fairly, Abbie felt _____ in keeping it.

Chapter Quiz

Answer the following questions in one or two complete sentences. Use a separate sheet of paper.

1. Escape! How would papers have helped the narrator?

2. Escape! Why does the narrator need to hide so often?

3. Escape! How does the woman at the tollgate help the narrator?

4. At Last I Kill a Buffalo Why is the narrator excited at the beginning of the story?

5. At Last I Kill a Buffalo Why is the boy told to hunt a small buffalo?

6. At Last I Kill a Buffalo What does the narrator's father do to show how proud he is?

Critical Thinking

7. Escape! What might have happened to the narrator if the Quaker had not helped him? Explain.

8. Both narratives in this chapter tell about dangerous adventures. Which one is more dangerous? Why?

Chapter Activity

Choose one of the stories from this chapter. Write four questions you would like to ask the narrator.

Giant Jack-in-the-Box by Jeremy Hauser

How might this painting relate to the theme of danger and adventure?

Chapter 17 / Short Stories
DANGER AND ADVENTURE

Learning Objectives

- Explain what a simile is.
- Understand onomatopoeia.
- Recognize the importance of setting.
- Identify the narrative hooks in a story.

Preview Activity

In some stories, adventures take place in the minds of the characters. Something in real life triggers, or starts, a daydream. With a partner, make a list of some ordinary things people say and do. Then, write a daydream that could start from these words or events. For example, playing basketball could start a daydream about winning a championship.

Short Stories of Danger and Adventure

A short story is one the author makes up. The characters and setting may seem realistic, but they are invented by the author. Short stories have

characters: the people (or animals) in the story.

setting: the place and time of the story.

plot: the actions or events of the story. A short story plot is usually simple. It has a beginning, rising action, a climax, and a conclusion.

In the two stories in this chapter, what the characters imagine is more important than what actually happens.

Keys to Literature

simile: a comparison of two things using the word *like* or *as*

> Example: The man was strong **as** an ox.

onomatopoeia: the use of words that imitate sounds

> Example: *Rat-tat-tatting* is a word that sounds like a machine gun firing.

Did You Know?

The character Walter Mitty has become so well known that he is now a symbol of ordinary people who dream of being heroes. If someone is called "a Walter Mitty," it means this person has fantasies about escaping everyday life.

Words to Know

auxiliary	back-up; something used when support is needed
turret	a section of a warplane shaped like a bubble
hydroplane	an airplane that can land on water
overshoes	rubber boots worn over regular shoes in wet or cold weather
aimlessly	without a goal or a purpose
intern	a doctor who is in training
objection	in a court of law, a complaint or argument against something said
defendant	a person on trial for a crime
sergeant	an officer in the armed forces
undefeated	never having lost or been beaten

The Secret Life of Walter Mitty

JAMES THURBER, *Adapted*

READ TO FIND OUT...
Who is the real
Walter Mitty?

Keys to Literature

In a **simile**, two things
are compared, using the
word *like* or *as*. What is
the Commander's voice
compared to?

"WE'RE GOING THROUGH!" The Commander's voice was like thin ice breaking. He wore his full-dress uniform. He had his white cap pulled down over one cold, gray eye.

"We can't make it, sir. A hurricane is coming, if you ask me."

"I'm not asking you, Lieutenant Berg," said the Commander. "Throw on the power lights! Rev her up to 8500! We're going through!"

The pounding of the engines increased: ta-pocketa-pocketa-pocketa-*pocketa-pocketa*. The Commander stared at the ice forming on the pilot's window. He walked over and twisted a row of dials.

"Switch on Number 8 **auxiliary**!" he shouted. "Switch on Number 8 auxiliary!" Lieutenant Berg repeated.

"Full strength in Number 3 **turret**!" shouted the Commander. "Full strength in Number 3 turret!" Berg repeated.

The crew went at their various tasks inside the huge, eight-engine navy **hydroplane**. The men looked at each other and grinned. "The Old Man will get us through," they said to one another. "The Old Man ain't afraid of nothing!" ...

"Not so fast! You're driving too fast!" said Mrs. Mitty. "What are you driving so fast for?"

"Hmm?" said Walter Mitty. He looked at his wife with shock. She was sitting in the car beside him. She seemed very unfamiliar. She was like a strange woman who had yelled at him in a crowd.

"You were up to fifty-five," she said. "You know I don't like to go more than forty. You were up to fifty-five."

Walter Mitty drove on toward Waterbury in silence. The roaring of the SN202 hydroplane through the worst storm in twenty years of navy flying faded in his mind.

"You're tensed up again," Mrs. Mitty said. "It's one of your days. I wish you'd let Dr. Renshaw look you over."

Walter Mitty stopped the car. They were in front of the building where his wife went to have her hair done. "Remember to get those **overshoes** while I'm having my hair done," she said.

"I don't need overshoes," Mitty said.

"We've been all through that," she said, getting out of the car. "You're not a young man any longer." He raced the engine a little. "Why don't you wear your gloves? Have you lost your gloves?"

Walter Mitty reached in a pocket and brought out the gloves. He put them on. After she'd gone into the building, and he'd driven off to a red light, he took them off.

> ▶ When Walter Mitty's wife says, "Not so fast!" he suddenly returns to everyday life.

Think About It

How do you know that Walter Mitty is only daydreaming about flying a hydroplane?

"Hurry up, brother!" a cop snapped as the light changed. Mitty quickly put his gloves back on and drove off. He drove around the streets **aimlessly** for a time. Then he drove past the hospital on his way to the parking lot.

... "It's the millionaire banker, Wellington McMillan," said the pretty nurse.

"Yes?" said Walter Mitty. He removed his gloves slowly. "Who has the case?"

"Dr. Renshaw and Dr. Benbow. But there are two specialists here. Dr. Remington came in from New York. Mr. Pritchard-Mitford flew over from London."

A door opened down a long, cool hallway. Dr. Renshaw came out. He looked upset and tired. "Hello, Mitty," he said. "We're having a terrible time with McMillan. He is the millionaire banker and a close friend of President Roosevelt. Obstreosis of the ducal tract. I wish you'd take a look at him."

"Glad to," Mitty said.

In the operating room, everyone was introduced to each other in whispers. "I've read one of your books," said Pritchard-Mitford, shaking hands with Mitty. "A brilliant performance, sir."

"Thank you," said Walter Mitty.

A huge machine, with many tubes and wires, was connected to the operating table. At this moment, it began to go *pocketa-pocketa-pocketa*.

"The new anesthetizer is giving way," an **intern** shouted. "There is no one in the East who knows how to fix it!"

"Quiet, man," Mitty said, in a low, cool voice. He went over to the machine. It was now going *pocketa-pocketa-queep-pocketa-queep*. He began softly touching a row of dials. "Give me a fountain pen!" he snapped.

Predict

When Walter Mitty drives past a hospital, what will he daydream about?

▶ There is no such thing as *obstreosis of the ducal tract.* The author made it up. It is supposed to sound like something a doctor would say.

Keys to Literature

The author uses **onomatopoeia** to imitate sounds. What does *pocketa-pocketa-queep-pocketa-queep* sound like?

Someone handed him a fountain pen. He pulled a broken part out of the machine. Then he put the fountain pen in its place. "That will hold for ten minutes," he said. "Get on with the operation."

A nurse hurried over and whispered to Renshaw. Mitty saw the man turn pale. "Coreopsis has set in," Renshaw said nervously. "If you would take over, Mitty?"

Mitty looked at him and at the cowardly figure of Benbow. The two great specialists looked grave and uncertain. "If you wish," Mitty said. They slipped a white gown on him. He adjusted a mask and put on thin gloves. Nurses handed him …

"Back it up, Mac! Look out for that Buick!" Walter Mitty jammed on the brakes. "Wrong lane, Mac," said the parking-lot attendant, looking at Mitty closely.

"Gee. Yeah," Mitty muttered. He began to carefully back out of the lane marked "Exit Only."

"Leave it there," said the attendant. "I'll put it away." Mitty got out of the car. "Hey, better leave the key."

"Oh," Mitty said, handing the man the car key. The attendant jumped into the car, backed it up, and put it where it belonged.

They're so high on themselves, Walter Mitty thought, as he walked along Main Street. They think they know everything. He kicked at the slush on the sidewalk. "Overshoes," he said to himself. He began looking for a shoe store.

A little while later, Walter Mitty came out onto the street again. He had the overshoes in a box under his arm. He began to wonder what the other thing was his wife told him to get. She had told him twice, before they left their house for Waterbury.

In a way, he hated these weekly trips to town. He was always getting something wrong. Tissues, he thought, razor blades? No. Toothpaste, toothbrush, medicine? He gave it up. But she would remember it.

Think About It

What makes Walter Mitty come out of this daydream?

Think About It

What does kicking the slush remind Walter Mitty to do?

Predict

Will Walter Mitty remember what else he is supposed to buy?

"Where's the what's-its-name?" she would ask. "Don't tell me you forgot the what's-its-name?" A newsboy went by shouting something about the Waterbury trial.

… "Perhaps this will refresh your memory." The District Attorney suddenly shoved a heavy automatic gun at the person on the witness stand. "Have you ever seen this gun before?"

Walter Mitty took the gun and examined it like an expert. "This is my Webley-Vickers 50.80," he said calmly. An excited buzz spread through the courtroom. The judge called for order.

"You are an expert with any sort of gun, I believe?" said the District Attorney.

"**Objection**!" Mitty's attorney shouted. "We have shown that the **defendant** could not have fired the shot. We have shown that he wore his right arm in a sling on the night of July 14th."

Walter Mitty raised his hand briefly. The arguing attorneys stopped talking. "With any gun, I could have killed Gregory Fitzhurst at 300 feet *with my left hand*," he said evenly.

A near riot broke loose in the courtroom. A woman's scream rose above the noise. Suddenly, a lovely dark-haired girl was in Walter Mitty's arms. The District Attorney hit her. Without rising from his chair, Mitty punched the man right on the chin. "You miserable dog!"…

"Puppy biscuit," Walter Mitty said. He stopped walking. The buildings of Waterbury rose up out of the imaginary courtroom and surrounded him again.

A woman who was passing laughed. "He said 'Puppy biscuit,'" she said to her friend. "That man said 'Puppy biscuit' to himself."

Walter Mitty hurried on. He went into a supermarket. "I want some dog biscuits for small, young dogs," he said to the clerk.

Think About It

What connection does Walter Mitty make that snaps him out of this daydream?

"Any special brand, sir?"

The greatest pistol shot in the world thought for a moment. "It says 'Puppies Bark for It' on the box," Walter Mitty said.

Mitty looked at his watch. His wife would be finished at the hairdresser's in fifteen minutes. She'd be done unless they had trouble drying her hair. Sometimes they had trouble drying it. She didn't like to get to the hotel first. She would want him to be there waiting for her as usual.

He found a big leather chair in the lobby of the hotel, facing a window. He put the overshoes and the puppy biscuits on the floor beside the chair. He picked up an old copy of *Liberty* magazine and sank down into the chair. He read, "Can Germany Conquer the World Through the Air?" Walter Mitty looked at the pictures of bombing planes and ruined streets.

Predict

Now that Walter Mitty is reading *Liberty* magazine, what might he daydream about?

… "Young Raleigh is too frightened by the enemy firing on us. He doesn't want to go, sir," said the **sergeant**.

Captain Mitty looked up at him. "Get him to bed," he said wearily, "with the others. I'll fly alone."

"But you can't, sir," said the sergeant anxiously. "It takes two men to handle that bomber."

"Somebody has got to get the weapons factory," Mitty said. "I'm going over." War thundered around the dugout and battered at the door. Then there was a shattering of wood, and splinters flew through the room.

"That was a bit close," Captain Mitty said carelessly.

"They're closing in," said the sergeant.

"We only live once, Sergeant," Mitty said with a slight smile. "Or do we?"

Captain Mitty stood up. He strapped on his huge Webley-Vickers automatic gun.

"It's twenty-five miles through hell, sir," the sergeant said.

"After all, what isn't?" Mitty said softly.

The pounding of the cannon increased. There was the *rat-tat-tatting* of the machine guns. From somewhere came the threatening *pocketa-pocketa-pocketa* of the new flame throwers. Walter Mitty walked to the door of the dugout humming a tune. He turned and waved to the sergeant. "Cheerio!" he said....

Predict

When Mrs. Mitty returns, how will she act toward Walter?

Something struck his shoulder. "I've been looking all over this hotel for you," Mrs. Mitty said. "Why do you have to hide in this old chair? How did you expect me to find you?"

"Things close in," said Walter Mitty.

"What?" Mrs. Mitty said. "Did you get the what's-its-name? The puppy biscuits? What's in that box?"

"Overshoes," Mitty said.

"Couldn't you have put them on in the store?"

"I was thinking," Walter Mitty said. "Does it ever occur to you that I am sometimes thinking?"

She looked at him. "I'm going to take your temperature when I get you home," she said.

They went out through the revolving doors. It was two blocks to the parking lot. At the drugstore on the corner, she said, "Wait here for me. I forgot something. I won't be a minute."

She was more than a minute. Walter Mitty waited. It began to rain, rain with sleet in it. He stood up against the wall of the drugstore ...

Think About It

What does Walter Mitty daydream about at the end of the story?

He put his shoulders back and his heels together. Then, with a slight, fleeting smile, he faced the firing squad. He stood straight, still, and proud. He was Walter Mitty the **Undefeated**, mysterious to the last.

Meet the Author

JAMES THURBER *(1894–1961)*

James Thurber was born in Columbus, Ohio. When he was young, he lost an eye playing bow and arrows with his brother. Later in life, he completely lost his eyesight.

Thurber was a writer and a cartoonist. He wrote books, articles, and short stories. He was also an editor at the *The New Yorker* magazine. Some of his writings and cartoons were made into movies and television shows. A movie was even made of "The Secret Life of Walter Mitty."

Check Your Predictions

1. Look back at the answers you gave for the Predict questions. Would you change your answers? Explain.

Understand the Story

2. What five things does Walter Mitty daydream about?

3. How do people treat the real Walter Mitty?

4. How do people treat Walter Mitty in his daydreams?

5. In three of his daydreams, Walter Mitty imagines something going *pocketa-pocketa*. What different things make this sound?

Think About the Story

6. What kind of person is Mrs. Mitty? Write a simile to describe her. Remember to use *as* or *like*.

7. Why is the last daydream a good ending for the story?

8. Do you think the ending of this story is happy or sad? Explain.

Extend Your Response

Almost everybody has at some time imagined being someone else and doing other things. Describe a scene you have imagined for yourself.

Learn More About It

SIMILES AND METAPHORS

Similes and metaphors are two ways to compare things. **Similes** use the word *like* or *as*. If you say, "This jacket is light *as* a feather," you are using the word *as* to link the jacket to the feather. It means that the jacket is light, too.

Metaphors suggest that one thing is actually the other. If you say, "This jacket *is* a feather," you do not mean that the jacket is really a feather. It is as light as one.

Similes and metaphors help to

- create pictures in your mind.
  Example: The clouds are like horses' tails.

- refer to emotions.
  Example: I was as angry as a tornado.

- say something in a new and fresh way.
  Example: Eyes are windows to the world.

Some well-known similes

busy as a bee	strong as an ox
brave as a lion	clean as a whistle
fresh as a daisy	gentle as a lamb
good as gold	big as a barn
neat as a pin	pretty as a picture
like a house on fire	like a breath of fresh air

Some well-known metaphors

No man is an island.

Life is just a bowl of cherries.

Apply and Connect

To what could you compare Walter Mitty? Make up a simile or metaphor to describe him.

Keys to Literature

setting: the time and place of a story

Example: This story takes place during a snowstorm.

narrative hook: a point in the story at which the author grabs your attention

Example: The narrator says he is telling *a strange story.*

Words to Know

actual	real
driving	strong
express	nonstop; high speed
departed	gone; dead
trance	a dreamlike state; a state of being unconscious
suffocating	making breathing difficult
aimless	pointless; without purpose
hoarsely	gruffly; with a husky voice

The Invalid's Story

BY MARK TWAIN, *Adapted*

READ TO FIND OUT...
How does a small package cause a lot of trouble?

I look like I am sixty years old and married. But that is because of my condition and my sufferings. I am really unmarried and only forty-one years old. It will be hard for you to believe that I was a healthy, strong man two short years ago. I used to be a man of iron, an athlete! Now I am only a shadow. This is the simple truth.

The way in which I lost my health is a strange story. I lost it when I was helping to take care of a box full of guns on a 200-mile train ride one winter's night. This is the **actual** truth, and I will tell you about it.

Keys to Literature

The author uses narrative **hooks** to get your attention. What narrative hook does he use in the first paragraph?

I live in Cleveland, Ohio. One winter's night, two years ago, I came home just after dark. I had arrived in a **driving** snowstorm. When I entered the house, I found out that my dearest boyhood friend, John B. Hackett, had died the day before. I also found out that in his last words he asked that I take his body home to his poor, old father and mother in Wisconsin.

I was very surprised and very saddened. But there was no time to waste in emotions. I had to start right away. I picked up the card marked "Deacon Levi Hackett, Bethlehem, Wisconsin." Then I hurried off through the whistling storm to the train station.

When I arrived there, I found the long, wooden box that had been described to me. I fastened the card to it with some nails. Then I watched a man put it safely aboard the **express** car. After that, I ran into the dining room in the train station to buy a sandwich.

When I returned in a little while, there was a box that looked just like my coffin-box *back again*! A young fellow was looking all around it. He had a card in his hands and some nails and a hammer! I was surprised and puzzled. He began to nail on his card. I rushed out

Predict

What happened to the narrator's box?

to the express car, in a terrible state of mind, to ask for an explanation. But no! There was my box in the express car. It hadn't been moved.

I didn't know it, but a huge mistake had been made. In my box was a load of *guns*. That young fellow owned them and had come to the station to ship them to a rifle company in Peoria, Illinois. But *he* had got in his box the body of my dead friend!

Just then the conductor sang out, "All aboard." I jumped into the express car and got a comfortable seat on a pile of buckets. The expressman was there hard at work. He was a plain man of fifty. He had an honest, happy face and a friendly way about him.

As the train moved off, a stranger skipped through the car. He set a package of very old and very stinky Limburger cheese on one end of my coffin box. I mean my box of guns. That is to say, *now* I know that it was Limburger cheese. But at that time, I had never heard of this cheese in my life. So, of course, I had no idea what it was like.

Well, we sped through the wild night with a terrible storm outside. Soon I became sad and miserable. My heart went down, down! The old expressman made a remark about the freezing weather. Then he slammed his sliding doors shut, locked them, and closed his window tight. He continued to busy himself here and there around the car. All the time, he happily hummed "Sweet By and By" in a low voice.

Keys to Literature

Which part of this paragraph is a **narrative hook** that gets your attention?

Soon I began to notice a terrible, stinking odor in the frozen air. This odor made me even more miserable. Of course, I thought the smell was the dead body of my dear **departed** friend. I was upset, too, because I thought the old expressman might notice it. However, he went humming happily on and gave no sign. For this I was grateful.

I may have been grateful, but I was still uneasy. Soon I began to feel more and more uneasy every minute. For every minute that went by, the smell thickened up more and more. It became more and more difficult to stand.

Soon the expressman got some wood and built a huge fire in his stove. This fire upset me more than I can tell, for I believed that it was a mistake. I was sure that the heat would harm the body of my poor departed friend.

Keys to Literature

The expressman seals the cracks and builds a fire. Why are these details about the **setting** important?

Thompson—that was the expressman's name—now went poking around his car. He stopped up whatever stray cracks he could find in the walls. He said that it didn't make any difference what type of a night it was outside. He was going to make us comfortable, anyway.

I said nothing. But I believed he was not choosing the right way. Meanwhile he was humming to himself just as before. Meanwhile, too, the stove was getting hotter and hotter, and the place stuffier and stuffier. I felt myself growing pale and slightly ill. But I was silent and said nothing.

Soon I noticed that the "Sweet By and By" was gradually fading out. Next, it stopped altogether. Then there was an uneasy stillness. After a few moments, Thompson spoke up.

"Pfew! It ain't no cinnamon I've loaded up this-here stove with!"

He gasped once or twice. Then he moved toward the cof—gun-box. He stood over the Limburger cheese for a moment. Then he came back and sat down near me. He looked a good deal changed.

After a pause, he pointed to the box. "Friend of yours?" he asked.

"Yes," I said with a sigh.

"He's pretty ripe, *ain't* he!"

Nothing further was said for perhaps a couple of minutes. Each of us was busy with his own thoughts. Then Thompson spoke up again in a low voice.

"Sometimes it's uncertain whether they're really gone or not. They *seem* gone, you know—body warm and limp. So, although you *think* they're gone, you don't really know. I've had cases in my car. It's perfectly awful, because *you* don't know what minute they'll sit up and look at you!" Then after a pause, he slightly lifted his elbow toward the box. "But *he* ain't in any **trance**!" he said. "No, sir."

▶ In Twain's time, doctors did not have the medical equipment we have today. They sometimes made a mistake and thought a person in a coma was dead. People were sometimes buried alive.

We sat for some time, thinking. We listened to the wind and the roar of the train. Then Thompson spoke again with a good deal of feeling.

"Well-a-well, we've all got to go. There's no getting around it. Man that is born of woman is of few days and far between, as the Bible says. Yes, you look at it any way you want to. There isn't anybody can get around it. *All's* got to go—just *everybody*, as you may say. One day you're healthy and strong."

Here he got to his feet and broke a window pane and stretched his nose out for a moment or two. Then he sat down again while I got up and thrust my nose out at the same place. We kept on doing this every now and then.

"The next day he's cut down like the grass. Yes'n deedy, we've all got to go, one time or another. There's no getting around it."

Think About It

What does the expressman mean when he says, "All's got to go"?

There was another long pause. Then he said, "What did he die of?"

I said I didn't know.

"How long has he been dead?"

It seemed wise not to tell him it was only yesterday. So I said, "Two or three days."

However, it did no good. For Thompson received it with a hurt look. It was a look that plainly said, "Two or three *years*, you mean." Then he went right along, like he hadn't heard my statement. He gave his views at great length upon the foolishness of putting off burials too long. Then he walked off toward the box. After a moment, he came back at a sharp trot and visited the broken window pane.

"It would have been a darn sight better if they'd started him along last summer," he said.

Thompson sat down and buried his face in his red silk handkerchief. He began to slowly rock his body. He looked like someone suffering to put up with something impossible.

By this time, the smell was just about **suffocating**. Thompson's face was turning gray. I knew mine didn't have any color left in it. Soon Thompson rested his forehead in his left hand, with his elbow on his knee. He sort of waved his red handkerchief toward the box with his other hand.

"I've carried a many a one of 'em," he said. "Some of them were really ripe, too. But, lordy, he just lays over 'em all!—and does it *easy*. Cap, they were sweet roses compared to *him*!"

Thompson began to mumble in an **aimless** and low-spirited way. He started calling my poor friend by different titles. Sometimes he gave him military titles, sometimes civil ones. I noticed that as my friend's odor grew, Thompson gave him a bigger title.

Think About It

Why does Thompson think the man has been dead for a long time?

Finally, he said, "I've got an idea. Suppose we give the Colonel a shove toward the other end of the car? Say about ten feet. We wouldn't smell him so much then, don't you think?"

I said it was a good plan. We took in a good fresh breath at the broken window pane and held it. Then we went there and bent over that deadly cheese. We grabbed onto the box. Thompson nodded, "All ready." Then we threw ourselves forward with all our might.

Thompson slipped, however. He fell down with his nose on the cheese and his breath got loose. He choked and gasped and made a break for the door. "Don't stop me," he said **hoarsely**. "Gimme the road! I'm dying, gimme the road!"

Out on the cold platform, I sat down and held his head awhile. In a moment, he felt better. Presently he said, "Do you think we moved the General any?"

I said no, we hadn't moved him a bit.

"Well, then, that idea's up in smoke. We got to think up something else. He likes it where he is, I guess. He's made up his mind he don't wish to be troubled. If that's so, you bet he's going to have his own way. Yes, better leave him right where he is. Because he holds all the cards. It stands to reason that the man that lays out to change his plans for him is going to get left."

However, we couldn't stay out there in that mad storm. We would have frozen to death. So we went in again and shut the door. We began to suffer once more and took turns at the break in the window. Soon, we began to move away from a station where we had stopped for a moment.

Thompson danced in happily and shouted, "We're all right, now! I think we've got the Commodore this time. I judge I've got the stuff here that will take the smell out of him."

Think About It

What is Thompson trying to do with the bottle of acid?

It was acid. He had a large glass bottle filled with it. He sprayed it all around everywhere. In fact, he soaked everything with it—rifle box, cheese, and all. Then we sat down feeling pretty hopeful. But it wasn't for long. You see, the two smells began to mix—and then. Well, pretty soon we made a break for the door. Out there, Thompson wiped his face with his handkerchief. Then he spoke up in an unhappy way.

"It's no use. We can't fight against *him*. He just uses everything we use to change him. He gives it his own flavor and plays it back on us. Why, Cap, it's 100 times worse in there now than it was when he first got going. I never *did* see one of 'em start to smell so. No sir, not as long as I've been on the road. And I've carried a many of one of 'em, as I was telling you."

We went in again after we were frozen pretty stiff. But my, we couldn't *stay* in now. So we just walked back and forth, freezing and warming up, and choking by turns. In about an hour, we stopped at another station. Thompson came in with a bag.

Predict

When the train stops at another station, what will happen?

"Cap, I'm going to give him one more chance," he said. "Just this once, and if we don't get him this time—. Well, the thing for us to do then is to just throw in the towel."

He had a lot of chicken feathers, and dried apples, and leaf tobacco, and rags. He also had some old shoes and some leaves from a plant. He piled everything on some sheet iron in the middle of the floor. Then he set fire to them.

When they got going, I couldn't see how anything could stand it. All that went before was nothing compared to that new smell. But mind you, the original smell stood up out of it just as strong as ever. The fact is, these other smells just seemed to give it a better hold. And my, how rich it was!

I didn't have these thoughts right there. There wasn't time. I had them on the platform. Breaking for the platform, Thompson suffocated and fell. Before I got him dragged out, I was almost gone myself. When we came to, Thompson spoke up again.

"We got to stay out here, Cap. We got to do it. There isn't any other way. The Governor wants us to leave him alone. He's fixed so he can make us do it."

Then soon, he added, "And don't you know, we're *poisoned*. It's *our* last trip. You can make up your mind to it. Typhoid fever is what's going to come of this. I feel it coming right now. Yes, sir, we're sick with the fever. Just as sure as you're born."

We were taken from the platform an hour later at the next station. We were frozen and senseless. I went straight off into a terrible fever and never knew anything again for three weeks.

I found out then that I had spent the night with a harmless box of rifles and a lot of smelly cheese. But the news was too late to save *me*. Imagination had done its work. My health was gone for good. Neither Bermuda nor any other land can ever bring it back to me. This is my last trip. I am on my way home to die.

▶ Typhoid fever is a deadly disease. It can easily spread from person to person. It was a common disease in Mark Twain's time.

Meet the Author

MARK TWAIN *(1835–1910)*

Mark Twain's real name was Samuel Clemens. He lived in Hannibal, Missouri, which is on the Mississippi River. He ran a newspaper with his brother. Twain became a steamboat pilot on the Mississippi until the Civil War ended river travel. Then, he joined the Confederate army.

Twain eventually became very famous. He traveled all over the world, writing about things and places he knew. Twain is known for his humorous writing and speeches. Some of his best-known books are *A Connecticut Yankee in King Arthur's Court*, *Life on the Mississippi*, and *The Jumping Frog and Other Stories*. Two of his most famous characters are Tom Sawyer and Huckleberry Finn.

Check Your Predictions

1. Look back at the answers you gave for the Predict questions. Would you change your answers? Explain.

Understand the Story

2. Why does the narrator take a coffin-box on the train?

3. What is really in the box the narrator is riding with?

4. What makes the terrible smell on the train?

Think About the Story

5. Which sentence in this story do you think is the strongest narrative hook?

6. Why do you think the author chooses a winter storm as the setting for the story?

7. Twain writes, "Imagination had done its work." What does this mean?

8. Do you think the characters would have felt as sick if they had known the smell was just cheese?

Extend Your Response

Write the first paragraph of a news article about the events in this story. Be sure your paragraph answers the questions *Who? What? Where? When?* and *Why?*

Summaries

The Secret Life of Walter Mitty Walter Mitty daydreams that he is a Navy Commander flying a hydroplane, a famous doctor, an expert gunman, a fighter pilot, and a man facing a firing squad. In his daydreams, he is brave and adventuresome. In reality, he is not.

The Invalid's Story The narrator takes the dead body of his friend home to be buried. He puts the coffin on a train, but it gets switched with another box. Someone leaves a package of smelly Limburger cheese on the box, and the narrator and the train expressman think the smell is coming from the dead body. To escape the smell, they go out onto the train platform in a snowstorm. At the end, the narrator is so sick from the cold that he thinks he is going to die.

aimlessly
undefeated
actual
departed
trance
express

Vocabulary Review

Match each word in the box with its meaning. Write the word and its matching number on a separate sheet of paper.

1. real
2. nonstop
3. a dreamlike state
4. with no purpose
5. unbeaten
6. gone

Chapter Quiz

Answer the following questions in one or two complete sentences. Use a separate sheet of paper.

1. The Secret Life of Walter Mitty How does Mrs. Mitty treat Walter?

2. The Secret Life of Walter Mitty What do all of Walter Mitty's fantasy characters have in common?

3. The Invalid's Story What is the narrator supposed to take on the train?

4. The Invalid's Story What do the narrator and the expresssman do to get rid of the terrible smell?

Critical Thinking

5. The Secret Life of Walter Mitty Why does Walter Mitty daydream so often?

6. The Invalid's Story Why does the narrator say that he will die because of his imagination?

7. In what way are "The Secret Life of Walter Mitty" and "The Invalid's Story" similar?

8. Which of the two stories do you think is funnier? Explain.

Chapter Activity

Describe the setting of one of the stories. When does the story take place? Where does the story take place? Why is the setting an important part of the story? How would changing the setting affect the story?

Unit 7 **Review**

On a separate sheet of paper, write the letter that best completes each sentence below.

1. In "Escape!" the narrator runs away in order to
   A. gain his freedom.
   B. get more food.
   C. see his brother.
   D. follow the North Star.

2. At the end of "Escape!" the Quaker
   A. captures the narrator.
   B. finds the narrator at a tollbooth.
   C. helps the narrator.
   D. gives the narrator his freedom.

3. In "At Last I Kill a Buffalo," the narrator
   A. lies to his father.
   B. tells his father the truth.
   C. kills more buffalo than his father.
   D. gives his father a horse.

4. In "The Secret Life of Walter Mitty," Mitty daydreams that he
   A. lives an ordinary life.
   B. has a nagging wife.
   C. is brave and smart.
   D. drives a car.

5. In "The Invalid's Story," the narrator gets sick because
   A. he sprays acid.
   B. he travels a short distance.
   C. he is carrying guns.
   D. None of the above.

6. In "The Invalid's Story," the narrator tells us
   A. he used to be healthy and strong.
   B. he is an old, married man.
   C. he lives in Wisconsin with his father and mother.
   D. he loves Limburger cheese.

Making Connections

On a separate sheet of paper, write your answers to the following questions.

7. Which selection in this unit is the best adventure story? Why?

8. Which selections in this unit are autobiographies? What makes them autobiographies?

Writing an Essay
Which of these stories did you understand better because of something similar that happened to you or that you knew about? Explain.

Appendix

Glossary of Words to Know   486

Keys to Literature:
A Handbook of Literary Terms   496

Index of Authors and Titles   498

Index of Fine Art and Artists   500

Acknowledgments   501

Photo and Illustration Credits   502

Glossary of Words to Know

Note: These definitions fit the way the word is used in the selection. See a dictionary for more information about the words.

accept admit; give in to

ached hurt

actual real

aimless pointless; without purpose

aimlessly without a goal or a purpose

alarmed very frightened; afraid

alien strange; coming from another place

ambush a surprise attack from a hidden place

amigo "friend" in Spanish

appliances household machines like dishwashers and refrigerators

apprehend capture or arrest

artillery large guns

assumed thought something was true

assurance confidence

assure make a person certain of something; comfort

astonished greatly surprised; amazed

authentic genuine; real

autograph something written in a person's handwriting, especially the person's name

auxiliary back-up; something used when support is needed

awl a sharp, pointed tool for making holes in leather

balance evenness

ballet a kind of dance, made up of graceful turns and jumps

barracks buildings used as temporary housing

barren empty

bayonets rifles with steel knives attached to the end

belongings personal items, often packed in luggage

betrayed lied to; broke someone's trust

blacksmith a person who shapes hot metal, such as iron, into horseshoes, pots, or other objects

bleak not cheerful; harsh, cold, and cutting

blurry not clear

bond money paid to free someone from jail before a trial

bouts fights, or matches, in boxing

brawn strength

brute a beast; a wild animal

cabinets cupboards

calloused hardened with thick skin

camouflage a disguise made by looking like your surroundings

capsules pills

captivity prison

captor someone who captures another person or animal

captors people who catch someone

casks barrels or kegs

cavern a large cave

ceremony a special event

challenger in boxing, the one who fights the champion

challenging daring someone to a contest

champion a winner of a match or a series of matches

channeled made into passageways

choir a singing group

choke clog or block

circuit a regular trip from place to place taken by people who do a certain kind of work

citizens people who have rights under the laws of the city or country in which they live

civic having to do with your fellow citizens

civil rights rights that are guaranteed to a person by the U.S. Constitution

claim a right

clawed dug into with fingernails

clerk an office worker; someone in charge of recording numbers and events

client a customer

clumsy awkward

coincidence two events that seem connected but are not

commence start; begin

commenced began

commodity something that can be traded or sold

communicate talk; make your thoughts and feelings known

comrades friends

contact two things or people coming together

coping dealing with something in a successful way

corpse a dead body

courteously politely; with good manners

courtesy good manners; kindness

craftiness cleverness

cremated burned a dead body

crisis a time of great danger; a turning point at which a major change takes place

crystal clear glass or stone that is expensive

curry clean an animal's coat with a brush

customary usual; normally done

debates thinks about; tries to decide

defendant a person on trial for a crime

defiance refusing to do something you are told to do

degrading insulting; embarrassing

departed gone; dead

derelict something left behind or thrown away

descendants children and grandchildren

desperate in terrible need; almost hopeless

destiny fate; what is likely to happen

determination having your mind set on accomplishing something

dignity pride; self-respect

discipline punishment; correction

disinfect sterilize; make clean

diverged separated

division a group at a certain weight or age level

dodge move quickly to get out of the way

drastic having a strong effect; harsh

draw a tie; when the fighters have equal points at the end of a match

drawn pulled on

dread great worry or fear

dreary gloomy and dull; depressing

drive force a piece of metal into a rock with a hammer

driving strong

drool let liquid run out of the mouth, as a baby does

dwell on think about all the time

efface wipe out, erase

elegant attractive and refined

emigrated left one country to settle in another

encircled surrounded

entreating asking

epidemic the quick spread of a disease to many people

etiquette good manners; rules of proper behavior

exaggerated made something seem better or worse than it really was

exotic unfamiliar, as if from another country

explicitly very clearly and plainly

explode blow up

exploits brave or daring actions

explosion a blast from a bomb

express nonstop; high speed

exulting rejoicing; showing great joy

farewell goodbye

fast held tight; fastened

fiends very evil or cruel people

fierce violent; strong

film a thin coating of something

flake a small, thin piece or chip

flushed forced out from a hiding place

fluttered moved like flapping wings

fly move quickly

forefinger the finger next to the thumb

forge a furnace or fire in which metal is heated and shaped

foul play dishonest behavior; murder

frail weak, thin

frenzy a wild, excited feeling

fugitive someone who is running away from people who are looking for him or her

furious very angry

furiously angrily

gait way of walking or running

gape stare in surprise with mouth open

gasped breathed in loudly and quickly after being shocked or surprised

gaunt thin and bony

generosity a willingness to give things to others

ghastly awfully

glimpse a peek; a quick look

gratification a feeling of pride or thankfulness

grenade a small bomb that can be thrown by hand

grimly in a gloomy or cold way

grisly terrifying; horrible

grooved having a long, narrow cut in a surface

groping searching blindly

grounds an area of land around a building

grub food

grunt a short, deep, hoarse sound

guardian protector

guilty proven to have committed a crime

harkened listened

harpoon a spear on a rope used for killing whales

hastens hurries

hatchet a small ax with a short handle

haunted came back again and again, often in a scary way

heed pay attention to

helm a ship's steering wheel

hoarsely gruffly; with a husky voice

hopper a grain bin

humor something funny

hydroplane an airplane that can land on water

hymn a religious song of praise

impetuous acting in a sudden way without thinking about what might happen

implore beg for; ask for in a serious way

impressed made someone think highly of something

impulse a sudden desire to act

influenza a disease usually called "the flu"

insulting disrespectful; hurting someone's feelings

intense very strong

intern a doctor who is in training

interpreter a person who explains the meaning of something to another person

intricate complicated; hard to understand

invalid a sick person

isolated alone; set apart from others

jerked gave a quick pull or twist

joint a place where two bones are joined

justified showed to be right

keel the center piece of timber along the bottom of a ship

kennels cages for dogs

knots a measurement of a ship's speed

lack absence; need

lame limping; disabled

lament a poem or song that expresses great sadness over a death

lantern a lamp that can be covered and carried or hung up

latching holding together tightly

latitude the distance north or south of the equator

lavishly in a way that is much more than enough

leaping jumping high into the air

leathery tough like leather

legible clear enough to be read easily

lightweight a weight class for boxers who weigh between 127 and 135 pounds

loathed hated

locomotive an engine used to pull railroad cars

longitude the distance east or west of Greenwich, England

lopsided uneven

luscious juicy; delicious

manifold many ways

mantel a shelf over a fireplace

marksmanship aim; accuracy in shooting

mighty very

mischievousness playfulness or naughtiness

mist fog or haze

moderately to do something somewhat, but not too much

molding the trim on a wall or ceiling

moorings a place where a boat is tied up

morality rules of right and wrong

mortals human beings

mortified ashamed; embarrassed

muffled less loud, as if covered up

murky dark or gloomy

mushing traveling on a sled pulled by dogs

muttered said softly

muzzle the front end of the barrel of a gun

neglected ignored; not taken care of

nicks small cuts, chips, or notches in something

nourishment food to keep you healthy and alive; something that provides good health, growth, and development

obeisance a sign of respect, such as a bow

objection in a court of law, a complaint or argument against something said

orbit an area that a person stays in

ought nothing

outlive last longer than someone or something else

overshoes rubber boots worn over regular shoes in wet or cold weather

paced walked back and forth again and again

pallid pale or light in color

parallel always being the same distance apart

passion a very strong or deep feeling

patiently calmly dealing with something

pause a stop or short wait

peril great danger

permit allow

persevere continue on

piercing making a hole through something

plantation a large piece of land where crops are grown by workers who live there

platform a raised area where people wait for a train

platoon a unit in the army

pneumonia a serious lung disease

ponder think about carefully

pout frown; be silent and unfriendly

powwow a Native American meeting or gathering

prairie a large area of land with rich soil, grass, and very few trees

preceding coming just before

prejudiced disliking people because they belong to a different group from one's own

procession people moving forward one after another

protection a guard against harm or danger

protest an action against something that seems unfair

pulpit a raised platform from which a person leads a worship service

pyramid a structure with a square base and four sides that meet at a point at the top

quaint old-fashioned, out of date

quarter an area; a section

quench stop or put out

racism the belief that one race is better than another

rack hardship; torture

reassuringly in a convincing way

recompense reward

referee the person who judges a match or a game

reflection an image, as from a mirror

refugee a person who leaves his or her country to find safety in another country

regiment a very large unit of soldiers made up of two or more large groups of soldiers

regretted felt sorry or guilty for something

relish foods, such as pickles, olives, and raw vegetables, served as an appetizer

reluctantly not wanting to do something; unwillingly

repellent something that keeps insects away, like a spray

reputation what most people think about a person

resistance fighting back

resolved decided

retreating running away from an attack

roomers people who pay to live in a room of a house

rut a track made in the ground by wheels

sacred holy, religious

salvation rescue

savagely fiercely; in an untamed way

scab the crust that forms on skin where a sore or cut is healing

sealed closed

seized grabbed suddenly

seldom not often; rarely

sergeant an officer in the armed forces

shack a small house built in a simple, rough way

sharecropper someone who works on a farm in exchange for a part of the crop

shutters wooden window covers that swing open and shut

simultaneously at the same time

slave catchers people who captured runaway slaves and returned them to their owners for money

slender thin

slithered slid or glided like a snake

slugger hitter

slurp make a loud sipping or sucking sound

snarled growled angrily, showing the teeth

sparring boxing for practice without throwing blows

spectators people who watch something without taking part

spine the part of a book where the pages are bound together

splinters thin, sharp pieces of wood that can stick into your hands or feet

sputtering making fast, spitting sounds

stagger sway or wobble

staggered walked in an unsteady way, as if about to fall

stamp to bring one's foot down hard

stately appearing important and worthy of respect

steam drill a steam-powered machine used to cut through rock

steeds horses

steel-drivin' using a hammer to pound a pointed piece of steel into rock

steep slanting sharply; sloping

steward the person in charge of food and equipment on a ship

stooped hunched over; bent forward and downward

straightening organizing; putting things in order; making things neat

stroke a sudden illness that is caused when a blood vessel in the brain is blocked or broken

stumped walked in a stiff way with heavy feet

submerged hidden or buried

subway a train that runs underground

suede leather with the rough side rubbed until it is soft

sufficient enough; as much as is needed

suffocating making breathing difficult

surcease end

surplus more than what is needed

tackle begin to or try to do something difficult

tainted damaged, ruined, or spoiled

temptation thinking about doing something wrong

tenement an apartment building that is rundown

termites small insects like ants that eat wood and damage buildings

thrashing tossing about

thundered moved noisily

timid shy

token sign

tolerably fairly; pretty much

tollgate a place where you pay to travel on a road or cross a bridge

trance a dream-like state, a state of being unconscious

tread step; walk

trembling shaking

trice a very short time; a moment

triumph an important success

turret section of a warplane shaped like a bubble

undefeated never having lost or been beaten

undergrowth small trees and bushes that grow under large trees

unfortunately without luck; unhappily

unison together and at the same time

unnerved caused someone to lose courage

untapped not used

vague unclear

varnished smoothed over with a glossy surface

vaults safes where money or jewels are kept

viciously cruelly; evilly

victor winner

vinyl a material made of strong plastic

volley a burst of bullets

vulture a bird of prey

weary tired; worn out

weather'd passed through safely (This word is a contraction for *weathered*.)

whereupon after which

whimper whine or cry

yonder in the distance; over there

youth a young person

Keys to Literature: A Handbook of Literary Terms

alliteration repeating the same consonant sound

analogy comparing something unknown with something you already know

atmosphere the general mood of a piece of literature

autobiographical essay writing that focuses on one event in the writer's life

ballad a song that tells a story

biography the story of a person's life written by another person

character a person in a story

character clues the thoughts, actions, and words in a story that help you understand what a character is like

character traits qualities that a person has like bravery or honesty

climax the high point of a story when the outcome is decided

coined words words that are made up

colloquial language everyday language people use when talking to friends

comparison showing how two things are alike

conflict problems in a story that need to be solved

connotation an idea or feeling suggested by a word

denotation the actual meaning of a word

details pieces of information that help to create a picture for the reader

dialect the form of a language that is spoken by people living in a certain place

dialogue a conversation between characters in a story or play; words that characters actually say

exaggeration making something seem better or worse than it really is

external conflict a struggle that a person has with another person, with society, or with nature

fable a short story that teaches a lesson. In fables, animals and other natural things act and talk like people.

figurative language words that describe something by comparing it to something else. It is used to add color and interest to a story.

first-person point of view a story character tells the story, using *I* to refer to himself or herself

foreshadowing hints about what might happen later in a story

free verse poetry that is not written in a regular pattern; the words do not rhyme

idiom a phrase or an expression that has a different meaning from what the individual words usually mean

imagery colorful words that appeal to the senses

internal conflict a struggle a person has within himself or herself when trying to make a decision

irony a result that is the opposite of what is expected

metaphor a comparison of two things that does not use the word *like* or *as*

meter the rhythm, or beat, of a poem

mood the feeling you get from reading a story

motivation the reason a character behaves as he or she does

myth a story, handed down through the years, that explains how something in nature came to be

narrative a story; a report of what has happened

narrative hook a point in a story at which the author grabs your attention

narrative poem a poem that tells a story

narrator the person telling the story

omniscient point of view when the narrator knows what all the story characters do, say, and feel. An omniscient narrator uses *he, she,* and *they* to refer to the characters.

onomatopoeia the use of words that imitate sounds

paradox a statement that seems impossible but that may actually be true

personification giving human characteristics to something that is not human

plot the action of a story or play. Most stories have a problem and, at the end, a solution.

quatrain a stanza made up of four lines

realism a style of writing in which people and events are presented the way they actually are in life

repetition words or sentences used over and over to create a feeling or mood

rhyme words that sound alike

rhyme scheme the pattern of words that sound alike

rhythm a sound pattern of stressed syllables, or beats, in a poem

rising action the buildup of excitement in a story

sensory details details that show how something looks, sounds, smells, tastes, or feels

setting the time and place of a story

simile a comparison of two things using the word *like* or *as*

slang very informal language

stanza a group of lines in a poem set apart from other groups of lines

symbolism using something to stand for something else

theme the main idea of a story, novel, play, or poem

tone the feeling a writer shows toward the subject of a poem or story

turning point the event in a story that leads to a solution to the problem

Index of Authors and Titles

A

After Twenty Years, p. 4
The All-American Slurp, p. 82
Ambush, p. 330
Amigo Brothers, p. 320
An Appointment, p. 12
At Last I Kill a Buffalo, p. 440

B

Ballad of Birmingham, p. 358
The Ballad of John Henry, p. 178
Birdfoot's Grampa, p. 284
Bradstreet, Anne, p. 414
Bruchac, Joseph, p. 284

C

from *The Call of the Wild*, p. 262
Chase, Owen, p. 226
from *Childtimes*, p. 376
The Circuit, p. 136
Colon, Jesus, p. 298
Crane, Stephen, p. 162
The Cremation of Sam McGee, p. 34
cummings, e.e., p. 280

D

A Day's Wait, p. 128
Dickinson, Emily, p. 278
Douglass, Frederick, p. 304

E

Escape!, p. 426

F

Fire, John/Lame Deer and Richard Erdoes,
    p. 98
Fletcher, Lucille, p. 58
Frost, Robert, p. 288

G

Giovanni, Nikki, p. 416
Greenfield, Eloise, p. 184, 206
Greenfield, Eloise and Lessie Jones Little,
    p. 376

H

Harriet Tubman, p. 184
Hawthorne, Nathaniel, p. 252
from *Helen Keller: The Story of My Life*,
    p. 216
Hemingway, Ernest, p. 128
Henry, O., p. 4
Housecleaning, p. 416
Hughes, Langston, p. 154, 406
Hunt, Evelyn Tooley, p. 362

I

in Just-, p. 280
The Invalid's Story, p. 470

J

The Jacket, p. 120
Jiménez, Francisco, p. 136

K

Keller, Helen, p. 216

L

Lame Deer Remembers, p. 98
Lament, p. 410
Little Things Are Big, p. 298
London, Jack, p. 262
Longfellow, Henry Wadsworth, p. 30, 192

M

The Medicine Bag, p. 386
Millay, Edna St. Vincent, p. 410
Mother to Son, p. 406

N

Namioka, Lensey, p. 82
from *Narrative of the Life of Frederick Douglass*, p. 304

O

O Captain! My Captain!, p. 188
O'Brien, Tim, p. 330

P

Paul Revere's Ride, p. 192
Pennington, James W. C., p. 426
Piercy, Marge, p. 366
Pijoan de Van Etten, Teresa, p. 244
Poe, Edgar Allan, p. 16, 42
from *Prisoner of My Country*, p. 104

R

Randall, Dudley, p. 358
The Raven, p. 42
from *The Red Badge of Courage*, p. 162
Ribbons, p. 338
River Man, p. 244
The Road Not Taken, p. 288
from *Rosa Parks*, p. 206

S

The Secret Life of Walter Mitty, p. 458
Service, Robert W., p. 34
Shipwreck of the Whaleship *Essex*, p. 226
Simple-song, p. 366
The Sky Is Low, p. 278
Sneve, Virginia Driving Hawk, p. 386
Sorry, Wrong Number, p. 58
Soto, Gary, p. 120
Standing Bear, Luther, p. 440

T

Taught Me Purple, p. 362
The Tell-Tale Heart, p. 16
Thank You, M'am, p. 154
Thomas, Piri, p. 320
Thurber, James, p. 458
The Tide Rises, the Tide Falls, p. 30
To My Dear and Loving Husband, p. 414
Twain, Mark, p. 470

U

Uchida, Yoshiko, p. 104

V

A Visit to the Clerk of the Weather, p. 252

W

Wharton, Edith, p. 12
Whitman, Walt, p. 188

Y

Yep, Laurence, p. 338

Index of Fine Art and Artists

Abolitionist, statesman, p. 315

Acrobats, p. 204

Anonymous, pp. 315, 417

Benton, Thomas Hart, p. 242

Brackman, Robert, p. 363

Brandt, Helene, p. 367

The Buffalo Hunt, p. 441

The Buffalo Hunter, p. 446

Cannon, T. C., p. 424

Catlin, George, pp. 443, 451

Circle of Love, p. 404

Demuth, Charles, p. 204

DeNapoli, Daniel, p. 318

Dunn, Harvey, p. 409

Eastman, Seth, p. 446

Entrance to Subway, p. 301

Escoffery, Michael, p. 404

Faces in Closet, p. 318

Farm, p. 276

Ferry Boat Trip, p. 80

Fruits of the Earth, p. 118

Ghosts, p. 296

Giant Jack-in-the-Box, p. 456

The Hailstorm, p. 242

Hauser, Jeremy, p. 456

Hirsch, Stefan, p. 56

His Hair Flows Like a River, p. 424

Johnson, William H., p. 80

Kids on Bikes, p. 152

Kurtz and Allison, p. 173

Once It Chased Doctor Wilkinson into the Very Town Itself, p. 28

Marian Anderson, p. 385

Memories of Childhood, p. 367

Mollica, Patricia, p. 299

Ong, Diana, pp. 296, 356

Parks, David, p. 152

Passing into Womanhood, p. 374

The Prairie Is My Garden, p. 409

The Propagandist, p. 137

Pyle, Howard, p. 28

The Race Track (Death on a Pale Horse), p. 13

Ringgold, Faith, p. 176

Rivera, Diego, pp. 118, 137, 142

Rothko, Mark, p. 301

Russell, Charles Marion, p. 441

Ryder, Albert Pinkham, p. 13

Scott, Jane Wooster, p. 281

Sioux Encamped on the Upper Missouri, Dressing Buffalo Meat, p. 451

Sioux Village, Lake Calhoun, near Fort Snelling, p. 443

Somewhere in America, p. 363

Sonny's Quilt, p. 176

Springtime in Central Park, p. 281

Storming of Fort Wagner, p. 173

Street in Saverne, p. 2

Subway, p. 299

Terpning, Howard, p. 374

The Tortilla Maker, p. 142

Waring, Laura Wheeler, p. 385

Weeper, p. 356

Whistler, James Abbott McNeil, p. 2

Winter Night, p. 56

Wyeth, N. C., p. 276

Acknowledgments

page 104: Adapted with the permission of Simon & Schuster Books for Young Readers, an imprint of Simon & Schuster Children's Publishing Division from THE INVISIBLE THREAD by Yoshiko Uchida © 1991 Yoshiko Uchida.

page 120: "The Jacket," from *The Effects of Knut Hamson on a Fresno Boy: Recollections and Short Essays* by Gary Soto. Copyright © 1983, 2001 by Gary Soto. Reprinted by permission of Persea Books, Inc. (New York).

page 128: "A Day's Wait." Reprinted with permission of Scribner, an imprint of Simon & Schuster Adult Publishing Group, from THE SHORT STORIES OF ERNEST HEMINGWAY. Copyright © 1933 by Charles Scribner's Sons. Copyright renewed © 1961 by Mary Hemingway.

page 136: Francisco Jiménez. Adaptation of "The Circuit." First published by *The Arizona Quarterly* (Autumn, 1973). Copyright © 1973 by Francisco Jiménez.

page 154: "Thank You M'am" from SHORT STORIES by Langston Hughes. Copyright © 1996 by Ramona Bass and Arnold Rampersad. Reprinted by permission of Hill and Wang, a division of Farrar, Straus and Giroux, LLC.

page 184: Unabridged Text of "Harriet Tubman" *Honey, I Love* by Eloise Greenfield. Text Copyright © 1978 by Eloise Greenfield. Used by permission of HarperCollins Publishers.

page 206: "Rosa Parks" by Eloise Greenfield. Copyright © 1973 by Eloise Greenfield. Used by permission of HarperCollins Publishers.

page 244: From "River Man" by Teresa Pijoan de Van Etten in *Spanish American Folktales*. Copyright © by Teresa Pijoan de Van Etten. Used by permission of Marian Reiner for August House Publishers, Inc. All rights reserved.

page 280: "in Just-." Copyright 1923, 1951, © 1991 by the Trustees for the E.E. Cummings Trust. Copyright © 1976 by George James Firmage, from COMPLETE POEMS: 1904–1962 by E.E. Cummings, edited by George J. Firmage. Used by permission of Liveright Publishing Corporation.

page 284: Joseph Bruchac. "Birdfoot's Grampa," from *Entering Onondaga* by Joseph Bruchac. Copyright © 1978 by Joseph Bruchac. Published by Cold Mountain Press. Used by permission of the author.

page 298: Jesus Colon. Adaptation of "Little Things Are Big," from A Puerto Rican in New York. First published in 1961 by Masses and Mainstream. Copyright © 1982 by International Press. Reprinted by permission of International Publishers Co. Inc., New York.

page 320: "Amigo Brothers" from STORIES FROM EL BARRIO by Piri Thomas. Copyright © 1978 by Piri Thomas. Reprinted by permission of the author.

page 330: "Ambush" from THE THINGS THEY CARRIED by Tim O'Brien. Copyright © 1990 by Tim O'Brien. Reprinted by permission of Houghton Mifflin Company. All rights reserved.

page 338: Laurence Yep. Adaptation of "Ribbons" from *American Girl* premier issue 1992, pp. 32–39.

page 358: Dudley Randall. *Ballad of Birmingham*. Reprinted by permission of Broadside Press.

page 362: Evelyn Tooley Hunt, "Taught Me Purple" (3 stanzas). Published in *Negro Digest*, February 1964, reprinted by permission.

page 366: "Simple-song" from *Hard Loving*. © 1969 by Marge Piercy and reprinted by permission of Wesleyan University Press. All rights reserved.

page 376: Unabridged excerpts: "Mama Sewing," "Pa," "Martha Ann Barnes Ridley," & "Family," from *Childtimes: A Three-Generation Memoir*. Copyright © 1979 by Eloise Greenfield and Lessie Jones Little. Selection reprinted by permission of HarperCollins Publishers.

page 386: Virginia Driving Hawk Sneve. Adaptation of "The Medicine Bag." Reprinted by permission of the author. Copyright © 1975.

page 406: "Mother to Son" from THE COLLECTED POEMS OF LANGSTON HUGHES by Langston Hughes, copyright © 1994 by The Estate of Langston Hughes. Used by permission of Alfred A. Knopf, a division of Random House, Inc.

page 410: "Lament" by Edna St. Vincent Millay. From *Collected Poems*, HarperCollins. Copyright © 1921, 1948 by Edna St. Vincent Millay. All rights reserved. Reprinted by permission of Elizabeth Barnett; literary executor.

page 416: "Housecleaning" from THE SELECTED POEMS OF NIKKI GIOVANNI by NIKKI GIOVANNI. Compilation Copyright © 1996 by Nikki Giovanni. Reprinted by permission of HarperCollins Publishers Inc.

page 440: Reprinted from *My Indian Boyhood*, by Luther Standing Bear, by permission of the University of Nebraska Press. Copyright 1931 by Luther Standing Bear. Copyright © renewed 1959 by May M. Jones.

page 458: "The Secret Life of Walter Mitty" from MY WORLD—AND WELCOME TO IT by James Thurber. Copyright © 1942 Rosemary A. Thurber. Reprinted by arrangement with Rosemary A. Thurber and The Barbara Hogenson Agency. All rights reserved.

Note: Every effort has been made to locate the copyright owners of material used in this textbook. Omissions brought to our attention will be corrected in subsequent editions.

Photo and Illustration Credits

Cover: *books* Will Crocker/The Image Bank/Getty Images; *raven* Gerard Lacz/Animals Animals/Earth Scenes; *trumpet* Photodisc/Getty Images, Inc.; *gloves* Eyewire/Getty Images, Inc.; *horse* James L. Stanfield/National Geographic/Getty Images, Inc. 2: Hermitage, St. Petersburg, Russia/The Bridgeman Art Library. 10: © Bettmann/Corbis. 13: Albert Pinkham Ryder, American, 1847-1917. The Race Track (Death on a Pale Horse). Oil on canvas, ca. 1886-1908, 70.5 x 90 cm. © The Cleveland Museum of Art, Purchase from the J.H. Wade Fund, 1928.8. 14: © Bettmann/Corbis. 23: Courtesy, Library of Congress. 28: Private Collection/ The Bridgeman Art Library. 31: Image Bank/Getty Images, Inc. 32: © Bettmann/Corbis. 40: *t.* © Bettmann/Corbis; *b.* Library of Congress. 51: © Bettmann/Corbis. 53: © Joe McDonald/Corbis. 56: The Newark Museum/Art Resource, NY. 75: Lucille Fletcher. 80: © Smithsonian American Art Museum, Washington, DC/Art Resource, NY. 96: Courtesy, Lensey Namioka. 102: unknown. 107: Culver Pictures Inc. 108: © Corbis. 111: Anthony Potter Collection/Hulton Archive/Getty Images Inc. 113: Prentice Hall School. 115: © Corbis. 118: Diego Rivera/Banco de Mexico Trust/ Schalkwijk/Art Resource, NY. 126: Diane Trejo. 134: © Hulton-Deutsch Collection/Corbis. 137: © Banco de Mexico Trust © Schalkwijk/Art Resource, NY. 142: Diego Rivera. "Tortilla Maker." 1926. University of California, San Francisco School of Medicine. Banco de Mexico Diego Rivera & Frida Kahlo Museums Trust. Av. Cinco de Mayo No. 2, Col. Centro, Del. Cuauhtemoc 06059, Mexico, D.F. Reproduction authorized by the Instituto Nacional de Bellas Artes y Literatura. 145: Francisco Jimenez Ph.D. 147: © Najlah Feanny/Corbis. 151: *m.* William H. Johnson/ Smithsonian American Art Museum, Washington, DC/Art Resource, NY; *b.* Art Resource, NY. 152: David Parks/ Curtis Galleries, Inc. 160: National Portrait Gallery, Smithsonian Institution/Art Resource, NY. 170: The Granger Collection. 173: Kurz & Allison/Library of Congress. 176: Faith Ringgold/Faith Ringgold Inc. 183: © Bettmann/ Corbis. 185: William H. Johnson/Smithsonian American Art Museum, Washington, DC/Art Resource, NY. 186: Courtesy, Eloise Greenfield. 189: Cornelis de Vries/The Picture Desk/The Art Archive/Kobal. 190: The Granger Collection. 199: © Corbis. 201: Paul Revere. ca 1768-70. John Singleton Copley, U.S., 1738-1815. Oil on Canvas, 35 1/8 x 28 1/2 in. (88.9 x 72.3 cm.) Gift of Joseph W. Revere, William B. Revere and Edward H.R. Revere, 30.781. Courtesy, Museum of Fine Arts, Boston. Reproduced with permission. © 1999 Museum of Fine Arts, Boston. All Rights Reserved. 204: © The Museum of Modern Art/ Licensed by Scala/Art Resource, NY. 208: AP/Wide World Photo. 210: © Bettmann/Corbis. 213: AP/Wide World Photo. 214: *t.* Courtesy, Library of Congress; *b.* Courtesy, Eloise Greenfield. 218: *t.l.* © Bettmann/Corbis; *t.r.* © Bettmann/Corbis; *b.l.* © Corbis; *b.r.* © Bettmann/ Corbis. 223: *t.l.* © Hulton-Deutsch Collection/Corbis; *t.r.* © Corbis; *b.l.* © Bradley Smith/Corbis; *b.r.* © Bettmann/ Corbis. 224: © Bettmann/Corbis. 227: Musee de la Marine

Paris/Dagli Orti/The Picture Desk/The Art Archive/Kobal. 229: Private Collection/Dagli Orti/The Picture Desk/The Art Archive/Kobal. 233: Scala/Art Resource, NY. 235: Nantucket Historical Association. 237: David Ward/DK Images. 250: Teresa Pijoan. 260: © Bettmann/Corbis. 271: Hulton Archive Photos/Getty Images, Inc. 273: © Paul A. Souder/ Corbis. 276: Art Resource, NY. 281: Jane Wooster Scott/ SuperStock, Inc. 282: *t.* The Granger Collection; *b.* © Bettmann/Corbis. 286: Prentice Hall School. 289: Dale Jorgensen/SuperStock, Inc. 290: © Bettmann/Corbis. 295: *b.* © Bettmann/Corbis. 296: Diana Ong/SuperStock, Inc. 299: © Patricia Mollica/SuperStock. 301: Art Resource, NY. 302: Facing History and Ourselves. 313: National Portrait Gallery, Smithsonian Institution/Art Resource, NY. 315: Hulton Archive/Getty Images, Inc. 319: Daniel DeNapoli/ADS 2GO. 328: The New York Public Library/Art Resource, NY. 335: Jerry Bauer. 352: BridgeWater Books. 356: © Diana Ong/SuperStock, Inc. 359: © Bettmann/Corbis. 360: © Yancey Hughes. 363: © Smithsonian American Art Museum, Washington, DC/Art Resource, NY. 364: Evelyn Tooley Hunt. 367: © Helene Brandt, Memories of Childhood #3, 1994 third work in a series of 10 images prismacolor and graphite on paper 14"x17". Steinbaum Krauss Gallery, NYC. 368: AP/Wide World Photo. 374: "Passing into Womanhood" by Howard Terpning. © 1994, licensed by The Greenwich Workshop, Inc. 383: Courtesy, Eloise Greenfield. 385: © National Portrait Gallery, Smithsonian Institution/Art Resource, NY. 387: Marilyn "Angel" Wynn/Nativestock.com. 389: Claudia Kunin/Allstock/Getty Images, Inc. 393: Marilyn "Angel" Wynn/Nativestock.com. 395: Werner Forman/Art Resource, NY. 396: Judith Miller & Dorling Kindersley/DK Images. 400: Virginia Sneve. 404: © Michael Escoffery/Art Resource, NY. 408: © Corbis. 411: Harvey Dunn/South Dakota Art Museum. 412: Brown Brothers. 415: Eyewire Collection/ Photodisc/Getty Images, Inc. 417: Omni-Photo Communications, Inc. 418: *t.* The Art Archive/St. Biddolph, Boston/Eileen Tweedy; *b.* Prentice Hall School. 424: T. C. Cannon/The Philbrook Museum of Art. 437: The African American Registry/Media Business Solutions. 441: © Art Resource, NY. 448: © Geoffrey Clements/Corbis. 451: George Catlin. © Smithsonian American Art Museum, Washington, DC/Art Resource, NY. 452: © Corbis. 456: Jeremy Hauser (20th century American)/Private Collection/SuperStock, Inc. 467: © Bettmann/Corbis. 469: Stone Allstock/Getty Images, Inc. 480: Library of Congress.

Illustrations: 473, 475, 479: James Bernardin. 1 *t.*, 17, 19, 21, 22, 263, 267, 269, 285: Denny Bond. 241 *b.*, 279: Mary Chandler. 423 *b.*, 459, 462: Dennis Dittrich. 295 *t.*, 305, 307, 311: John Dyess. 35, 38: William Farnsworth. 151 *t.*, 163, 167, 171, 295 *m.*, 331, 332: Ron Himler. 1 *b.*, 43, 46, 49, 61, 63, 66, 73, 193, 195, 196, 373 *b.*, 407: Joel Iskowitz. 5, 9: David Lantz. 99, 101, 245, 247, 249: Diana Magnuson. 83, 85, 91, 95: Yoshi Myoshi. 79 *b.*, 130, 133: Pat Porter. 121, 123, 125: Stacey Schuett. 179, 180, 321, 326, 423 *t.*, 427, 430, 436: Marc Scott. 25: Ben Shannon. 241 *t.*, 253, 255, 257, 259: Valerie Sokolova. 339, 342, 347: Meryl Treatner. 155, 157, 373 *t.*, 377, 379, 382: Fred Willingham.